SCORING AT HALF-TIME

To Professor Roger Williams for his faith in me,
Mr Nigel Heaton for his amazing skills as a surgeon
and the family of the donor who made my new life possible.
To my wife Alex for her continued love and support.
And lastly to Shay Brennan the friend who I
remembered so fondly while writing this
book – gone but not forgotten.

GEORGE BEST

WITH MARTIN KNIGHT

SCORING AT HALF-TIME

ADVENTURES ON AND OFF THE PITCH

EBURY
PRESS

1 3 5 7 9 10 8 6 4 2

First published 2003 by Ebury Press,
An imprint of Random House,
20 Vauxhall Bridge Road, London SW1V 2SA

Random House Australia (Pty) Limited
20 Alfred Street, Milsons Point, Sydney,
New South Wales 2061, Australia

Random House New Zealand Limited
18 Poland Road, Glenfield, Auckland 10, New Zealand

Random House South Africa (Pty) Limited
Endulini, 5a Jubilee Road, Parktown 2193, South Africa

The Random House Group Limited Reg. No. 954009

www.randomhouse.co.uk

Printed and bound in Great Britain by Clays Ltd, St Ives plc

A CIP catalogue record for this book is available from the British Library.

Front cover picture © Empics
Back cover picture © PA Photos
All plate section pictures are credited to the relevant picture libraries.
All other pictures are from the author's private collection

Cover designed by Two Associates
Interior by seagulls

ISBN 0 09188 927 8

CONTENTS

INTRODUCTION   1

PART I   ON THE PITCH   4

1   PLAYERS   5
2   BOSSES   75
3   OVER LAND AND SEA   129

PART II   OFF THE PITCH   152

4   THE DRINK   153
5   THE FAME   209
6   THE MEDIA   232
7   THE FAIRER SEX   265

ACKNOWLEDGEMENTS

To my father and family, Dr Akeel Alisa, all the nurses and staff at the Cromwell hospital, Phil Hughes, Martin Knight, Andrew Goodfellow, Jake Lingwood, Stina Smemo and everyone at Ebury Press, Paul Collier, Martin Noble and well-wishers everywhere for their continued support.

INTRODUCTION

I am truly blessed. I am. Once I had the world at my feet and then I almost had nothing. No wife, no home, no money, no self-respect, and more or less no liver. Then I met my wonderful Alex and slowly and painfully we began rebuilding me. It's been a long haul and the story has been told in my autobiography *Blessed* but as at 30 July 2002 a new chapter has begun. For on that day I went into the Cromwell Hospital, London, and received a new liver. A new liver that I hope and believe will allow me the opportunity to enjoy the rest of my life. You may have heard this before but I *will* respect this liver. After all, it's not mine.

After my transplant and when I had been able to return home permanently, it was obvious that I was incredibly weak and my recuperation therefore was going to take longer than the optimistic estimates. While I was happy to savour being alive and in the bosom of my family, I needed to keep mentally active while my body was busily engaged in adapting to its new organ. I knew this, but the doctors also advised it. I loved working on *Blessed* and writing my newspaper column and started to toy with the idea of taking a stab at a novel. But my mind kept coming back to all the humorous stories and experiences that have happened to me or which I have heard about during my years in the game and beyond. I decided it would be good therapy to start writing them down and, maybe, at some later date put them into a book. Here we are now at that later date and here is that book.

If any one thing defined for me what football was about when I was playing it was the fun. Great fun. Of course there was the buzz, the adulation, the money, the satisfaction, the glory ... I could go on all night, but the one thing that was consistent was that we always had a laugh. Talk to any old retired footballer now and they will tell you, if they think about it for a minute, it is the fun they miss most of all. The game was full of larger than life characters, whether they were players, managers, chairmen or supporters, and we all enjoyed a camaraderie and rapport that bred a wealth of pranks, incidents, escapades and fun. I'm not sure any other sport or walk of life can claim such a culture; a culture that has spawned, for example, a whole industry of after-dinner speaking where many of us have been able to make a living recounting these tales to appreciative audiences up and down the country and beyond.

Many of the stories and anecdotes collected in this book are from my direct experience, the rest have been told to me, or I have read of them or they have entered my consciousness in some other way. I apologise in advance if I have got any stories or memories slightly wrong, or, even worse, if I have pinched anyone's after-dinner material. But plenty pinch mine and let's remember – it's fun!

PART
I

ON THE
PITCH

1

PLAYERS

KICK-OFF

Rodney Marsh didn't win many England caps during his career, nine in fact, but neither did many of the flair players of his period. Managers Sir Alf Ramsey and Don Revie after him seemed to have largely had a mental block about the more creative and flamboyant characters of the period, preferring their solid, dependable but not always multi-skilled peers. When Ramsey did play Rodney, he was a touch nervous about how he might perform. Just before kick-off in an important international Sir Alf gave his team-talk in the dressing room. He turned to Marsh and said, 'Rodney, if you're not playing well I will have to pull you off at half-time.'

Rodney Marsh grinned impishly, 'That sounds interesting, boss. At Manchester City we just get some oranges and a cup of tea.'

HEROES

As a boy I didn't get to see any of the footballing greats in the flesh. Visits to Belfast by top teams were few and far between and I can't recall watching much football on the television; a mod con that didn't arrive in our household until only a couple of years before I was whisked over to England. Wolverhampton Wanderers, however, were my team as a small boy because I *did* get to see them on the television set of a neighbour when they played a series of friendlies against European sides. Billy Wright was the Wolves captain and at the time the most famous footballer in Britain. With the passage of time it is easy to forget just how idolised he was. He really was the David Beckham of his day; even marrying a member of the 1950s Spice Girls equivalent – one of the Beverley Sisters. I always thought they were identical twins until someone pointed out there were three of them. As I recall, he advertised hair products and household soaps in the same way that Becks (and myself come to that) has endorsed various products. I don't know if Billy went as far as wearing a sarong and a bandana but who knows what he and the Beverley sister got up to in the privacy of their own home.

Recently I came across Billy's autobiography *The World's My Football Pitch*, written in 1954. One small extract illustrates just how much football and indeed the world has changed over the near fifty years that have passed since its publication.

'I said to Neil Franklin, as we lay in bed that evening

talking over our humiliating defeat by the Irish League ...'
writes Billy.

Imagine the furore now if David Beckham said, 'As Paul
Scholes and I lay in bed the other night ...'

Billy collected 105 caps for England, many as captain, a
record that most believed would never be surpassed, but Bobby
Moore did just pip him. He finally ended up with 108. Only
when I arrived in Manchester as a spotty under-developed kid
did I see the likes of Billy Wright, Denis Law, Johnny Haynes,
Bobby Charlton and the other greats in the flesh. And I was
actually playing on the same pitch as them, not watching from
the terraces, which made it all the more surreal.

As a really small boy I used to take the *Dandy* comic featuring Korky the Cat on the cover and Desperate Dan on the
inside cover. All boys took the *Dandy* or the *Beano* or both; a handful of the more studious kids bought the *Eagle*. Every week my
comic featured a footballer from the past and it was this page I
devoured eagerly. One of the earliest footballing 'true' stories I
remember reading was in there. It was illustrated with lifelike
pictures and concerned the great Dixie Dean of Everton and
England. Dixie scored sixty League goals in one season (1927/28)
– these days entire teams struggle to get this many. At the time, as
a young boy, I believed every word of the legendary centre forward's anecdote in my favourite comic and only now as I recall
this can I see that it was obviously not true. I wish it were though.

In his heyday Dixie Dean's greatest rival was, naturally, the
Liverpool goalkeeper of the time, one Elisha Cook. The two men

locked horns in the great Merseyside derbies for many years and it has to be said that Elisha, while a great keeper was punished by the unfailing accuracy of Dixie's head and left foot many times. He feared his encounters with Dixie Dean more than any other centre forward of the time.

One day Dixie was out shopping in Liverpool city centre with his wife and he spotted Elisha on the other side of the road, also leisurely shopping with his own wife. A look of mild fear spread across Elisha's face as he registered his rival. As Dixie nodded to greet him, Elisha unlocked himself from his wife's arm and dived instinctively and acrobatically into the road ...

I have a photographic memory of the illustration that accompanied this story – Dixie Dean standing by the kerb with his trademark centre parting and a bewildered look on his face as Elisha Cook, in a suit, is prostrate in the road, arm outstretched with cans of beans and the rest of the contents of his wife's shopping bag scattered around him.

As I write, Evertonians think they have a hero worthy of inheriting Dixie Dean's crown – Wayne Rooney. I hope he is. It is hard for me to judge because the boy has only played a handful of senior games and I have not seen them all. What I have seen though is promising and I can understand the excitement. But, I fear for Wayne, because the fanfare surrounding him is totally out of proportion and the press has already placed the footballing aspirations and frustrations of a nation firmly on his shoulders. Be sure that as soon as he falters he will be pilloried and abused. All this before he has put down his Gameboy.

That is the problem nowadays. Brilliant players are few and far between and when one comes along they are pounced upon, lauded and sucked dry. It happened to Michael Owen to an extent. The media perception of him today is now one of almost any other England international. Yet here is a player who is still only in his early twenties and has yet to reach his peak and whose arrival on the scene mirrored the welcome Rooney is now receiving.

When I played, every First Division club had at least one brilliant player to spread the focus of attention. Arsenal had Charlie George; Birmingham had Trevor Francis; Chelsea had Osgood; West Ham had Bobby Moore; Liverpool had Keegan; Manchester City had Colin Bell; Queens Park Rangers had Rodney Marsh; Sheffield United had Tony Currie; Stoke had Gordon Banks and Spurs had Jimmy Greaves. I can't think of one at Leeds because I don't want to. In 2003 one turns up at Everton and the country wets itself.

B ert Trautmann was another player I had huge admiration for during my childhood. He was a German prisoner of war in England during the Second World War and stayed around when peace was restored, becoming the first team goalkeeper for Manchester City. He is now best remembered for playing part of the 1956 FA Cup Final against Birmingham with what was later discovered to be a broken neck. Apparently he never looked back after that. By the time one of my old adversaries, the tough defender Mike Doyle, started as an apprentice at Maine Road, Bert's days at the club were coming to a close. Mike was never shy in coming forward and while cleaning the great man's boots he quipped, 'How's your back today, Mr Trautmann?'

Doyle was mischievously referring to the previous match when City had been thrashed 6–0 and Bert had spent some considerable time bending down picking the ball out of the net. Trautmann looked at the impertinent young boy and promptly smacked him around the head.

One of the other reasons I admired Bert was a story I read about him regarding something that happened in the dying embers of his playing career. He was past his best and in this particular game a forward scored against him but Bert felt that the player had unfairly barged or impeded him. The referee was not listening to Bert's protests and turned and trotted back to the halfway line. Bert followed, still clasping the ball he had picked out of the net and in sheer frustration and anger kicked the ball as hard as he could at the referee's back. He got into a lot of trouble over that and I think his career more or less stopped there. This appealed to the rebel in me. I never really emulated his action but I did get suspended once for knocking the ball out of the referee's hands. Stupid, but fun at the time.

Derek Dooley was another name that resounded around football when I was a lad because he represented everything good and courageous about the game. He was a brave centre forward for Sheffield Wednesday and England who suffered a bad leg-break and then tragically gangrene set in and his leg was subsequently amputated. Instead of crumbling as most of us would Derek was determined to stay in the game and indeed he did as a writer, a manager and a chairman. The comment he made when he first came out of hospital after losing his leg has stayed with me ever since I first read it as a boy. It's sad but it also epitomises the footballing sense of humour in the face of adversity. Derek said, 'They can stick me in the ground and use me as a corner flag just as long as I can stay in football.'

STAN THE MAN

When I first began to get noticed as a young boy at Manchester United I was often compared to Stanley Matthews. The media called us both the Wizard of the Dribble for a while. (I was called it again by some when my drinking took hold years later.) I never saw Stanley in his prime, although I did play against him at the end of his career. Like everyone though I was familiar with the newsreels of the so-called Stanley Matthews Cup Final in 1953 when the other Stanley (Mortensen) scored a hat-trick for Blackpool when the Seasiders beat Bolton Wanderers 4–3. This, together with other footage from England matches, was interspersed with Flash Gordon, Abbott and Costello and the cartoons we religiously watched at the cinema every Saturday morning. Stan Mortensen, probably justifiably, lamented years later that he must be the only player to score a hat-trick in the FA Cup Final only to see the game remembered and named after another player. He worried that when he died his burial would be called the Stanley Matthews Funeral.

Mortensen obviously possessed a good sense of humour. He used to tell the story about when he was playing in a match for Blackpool against Arsenal. He was running down the wing and a man in the crowd was roaring at him, 'Give it to Taylor. Give it to Taylor, for Christ's sake.'

He looked up and Taylor was well placed so he tapped it to him with the side of his foot. The defender scooted after Taylor and he passed the ball back to Stan. Stan held it close for a few seconds as he liked to do. The man in the crowd was in his ear again.

'Pass it to Matthews. Matthews!' he screamed. The other Stanley was screaming up on his inside and Mortensen released the ball to him. Matthews kept running and played a lovely ball down the line back to Mortensen. This time two Arsenal defenders were bang on him. Options were limited. Mortensen looked over and searched the crowd for the vocal spectator. This time he wasn't shouting but when Stan did alight on his face he said casually, 'Use your own discretion.'

Matthews was just packing up as I started, at the unbelievable age of fifty, but he was absolutely revered. Beckham is appreciated, Moore was respected, but Stanley was revered by those who played and by those who watched. It was like a member of the Royal Family was out there on the pitch. For the benefit of our younger readers the Royal Family were generally loved and treated like gods in those days. I don't think there has been a player since who I could describe in that way.

I heard the great man speak once and he told a nice story about when he guested for Arsenal in a match against Moscow Dynamo just after the Second World War ended. Although the match was a friendly, the Russians were not treating it as such and the crowd at a packed White Hart Lane (Highbury had been closed during the war) were shocked at some of the dirty play and time-wasting tactics on display. The Arsenal right half (Stan was too much of a gentleman to name him fifty years on) got particularly annoyed by the Dynamo goalkeeper, who insisted on holding and bouncing the ball for an inordinately long time to allow the minutes to tick away. His team were in front and he wanted to keep it that way. At the same time a fog was beginning to descend and this was making visibility poor.

The right half told his team-mates at half-time that he was going to hammer the goalie in the second half if he persisted in time-wasting. Despite the Arsenal captain, Bernard Joy (in my day a respected journalist), warning against any such action the player went out there and did just that, clattering the Russian to the ground within minutes of the kick-off. The referee had no hesitation in sending the Arsenal player straight off. Joy asked Stanley to drop back into the right half position as they were now down to ten men. Meanwhile the fog thickened. Some ten minutes later and with twenty minutes still remaining Stan heard someone behind him hiss, 'Get back on the wing, I'm back!' The errant right half had used the cover of the fog to creep back on to the field and complete the game. The referee never noticed.

Stan played in what must have been the most awesome forward line for England ever: Stanley Matthews; Wilf Mannion; Tommy Lawton; Stan Mortensen; Tom Finney. I was never lucky enough to see them play in their prime but I met with enough people that did: men whose opinions I respected and many of whom did not give praise easily. Each one of them was considered a genius. Sadly only Tom Finney survives. I read a poignant story about Wilf Mannion. It was after the 1973 dumping of England by underdogs Poland in the World Cup qualifiers and a group of workers at the ICI factory on Teeside were lamenting their national team's failure. Their tea-boy, who was in fact a man in late middle age and pushing retirement, hesitantly joined in the conversation.

'It can be daunting playing at Wembley,' he volunteered in defence of the defeated players.

'Oh really?' chuckled one of the young workers. 'And what would you know about it?'

'I played there a few times.'

One of the older chaps nudged the young worker and said that the 'tea-boy' was Wilf Mannion, the former Middlesbrough and England icon. There was no question that the young man would not know who Mannion was. In those parts he was (and is) still revered. It just defied logic that he would be performing such a menial job in such reduced circumstances.

Tommy Lawton suffered similar indignity in his post-playing life. He had problems finding work and along the way fell foul of courts, debt-collectors and bailiffs. Times became so hard that at one time he seriously contemplated suicide. Hughie Gallacher, a Scottish contemporary of Tommy's, did exactly that by walking on a crossing in front of a train when he was beset by personal problems when his career was over. Situations like these were sad to see and it is a stain on our national game that we have been unable to provide a safety net for our footballing idols who have fallen on hard times and were unlucky enough to play in the days of a maximum footballing wage.

BACK OF THE NET

Ferenc Puskas was the biggest overseas footballing name when I was a youngster. His Hungarian side had historically beaten England at Wembley by six goals to three, becoming the first international side to inflict defeat on England at Wembley Stadium. He scored a staggering eighty-three goals in eighty-four internationals and figured prominently in various European Cups for Real Madrid after he left humble Honved. He had an unlikely build for a forward being barrel-like to the point of being fat, but for a time nobody could deny that he was the best player in the world. I only knew of his reputation and witnessed his performances in grainy black and white newsreels so it was a great honour to meet him years later when Denis Law and myself were doing a spot of kids' coaching out in Australia.

I guess Puskas was in his early fifties by this time and the years hadn't been particularly kind. His pot belly was now even more pronounced. He was working on one pitch with a bunch of students and we were on an adjacent pitch with our group of boys. I noticed that our lads were nudging each other and giggling as they looked at this late middle-aged, portly fellow trotting among them in his kit. On first glances, I have to confess, Brian Glover, playing the schoolmaster dreaming he was Bobby Charlton in the film *Kes*, sprang to mind.

'That guy you're taking the piss out of was the greatest footballer in the world,' I rebuked them.

'Yeah, and I'm the Fonz,' drawled one of the bigger lads. I

asked Ferenc if he would join us for a few minutes and then encouraged him to take ten shots against the mouthy lad, who I told to stand in goal, from the eighteen-yard line. Ten times the 'old man' had the lad diving this way and that, and each time the ball thundered into the back of the net. He then proceeded to shoot and deliberately hit the bar successively and demonstrated his still magical ball-juggling skills. It really was a case of mouths hanging open. Including mine. The skill, ball control and precision were a pleasure to behold and I knew those boys then realised they were in the presence of greatness. I am sure none of them has ever forgotten it.

It was when Denis and I were out in Oz that we bumped into Frank Haffey. Frank who? I hear you ask. Frank Haffey was the Celtic goalkeeper who conceded nine goals against England when playing for Scotland in a home international tie at Wembley in April 1961. This was an absolute embarrassment for the Scottish team, and the Scottish race generally, losing like this to the auld enemy and the blame was put squarely on poor Haffey's broad shoulders. 'Slap Haffey', the press dubbed him. I know from Denis how much this drubbing hurt because he played in the game. Denis was the only man I knew personally who was willing England to lose against West Germany, three years later in the 1966 World Cup Final. Haffey didn't help his cause when he refused to let the defeat get him down and even wisecracked in the dressing room after the game. 'That's not the first time I've had one over the eight,' he is reputed to have said. The vitriol against him was such that, not so long afterwards, he emigrated to the other side of the world where nobody knew him.

It was nearly twenty years later when Denis and I met Haffey in the car park of a hotel in Sydney. He and Denis exchanged a bit of small talk until, as we were parting, Frank looked at Denis intently and said, 'Denis, tell me straight, is it safe for me to go home yet?'

'Not yet, Frank,' said Denis solemnly.

UNITED WE STOOD

Harry Gregg was a massive hero to all us football-loving kids in Belfast and to be cleaning his boots when I arrived at United in 1961 really was an honour. Only three years before he had been part of the Irish side that had battled to the last eight of the 1958 World Cup Finals and made our little country so proud. You have to be Irish to really appreciate what a massive achievement this was. He was a big man and the bravest goalkeeper I ever saw or played with and, believe me, in those days goalies were knocked around something terrible. But Harry had been through much more having not only survived the Munich air disaster but selflessly dragging some of his colleagues to safety from the burning aircraft and saving the lives of a pregnant lady and her child. Thinking about it, all these players I have talked about who impacted upon me as a boy were idols. Harry alone was the hero.

Harry went on to become a manager before eventually retiring to Ireland where he still keeps tabs on my dad, which is typical of his thoughtfulness. I nearly played for him once when he was in charge at Swansea but that was at the height of my unreliability. Sorry Harry. Alex Stepney was the keeper I played with the most during my golden years at Manchester United. He was a fine goalkeeper who unluckily for him played at a time when there was a feast of brilliant English goalkeepers (Gordon Banks, Peter Shilton and Peter Bonetti to name just three) who prevented him from enjoying a spell between the sticks for his country. I saw him make the most fantastic save ever in a match against Leeds United.

Peter Lorimer, their Scottish target man, who was feared for his cannonball shot up and down the country, let rip with a sizzling drive that nigh on smashed the crossbar. It came so fast and with such velocity that before I registered the shot it had rebounded back off the bar and back into his path for Lorimer to volley again, this time towards the left-hand corner of the net. Alex somehow managed to arch his body backwards and to tip the ball over the bar. As I ran to congratulate him I checked for fingers on his hand.

'Alex, that was brilliant. Absolutely brilliant.'

Alex didn't look at me as he was concentrating on Eddie Gray, preparing to take the corner, but from the side of his mouth he hissed, 'Piss off, Bestie, I was still going for the first shot.'

A few years later when I was depressed over Manchester United's decline in fortunes Alex made me feel even worse. Unusually for a goalie he took a couple of penalties in the second season of Tommy Docherty's tenure and scored them both. After twelve games he was still the club's joint leading marksman. What hope was there? Ian Storey-Moore was signed eight months earlier from Nottingham Forest amid great fanfare but he never reproduced the goal-scoring potential he had shown at the County Ground. To be fair he was dogged by injury; it was that bad he'd pull a hamstring if he appeared on *A Question of Sport,* and injury in the end would cut his career sadly short.

I love Nobby Stiles dearly. When I heard while doing this book that he was quite ill I was on the telephone immediately. It turned out to be one of those occasions when I was pleased that the press had exaggerated – he was okay. His reputation was that of a hard man, and he was, but he wasn't an executioner like some of them and his cry of 'I was going for the ball, ref' wasn't as cynical as it was with the others. For Nobby, as most people know, was almost blind – and his contact lenses on the field didn't improve things much either – most of the time he *really was* going for the ball. He wasn't called Inspector Clouseau for nothing. He had tried glasses but his poor eyesight must have contributed to his choice because he plumped on the biggest pair of spectacles I have ever seen. Only Deirdre Barlow of *Coronation Street* circa 1980 came close. His other nickname among the boys was Happy for obvious reasons.

After the historic European Cup final win in 1968 we had a celebratory dinner back in Manchester at a top hotel. The European Cup itself stood gleaming imperiously and bedecked with ribbons at the top of the dinner table. Nobby was sitting opposite me and at one point in the meal I registered that he had got up and gone off to the toilet. After about fifteen minutes I began to wonder why he had not returned to his seat so I went out to the lavatories to look for him. All the doors were open and there was no one washing their hands or standing around the area. I checked back in our dining room to see if he had returned meanwhile but his chair remained empty. I wondered if for some reason he had decided to go home. I couldn't imagine why but Nobby could be unpredictable. I went to the reception desk to see whether anyone had noticed him leaving the building. No one had. On the way back, thoroughly baffled, I noticed that the dining room next to ours had a sign up saying it was a Rotary Club dinner and the door was slightly ajar. Something made me peep in. There he was, Nobby, not only sitting among the Rotarians but eating someone else's dinner. The gentleman opposite him, looking somewhat puzzled, bore no resemblance to me either.

He is one of those men who are accident-prone and even if you dressed him in the best Savile Row gear he'd still look like someone on his first day of being released from Strangeways Prison. I remember one evening when we were playing away for United in a hotel in Hamburg and we were all getting ready to go out for a drink. We went to Nobby's room to collect him. He was walking around the room in his pants, the buttons on his shirt were done up out of synch and his face was peppered with small bits of paper where he had butchered himself shaving. At one point he pulled on a cord to lower the window blind and the whole thing fell off, then he couldn't find where he had put his trousers and so on. By the time he was ready we properly needed a drink.

At dinner, woe betide those who are sat next to Nobby. He cuts the meat and the gravy splashes over him (or worse still, over you), the top falls off the salt pot and he drinks from your glass. This was Nobby.

Maurice Setters was another so-called 'hard man' but he too was a good footballer and nobody's fool. He enjoyed further success when he teamed up managerially with Jackie Charlton and did wonders for the Irish national side long after his playing days were over. One day he and Denis Law had decided to go and see the boss about their wages. Maurice said to Denis they must stick together and be honest with each other over what they had negotiated. In those days there were two rates of pay – one for the season and one for the close season. Denis and Matt Busby finally struck a deal at £150 per week during the season and £95 off-season. Denis told Maurice before he went in to the office what he and the gaffer had agreed. Matt offered Maurice £125 during the season and £75 off.

'With all due respect, boss, I don't think that is fair,' Maurice reasoned. 'You have just agreed with Denis a much higher figure.'

Matt pondered a little but finally said rather bluntly, 'He's better than you, Maurice.'

Sharp as a razor Maurice retorted, 'Not in the close season he isn't, boss.'

That story reminds of a time when a chap – and I really do not remember his name – was trying to get me to play for his club in America. 'George, we'll pay you $20,000 this year and $30,000 next year,' he drawled.

'Okay, I'll sign next year then,' I replied.

I don't know if the following recollection says more about the negotiating skills of Matt Busby or Denis Law's lack of them. It happened before my arrival but I heard the boys tease Denis over it enough times. They were generally unhappy about their wages and, having just won an FA Cup, felt they should be entitled to a meaningful salary increase. This time they decided it would be more effective to negotiate as a team and Denis was nominated (knowing him he probably volunteered) to go and hammer out a deal with Matt. An hour later he left the boss's office smiling. The boys thought he must have got a result. Denis thought he had. Matt had wanted to reduce wages by a £1 a week but Denis had limited it to ten bob.

I still think of Shay Brennan every day although he has now been dead a couple of years. It was a real thrill for me when his wife Liz flew in for my recent *This Is Your Life* tribute. He was a wonderful, wonderful, kind and decent man and one of the funniest people I have known in or out of the game. He didn't always mean to be comical – he just was. I remember once sitting with him on a coach coming back from a game. He was engrossed in filling out a form for a credit card or a mortgage, if I remember rightly.

He said to me, 'It's asking me for *Company*. What do I put?'

'Put Manchester United, Shay,' I said. 'They employ you.'

He nodded and continued to fill out the form quietly and when he finished he handed it to me to check over. I collapsed into convulsive laughter when I read through it, for under *Position* he had written Full Back.

Another time years after we had retired from playing football we appeared on TV AM together to be interviewed by Anne Diamond. On driving to the studios we passed a road sign – BOROUGH OF LAMBETH – NUCLEAR-FREE ZONE – it announced almost triumphantly.

'Lucky bastards – I think I should live here, at least it's safe,' muttered Shay. He had a thing about road signs and reading them out. One time he pointed at one that said CAUTION – LOW-FLYING AIRCRAFT as we passed alongside some airbases in East Anglia.

'What are we meant to do – duck?' asked Shay.

And another that was funny the first time he said it to me (maybe not on the next twenty occasions) was when he saw a POLICE SLOW sign and commented, 'That goes without saying.'

That morning at TV AM Anne Diamond had the singer Julio Iglesias on a video link. What the tenuous connection was between him and us I'm not sure, although apparently he had been the reserve team goalkeeper at Real Madrid when he was a younger man. Julio mentioned the word *mañana* and Anne asked him to explain what it meant.

'In Spain the word *mañana* means the job will get done tomorrow, maybe the next day, maybe next month or even next year.'

Anne saw this an opportunity to bring Shay and me into the conversation. 'Do the Irish have an equivalent to the word *mañana*?'

It was early in the morning and my brain wasn't at its sharpest. Shay leant back on the settee trying to look as laid-back as Julio himself.

'In Ireland, Anne, we don't have a word that describes that degree of urgency.'

Paddy Crerand looked after me on the field at Old Trafford and off it. As soon as I became known defenders came looking for me and he started looking out for them. Paddy was my minder. And he was a fearsome prospect I can tell you. He had a temper on him that opponents and team-mates alike would think twice about stoking. He also spoke his mind and had no time for all the niceties and false politeness that underpins much social interaction. He was a great pundit after his playing career was over and was one of the first 'experts' to sit alongside Brian Moore and talk about the game. If I remember correctly Bob McNab, Derek Dougan and Malcolm Allison also sat on that first television 'panel'. How entertaining and refreshing they were compared to most of the TV pundits around today (and I include myself in that sweeping statement).

Brian Moore told me a great tale about that panel. It was during the 1970 World Cup and they were on live straight after *Police 5*; ITV's forerunner to *Crimewatch* presented by Shaw Taylor. The main felony that police wanted help with was the hijacking of a lorryload of fashionable flowery shirts. That makes you feel all warm and nostalgic, doesn't it? Thirty years ago we sat in our armchairs and shook our heads and tutted over appeals for help to nail Ben Sherman thieves when now it's accounts of Uzi-toting crack-cocaine addicts wreaking havoc across our cities. Shaw Taylor even had a mannequin model the shirts in the studio and walked around it pointing out their distinctive features – the button-down collar, the double-button sleeves and the discreet anchor motif on the pocket. Shaw ended the programme in customary style by looking straight into the camera and asking the public to come forward if they knew anything about the robbery or had been offered one of these shirts. The commercial break followed and then the TV cut straight to the World Cup studio in London where Bob McNab, always a dedicated follower of fashion, was introduced wearing a very loud shirt (for those with the new-fangled colour TVs), sporting a very familiar-looking anchor motif.

Back to Paddy. His abrasive personality made him murder to travel with. One time we were in Berlin, crossing from the West to the East at Checkpoint Charlie. We all had to disembark the coach and stand around in the pissing rain, in the dark, as heavily armed soldiers checked our passports. The passports were handed to the guards all together and they waved us through to board the coach on the other side of the gate, but as Paddy squeezed past they blocked his way and motioned him to stand to one side. Paddy had an Irish passport (even though he was a Scottish international) but so did some of the other lads so it wasn't clear what the guards didn't like about him. They fished his passport out from the bunch and looked him up and down and then did it again and again. We could see Paddy's cheeks reddening and started to worry a little. Then Paddy snatched the passport from the soldier's hand and shoved him, gun as well, to the ground, stepped over his prostrate body and boarded the coach. For some inexplicable reason the guard did not put Paddy up against the wall and shoot him.

It was on another of these cross-border trips with United that an Eastern European immigration official stepped on to our coach and worked through the bag of passports asking us to raise our hands as he called our names.

'Anthony Dunne ... Robert Charlton ...' His English was good but perhaps the writing in one of the passports was not too clear because the coach erupted when he looked up and asked next for 'Penis Law'.

Paddy was at it again years later when he and I were among a group of ex-players invited to attend a Liverpool versus Celtic exhibition match in Dubai. As we were leaving the country Paddy was stopped and the officials began to question him about his dreaded Irish passport. Paddy went nuts – shouting, swearing and throwing things around. Before we knew it he was surrounded by armed guards and was being led away. Denis Law and myself looked on in horror. As he was being frog-marched across the tarmac we could hear Paddy screaming for the sheik who had arranged our visit and had looked after us so well, but nobody was listening. We had to board the plane and our hearts sunk lower as we looked out of the window and saw them unloading Paddy's luggage from the hold beneath us. When we landed back in London I immediately phoned Paddy's wife, Noreen.

'Do you want the good news or the bad news?' I asked.

'You best give me the bad news,' said a worried Noreen and I then explained about Paddy's predicament. She wasn't too alarmed. I suspected that she must have had similar experiences with him.

'And what's the good news then?' she said resignedly.

'He's got you a really lovely chain from the souk.'

Paddy was not entirely blameless for the problems he encountered overseas. He had no patience for the amount of form-filling that was part and parcel of crossing borders. One time he was asked to leave the coach we were travelling on and when he came back an hour later, looking a bit sheepish rather than angry, it transpired that he had filled out the entry form that was tucked into his passport for review by the border guards like so: *Name*: James Bond; *Occupation*: Spy.

On one of these tours we played an exhibition match in Saudi Arabia. It was our first of the tour and we had been ferried from air-conditioned plane to air-conditioned car to air-conditioned hotel. Then from air-conditioned car again to the air-conditioned changing rooms of a large football stadium. Paddy decided to take a walk out on to the pitch still dressed in his suit. Out there it was 110 degrees and after a couple of minutes he re-entered the changing room breathless. The sweat was literally pouring off him and a puddle began to form around his feet. 'Turned out nice again,' he said.

Early in his career Paddy was introduced to the Duke of Edinburgh after a function. 'Your Highness, this is our wing half, Pat Crerand,' said Noel Cantwell.

'How you doing, Jimmy,' grinned Paddy. He then went on to engage the bemused Duke about when he was stationed in Derry during the war, claiming to have met some girls Prince Philip had taken out. Noel Cantwell, Bobby Charlton, Sir Matt and the rest stood there wincing and praying Paddy would shut up.

Albert Quixall was Matt Busby's first big signing for United after the Munich air disaster and in that period until I came along (when he moved on) he made a big impact at Old Trafford. He managed to score 56 goals in his 183 matches and helped the club take the FA Cup in 1963. By all accounts he was a joker and the players still recounted some of his japes long after he had left. One winter's night United were to play Tottenham Hotspur at White Hart Lane but at the last minute, and when the players were already on the pitch, the referee decided that the fog was too thick and abandoned the match. As both sides traipsed off some of the lads spotted Albert through the fog, standing with his legs apart and steam rising from the ground as he urinated on to the centre spot.

'What did you do that for?' asked David Herd when they were back in the changing rooms.

'Well, we don't often get a chance to piss all over Spurs,' replied a grinning Albert Quixall.

There was another Albert at the club when I joined and he too had a reputation as a character. Albert Scanlon was a local boy who had survived the Munich air disaster. Wherever United travelled in the world he'd like to sample the local delights and the thing I heard about him that really amused me was what he would do when the lads first arrived in a foreign city. He'd get hold of the local phone directory in the hotel and thumb through it until he found an English name. Then he'd ring the person and tell them who we were and would they like to come out for a drink with him and the United lads? Naturally these expatriates were normally up for it. They got to share a night with the United stars and Albert could tap straight into local knowledge of nightspots and other delights without wasting any time.

O nce I was in the public eye any other player who grew his hair over his ears or showed the slightest sign of keeping up with the fashions of the day was labelled the new George Best or the George Best of wherever. I can understand that this could be rather annoying for the players concerned but it wasn't me saying it. Willie Morgan, a winger making waves at Burnley and later to be signed by Manchester United, suffered this but I couldn't believe it when I came off the pitch at Turf Moor one afternoon and was accosted by a lady who, I was later told, was one of his relatives.

'Our Willie is a better player than you are and he had long hair before you, too,' she spat. I'm glad I didn't bump into his dad.

D enis Law is my great mate. We have probably become closer since our days at Old Trafford came to an end. Denis was only a few years older but he was well established by the time I arrived as a boy from Belfast and he was a married man. The guys in their mid and late twenties didn't really mix socially with the teenagers and the teenagers regarded the players in their thirties as from their father's gen-eration. Now, age differences are irrelevant. We're all old. Full stop. We are not in each other's pockets (no one gets in Denis's pockets, especially Denis) but I would say we are really great, great mates.

We sometimes meet up in Portugal when my wife Alex and I go out there and Denis is there with his family. One year he kept on at us to meet him at a restaurant he had 'discovered' in the Algarve. When we arrived we thought it was some kind of joke on us by Denis. The place was called the Chicken Shack and it was just that – a shack that sold chicken. But Denis was deadly serious and played the good host by telling us about the food and introducing us to the manager. I had chicken and chips, Alex had chicken and chips, Denis went for the chicken and chips and so did Di, Denis's wife. When the bill came, Denis waved it in front of my nose triumphantly. 'Look at that, where else on the Algarve can four people eat for that price? Includes wine, you know.'

I told Denis of a restaurant I used, one of my favourites in the world, called Gigi's nearby and arranged to meet him there the next night. Gigi's was a charming wooden restaurant on stilts with beautiful views out on to the Mediterranean. It could only be reached by a delicate walk over a picturesque little bridge, which was fine on the way in, but a little trickier on the way out. Inside the restaurant you could watch the fish swimming in a tank, select the one you like and the staff would weigh it and cook it for you there and then. Gigi himself is a lovely Brazilian man who, without being overpowering or fawning in any way, makes you feel warm and welcome. So we could watch the sunset – and also conscious of the fact of Denis's age and his need to get to bed reasonably early – I booked a table for four people early.

Denis was impressed but did point out that, besides us, the restaurant was empty save two men sitting together at a table on the other side of the room.

'It's normally packed,' I told him.

When the bill came, even though I was paying it, Denis

peered over my shoulder, shaking his head. 'Not cheap. Not cheap.'

'You pay for what you get, Denis.'

On the way out I stopped to chat to Gigi and thank him. I was curious about the lack of custom. 'Not many in tonight, Gigi?'

Gigi smiled. 'We don't open in the evenings, Mr Best,' and then he explained that they were a daytime business only, but when I had rung and asked for an evening booking, saying I was bringing Denis Law, he didn't want to let me down.

'Don't be silly, Gigi, you mustn't do that on my behalf.' Then I looked over at the table where the two men were still finishing their wine. 'Did they see the lights on and just come in?'

'Oh no, that is my brother and his friend. I told him that George Best and Denis Law were eating in my restaurant tonight and they just wanted to sit in. I hope you don't mind.'

Denis was at my wedding to Alex in 1995. We were wed in Chelsea Registry Office and we had the reception in a hotel that seemed as if it were built between two runways of Heathrow Airport. It was a great party but the roaring thunder of the comings and goings of jumbo jets punctuated all conversations and speeches. Denis delivered a lovely vote of confidence that afternoon by getting me in a corner on my own and saying, 'I give it six months, Bestie. I'll have £100 with you that it will all be over inside six months.'

I was not at all offended by this and never being able to resist a bet we shook on it. After six months I called Denis.

'You owe me one hundred quid,' I said.

'Double or quits?' suggested Denis. And we have carried on double or quitting every six months since. By my calculations he owes me around £800,000 now.

Much has been made about me and Bobby Charlton not getting along and I suppose for a time we did not. But in the context of the forty years we have known one another there was only a period of a couple of years when we didn't see eye to eye. This was when I was going on the missing list, drinking and not turning up for training. Bobby felt I was letting Manchester United down and I was. Childishly, I probably had the hump with him having the hump with me. I'm sure neither of us holds those views now and with the passage of time it doesn't really matter. Like with Denis, Bobby was older, married with a family and we were never going to be in the same clique. Yet he was not the sourpuss he was sometimes presented as. I do not believe, as the old story goes, that when he wakes up he looks in the mirror, smiles and says, 'Good, that's that out of the way for the day.' He had – still has – a sharp sense of humour and he got on well with everyone. He was always very well respected. We all called him Sir Bobby. And that was before he was knighted.

He and Denis both got fed up with my unwillingness to pass to them. This was nothing personal against them; it was just my game at the beginning. The sheer exhilaration of taking on and beating players was too strong for me; however, as I got older I learnt to release the ball if others were better positioned than me or unmarked. It hurt though. One time in a match against Southampton I collected the ball at the halfway line and beat one player, then another, then another. I was in their penalty area before I knew it and Bobby was close up next to me in plenty of space and Denis wide of him. Both were free, I had one man left to beat.

'*Pass! Pass!*' they screamed. I could hear more from Bobby though as he was nearest. He was angry and standing unmarked, hands on hips, yelling, '*George, for Christ's sake, pass it here you gre……………..at goal, George.*'

The following anecdote is not really comparable but it does say something about the kind of players Rodney Marsh and myself were. Rodney had beaten two or three defenders in a Queens Park Rangers match and was left with just one defender to beat and then the goalkeeper. However, John O'Rourke, a big centre forward, who could score goals, was loose and completely unmarked and hollering for the ball. Marsh ignored him and took the defender on, only to be beaten and the chance was lost. At half-time in the dressing room the recriminations flew like a projectile football boot from the shoe of Alex Ferguson.

'Why didn't you pass to John?' demanded Terry Venables, the captain, although inside he knew the answer.

'Because,' replied Rodney, 'I think I had a better chance of scoring with one defender to beat than John does with none.' It was this sort of self-confidence that didn't always endear Rodney to his fellow professionals.

Gordon Jago became Rangers' manager shortly after this incident and Rodney was unimpressed by his first address to his new players. He thought that Jago took himself a bit too seriously and his pleas for commitment and trust were a bit over the top. Rodney decided to puncture the moment with humour. He put his hand up and said, 'Mr Jago, I'd just like to say on behalf of the lads, we're forty per cent behind you.'

A few weeks later Rodney Marsh was transferred to Manchester City.

AIR RAGE

Ironically one of my best mates in the game during my playing days was not only not a Manchester United player but a player for our arch-rivals Manchester City. Mike Summerbee and I embraced the 1960s together and all it had to offer and went into business for better or for worse. He was and still is a real character. His son Nicky has also recently enjoyed a successful footballing career. Mike's father was also a professional footballer making the Sumerbees a true footballing dynasty. One of my favourite stories about Mike is one he does not often tell himself.

City were flying home from a European Cup Winners Cup tie in 1970 and Ken Mulhearn the goalkeeper was ferreting around furiously in his bag and in his pockets. He seemed to be panicking a bit. He said he was looking for something he had just bought in the duty-free shop before the plane had taken off.

'Who's pinched my perfume?' said an exasperated Ken, looking around the plane accusingly. Mike laughed, not at Ken but at something Alan Oakes, who was sitting next to him, had said.

'Have you had it, Mike?' said Ken looking daggers at his team-mate. The atmosphere changed, the chattering stopped and all eyes were on the two men.

'Are you calling me a thief?' said Mike, unclipping his seat belt and standing up.

'Yes I am.' Ken was now on his feet too.

Mike Summerbee thrust out his chest and chin, pointed at Ken and shouted, 'Right. Me and you. Outside. Now!'

JIM FIXED IT

Jimmy Greaves was undoubtedly the greatest goalscorer among my contemporaries at least and possibly the greatest ever in the domestic game. His goals per game ratio is unlikely ever to be equalled. He enjoyed a long and fruitful career with Chelsea, AC Milan, Tottenham Hotspur, West Ham United and England. Goalkeepers feared him more than anyone else because of his goal-poaching abilities. People think that Peter Bonetti, the Chelsea and England keeper, was nicknamed The Cat because of his acrobatic diving and jumping skills but it was not that at all. He was called The Cat because whenever he saw Jimmy Greaves in the penalty area he had kittens.

The low point of Jimmy's career came when he lost his England place in the 1966 World Cup tournament through injury and therefore missed the historic and victorious final.

Although Jim and I knew each other, being at opposite ends of the country, we were not special buddies and I had no idea that his social drinking (like mine) had become a problem after this disappointment, although Jimmy doesn't necessarily link the two. Jim was the first English star player to admit to being alcoholic and published a ground-breaking book called *This One's On Me*, charting his decline from the heights of the game to a hopeless drunk. He finished playing prematurely, his finances faltered and his marriage collapsed. However, Jim picked himself up, dried out, stayed dry and rebuilt his family. His bubbly, down-to-earth personality provided him with a second career as a television personality and he endeared himself to a whole new generation. The *Saint and Greavsie* show injected a welcome dose of humour into the Saturday morning football preview slot and he went on to become the resident TV critic on breakfast television.

Greavsie and I have worked together on the after-dinner circuit and in the theatres before, but as I write we have just started a tour, my first since I became too ill a couple of years before my transplant. I couldn't have had a better friend and colleague to ease me back into it. On our first night down in Bournemouth he opened the show.

'It's great to have George back,' he said. 'I can tell you he's a changed man. He's turned up for a start.'

NEW KID IN TOWN

Ian Hutchinson sadly died in September 2002. He spent most of his career with Chelsea where he became famous for his amazing long throw. He really could throw the ball from the halfway line into the goal – it was a wonder to see. He was also a fearless player who wouldn't shirk from any tackle and unfortunately paid a high price for such courage, spending much of his career on the treatment table and eventually having to retire in his late twenties. He was a big, easy-going lad who formed part of that hard-drinking Chelsea side of the 1970s. When Manchester United played in London I rarely went back with the United lads, preferring to go out on the town in London on the Saturday night and sometimes bumped into Huddy, Ossie, Charlie Cooke, Tommy Baldwin, Hutch and the crew. It was never a dull moment with that mob, I can tell you. But Hutch was not always so worldly-wise and his account of his introduction to Chelsea I think sums up the innocence of many young footballers when they hit the big time in those days.

Hutch originally came from Derby but at the time Chelsea discovered him he was playing non-League football for rural Cambridge. When Dave Sexton, Chelsea's then manager, invited him down to Stamford Bridge to see the set-up before signing him, Ian was totally overawed. He was a country boy and hadn't been to London before and as he looked around the stadium at Stamford Bridge his mouth hung open. The assistant manager Ron Suart was doing the honours and he took Ian out to the training ground at Mitcham before taking him on to somewhere else in Surrey where the Chelsea players were staging a cricket match for charity. Ron introduced him to the players and before he knew it he was playing cricket with the likes of Peter Bonetti, Peter Osgood and John Hollins. Ian said the whole day was like a dream; meeting and mixing with the superstars he had so far only seen on TV and in football magazines. Ossie was even calling him Hutch before the afternoon was out. When he heard Charlie Cooke talk about having a cortisone injection Hutch thought he was talking about a high performance car he owned. Ron Suart had to leave but before he went he gave Hutch a ten-pound note and told him to get a cab back into London when it was time to go home. He saw the afternoon out and when the minicab arrived his head was still spinning.

'Where to mate?' asked the driver.

'London, please.'

'Anywhere particular in London,' said the cabbie with more than a hint of sarcasm in his voice.

'To the station,' replied Hutch.

'Yes, mate, but which station is that?' The cab driver was becoming impatient now.

Hutch had to think about that one for a minute. The driver must want to know if I mean the bus station or the railway station, thought Hutch.

'The railway station ...'

'Are you taking the piss out of me?' growled the driver.

CAN DO BETTER

There are many examples down the decades of players who promised much but fizzled out for no apparent reason. Or players who had undoubted class but then hit a patch of bad form that they never re-emerged from. Sometimes it happened when they had moved to a club with a big transfer price on their heads. Steve Daley moving from Wolverhampton Wanderers to Manchester City in September 1979 is an example that springs to mind. Steve had shown great promise at Wolves when Malcolm Allison snapped him up for a then record fee but subsequently failed to shine. It can be a vicious circle. The crowd has high expectations that make the player nervous in his new surroundings. The nerves cause him to have a bad debut. The crowd gets on his case. The nerves get worse. And so on. I wonder if it was the example of Steve Daley that could have played a part in making Steve Bull stick faithfully with Wolverhampton Wanderers for the rest of his career despite there being numerous opportunities to join the bigger clubs?

There was another example of this at Manchester United during my time. As the old team was breaking up, Wilf McGuinness had taken on the mantle of manager from Sir Matt Busby. It was a difficult time, as every United fan will tell you.

Poor Wilf. He was on a loser when he took over at Old Trafford whichever way you looked at it. He was United through and through but when he was given the hottest managerial post in the English game he had no real managerial experience. He inherited an ageing side. He had to deal with a certain wayward Irishman and suddenly he was elevated from former colleague of half the first team to boss. Not everyone could or would take him seriously because of that. Results didn't improve and the worst thing that could have happened to the man happened.

When our form continued to falter, Sir Matt called him upstairs and sat him down. 'Wilf, you've been with us for nearly twenty years now, man and boy. I really don't know how we would get by without you ... But we're going to give it a try.'

The trauma devastated Wilf and he lost all his hair almost overnight and we all felt very sorry for him. Some of us, I'm sure, felt a bit guilty too. I see Wilf now, at functions, reunions and on the after-dinner circuit. The years have passed and he seems at ease with himself and laughs a lot.

'Does it still hurt?' I probed when I saw him recently.

'Definitely not,' he replied firmly. 'Thirty years have gone by, George. Thirty years, eight months, one day, six hours and seventeen minutes!'

Frank O'Farrell was the poor bastard who succeeded Wilf as manager. Frank had had mixed success as manager of Leicester City, taking them to an FA Cup Final in 1969 but also getting relegated from the First Division in the same season. Frank signed a lad called Ted MacDougall who had been banging the goals in by the hatful with Third Division Bournemouth. In one game down there against Margate he had managed an incredible nine goals. There was great excitement when Ted came to Old Trafford and it was generally assumed that his goal-scoring talent would transfer from the Third to the First effortlessly. Unfortunately this was not the case. Ted struggled a bit and was not finding the net in anything like the way he had with Bournemouth. The crowd was merciless in their barracking of him and this just made matters worse. The spiral continued. Ted lost confidence and sometimes could appear clumsy and awkward. Eventually some of his playing colleagues and some of the management were beginning to doubt his ability. In one game Ted jumped up to a ball and there was a clash of heads with the defender marking him. The smack could be heard around the ground and both men collapsed to the floor. I ran over to see how he was but it was clear that he had been knocked out temporarily and was not with it.

I shouted over to the bench, 'He's concussed, he doesn't know who he is.'

Dave Sadler, our sub that day, put his hand to the side of his mouth and shouted back, 'Tell him he's fucking Pele!'

I'm not sure he was particularly well suited for the job. I am sure he could have been a good team manager but I wonder if he might have lacked the extra resilience in the face of the unprecedented media scrutiny that that particular post demanded. Not many men did. Frank was a quiet, dignified man and when the heat was on he just retreated into himself and became more and more introspective. His old playing pal at West Ham United, Malcolm Allison, could see what was happening to him. Big Mal invited Frank to meet him for lunch at a Manchester restaurant he frequented. Mal says that Frank turned up in dark glasses looking extremely furtive and nervous. This was very un-Frank.

'You didn't tell me it was going to be busy,' hissed Frank as he glanced at around the tables of diners.

'It's a restaurant. It's lunchtime. They get busy Frank. Funny that.'

But Frank wasn't laughing. A few weeks later, he too had lost his job.

WHEN THE GOING GETS TOUGH, THE TOUGH GET GOING

Hard men. Every team had one in my day. Players whose function it was to stop good, creative and dangerous players. They
were as key as the goalkeeper and the goal-scorers. It became a
vicious circle really; Liverpool had Tommy Smith so Leeds
unleashed Norman Hunter. Spurs had Dave Mackay so Arsenal
developed Peter Storey and so on. Smith and Hunter were
among the two most famous of their era. Tom was like a Scud
missile – you could see him coming but there was nothing you
could do about it. He was probably the most famous of them all.
But he was a good bloke and he bore no malice. I would say
most of us forwards respected him. He just looked worse than
he was. He had a face like a careless beekeeper and loved to
wind you up. For example, he'd shout out to his goalkeeper Ray
Clemence, for my benefit obviously, 'If Bestie gets through, Ray,
chip him back to me will you?'

I never allowed myself to become intimidated or scared by
all this bluster. Indeed one time I gave Tommy a real mouthful.
'Tom, you're pathetic. You're a complete wanker to be honest.
You don't scare me. You can't get me. I just laugh at you.' He
didn't reply. He didn't get a chance. I put the phone down
straight away.

Norman earned the nickname 'Norman Bite Yer Legs
Hunter' although he never bit my legs or any other part of my

body; normally I was too quick for most of them and delighted in making them look stupid when I could. Leeds United, though, were a worry because unlike other teams more than half of their side were happy to kick lumps out of you. Besides Hunter, there was Billy Bremner, a decent man, but he would spend the whole match snapping away at your ankles like a bad-tempered terrier. I was grateful once when a referee saw how he was kicking lumps out of me off the ball and called Billy over.

'That tackle was late,' warned the ref.

'I got there as quickly as I could,' countered Bremner.

Jack Charlton was big and wasn't averse to dishing out a crafty clump when the ref wasn't looking. Paul Reaney and Terry Cooper, the full backs, both had skill but could put out big time. Then there was was Johnny Giles – he could be a tough customer who went in hard. Yet somehow he didn't seem to acquire that kind of reputation with the fans and was generally regarded as a creative player who commanded great respect among the journalistic fraternity.

JOHNNY COME LATELY

Johnny Giles of course had played for Manchester United before Leeds and had argued with Matt Busby when he was dropped from the first team and basically his career at Old Trafford was over. Although he had great success at Elland Road, he missed out on a European Cup. He missed out on being a part of one of the most loved teams of the century. He wrote once that he was disappointed with me as a professional footballer. He was particularly upset that Wilf McGuinness had captured me on the morning of a game in the hotel room of a lady. Why? Wilf may have had the right to be upset, but I'm not sure, even now, I can see the harm in having sex before a game.

Does sex really deplete your energy levels? Can it really negatively influence an athletic performance hours later? I don't think so. When you make love to your wife or girlfriend when you are a young man, are you really exhausted hours afterwards? Maybe I was unusual but I always fancied going again after about half an hour. Maybe at Leeds United it was different. Maybe having sex on a Friday night did exhaust some of those young, free and single Leeds boys although I suspect it wasn't the sex but the staying up on a Friday night looking for it that wore them out. Whatever, only for Leeds United did I wear shin pads. I knew I could avoid one, maybe two, hard players but not six or seven!

Sir Matt Busby, who it must be remembered was a patriotic Scot, ran through that Leeds team in a pep talk before one match against them. 'Gary Sprake, the keeper … on his day quite a piece of work. Couldn't catch a cold. Useless in the air. Worse on the ground. Right back, Paul Reaney … dirty. No skill. Left back, Terry Cooper … even dirtier. Likes going forward. Let him. John Giles …No better. Hates us. Centre half, Jackie Charlton … dirty big lump. Clumsy. Norman Hunter. No self-control. Play with him George. Watch him get himself sent off. Wee Billy Bremner,' his tone softened, 'good Scottish boy.'

Mind you, one thing about Giles is that for a little man you could not say he didn't have bottle. It's one thing for the big lads to throw their weight around, it is another for the little guys and Giles was scared of nobody. The lads told me how when he was with United he had fallen into an argument with our own gentle giant Bill Foulkes and had jumped up and clumped him. Bill looked down and said, 'Do that again, Johnny, and you are in serious trouble.'

Normal people would count their lucky stars they had got away with that but Johnny, by all accounts, jumped up and thumped him again.

In my debut match for Manchester United in September 1963 we were pitched against West Bromwich Albion and their resident hard man was a Welsh left back named Graham Williams. He was more of a tenacious tackler than a hard man really but nevertheless he was their steel at the back. I ran him ragged in that game and in many others after. Years later he caught up with me at a charity function. He came over and tapped me on the shoulder.

'Hello, George.'

Then he just stood there and stared at me with a strange grin on his face.

'Something wrong, Graham?' I asked.

'No, George, I just wanted to see what you look like from the front. I only ever saw you from behind on the pitch.'

My Northern Ireland debut came soon after my United debut and Derek Dougan, our big centre forward, gave me a bit of an education about the hard men. He had no respect for them at all and aware of my extreme youth he was trying to bolster my confidence against these fearsome-looking men and their reputations.

'They can't play football,' he said, 'they're jealous. They want to hurt us because we can do what we do and they can't. You'll beat them every time, George, I promise you. You know why they all have nicknames like Nobby and Chopper? Because they're pricks, that's why.'

CHOPPER –
THE AXE MAN

The master of cracking shins and taking your legs from beneath you was neither Tom nor Norman but the aforementioned Ronnie 'Chopper' Harris of Chelsea. Chopper held no ambitions to be appreciated as a class player or admired for his footballing skills, he was happy to be known for his hard-man qualities and revelled in his own notoriety. As a boy he became infamous for kicking lumps out of a fifty-year-old Stanley Matthews at the end of his illustrious career, an act that was as controversial at the time as it would have been to talk through Elton John singing 'Candle in the Wind' at Princess Diana's funeral. When even his fellow players bollocked him for his treatment of Sir Stanley, Chopper was dismissive: 'Oh he's all right.'

'No, Ron, he's not. He was rolling about there holding his leg.'

'That wasn't me,' protested Ron, 'that's his arthritis.'

I had many run-ins with Mr Harris and must say that of all the defenders I played against he was the only one who followed me home after the game. He was not the best by any means. He just worried me. I heard him on the radio recently talking about the incident where Lee Bowyer stamped on an opponent's head and he said 'it turned his stomach'. I hadn't seen the incident at that point but if it turned Chopper's guts I knew it had to be very, very bad.

In one clash at Stamford Bridge he nearly got me. I had

goaded him – calling him on like a bullfighter – and nutmegged him more than once. As we had walked out on to the pitch he had said something like, 'I'm going to do you, Bestie.' The intention was to psych you out, scare you, but with me it had the opposite effect and when they said these things I just became more determined to make them look stupid. It was getting towards the end of the game and we were drawing and Chopper hadn't got me once. I felt like rubbing it in and as he had the ball at his feet and looked up to see who to distribute it to, I slid in and took his legs from beneath him. He went over and fell awkwardly and I could tell by his face that I had really hurt him. I knew it was serious when he called me something beginning with C and ending in T. Footballers did not routinely call each other clot in those days. Straight away I knew I shouldn't have done it and was dreading playing out the final ten minutes. A way out, it seemed, was coming via the referee charging over to me blowing his whistle. Then there were no cards and the refs moved the players a few yards away from the incident while dispensing justice. I did not protest my innocence. I was feeling drawn to the safety of the dressing rooms. But, then, out of the corner of my eye I saw Chopper limping over with a malevolent smile and saying the words I didn't want to hear: 'Don't send him off, ref. It was an accident.'

They all had good, bluff, hard man names: Norman, Tommy, Ron, Nobby, Mick, and Wilf, etc. Never did I think we'd end up, a couple of decades later, with a hard case by the name of Vinny Jones. In the 1960s and 1970s anyone with a name like that would more likely have been a gay hairdresser from the Valleys than the most feared defender in the English Football League. Like Chopper, Vinnie loved his reputation but unlike Chopper he started to believe his own publicity to the point he took to biting the noses of inquisitive journalists. He firmly registered himself in the public eye when he was famously photographed clasping Paul Gascoigne's testicles while waiting for a free kick to be taken during a match. Again, in my day, an action like that would have convinced the watching public he was that gay Welsh hairdresser rather than a burgeoning hard man of the game. More worrying though was Gazza's appreciative smile while being handled in this way.

People often ask me how the Vinnie Joneses or Roy Keanes or any other of the hard men of recent times would fare against the characters talked about above. It is a natural reaction to say they would not have stood a chance, but really who knows? We are all guilty of looking back at our own eras, whether it be in sport, music, films or quality of life generally, through rose-coloured spectacles. I think Nat Lofthouse, the great Bolton Wanderers and England centre forward from the 1950s, got quite close to summing up the changing times when he said, 'In my day you could get your bollocks kicked off. The difference was that then the defender who did it would walk around the pitch with you afterwards and help you find them.'

THE CULT OF
THE COACH

When I started out the only coaches I came across were the bat-
tered old vehicles that took players and supporters to and from
away matches. They had no videos to watch then, and outside
toilets. Outside being the side of whatever road we were travelling on. Then we had managers and trainers; at Manchester
United it was Matt Busby and Jimmy Murphy, at Leeds it was
Don Revie and Les Cocker, at Liverpool Bill Shankly and Bob
Paisley and so on. The cult of the coach didn't really take hold
until the 1970s. Before we knew it coaching had become an
industry in its own right and eventually, in my opinion, it did
its very best to stifle the flair, spontaneity and talent that underpins the game as an entertainment sport. Training is vital but
coaching is dangerous in the wrong hands. Of course it can
only be to the good to help players build on their strengths and
limit or eradicate their weaknesses, but to instil systems, tactics
and styles of play that don't come naturally was and is very
damaging. It is no coincidence, in my mind, that the greatest
promoters of the cult of the coach are those people who have
never been professional footballers or if they had been were
notable by the fact that no one could remember them as players. Coaching schools and badges sprung up all over the place
and the game became overrun with what I saw as clueless silly
ideas. Charlie Hughes was at one time 'officially' responsible
for the development of the game in this country. I knew we

were doomed when he announced that Brazil, winners of World Cups and exponents of exciting football, had it all wrong.

I coached myself. When it was pointed out to me that I was better with my right foot than my left I worked on it until I was just as good with both feet. I did this when I was about ten years old. I am amazed that for all the coaching we do have now, even some of our top players are mainly one-footed. You see time and time again in matches where our leading household names take all sorts of risks so they can play the ball with their preferred peg. Sometimes, when they can't, the most horrendous mistakes ensue. So, if the coaches can't even get the boys to play with both feet, what *are* they doing?

COWBOYS

Malcolm Macdonald says it really hit him when he was at Newcastle United when the old-school manager Joe Harvey was considered past his sell-by date and replaced by the young flavour of the moment Gordon Lee. Supermac was happy to give the new man the benefit of the doubt, but his heart sank when in pre-season training he split the players into two teams and then instructed them to hop one-legged towards the goal. Left hand on hip and holding the ball above their head with their right. They then had to throw the ball against the bar and hop back again. Lee went berserk when Malcolm burst out laughing at the stupidity of it all.

Later when Gordon Lee was manager at Everton he rang the Northern Ireland team manager Billy Bingham to recommend his player Eamonn O'Keefe for the international side. Billy seemingly had already looked into the lad.

'He's not Irish. He was born and bred in Manchester.'

'What business has anyone got naming someone Eamonn O'Keefe if they're not Irish,' said Lee.

'The same business someone had naming you Lee when you're not Chinese,' laughed Billy.

The Gordon Lee balls on head story reminds me of an episode that Rodney Marsh told me about. Vic Buckingham was years ahead of his time as a manager. He won the FA Cup with West Bromwich Albion and then unusually for the time went abroad to manage Ajax and with them he won the Dutch title. In those days Englishmen only went abroad to invade countries or sunbathe. Vic came back to England to manage Sheffield Wednesday and then Fulham and the players were dumbfounded that he spoke to them in some peculiar half-English, half-Dutch accent. It was like he needed to remind everyone he had worked abroad. He told the squad they needed to be lighter on their feet and he proceeded to tap dance before them and encouraged them to do the same.

Maurice Setters, later a colleague of mine at Manchester United, would not take Vic seriously and made his life a misery when Vic was manager at West Bromwich Albion. It started when the team gathered at the beginning of the season for the traditional and mandatory crossed arm, wide angle, team photo. When the picture was released in the press Vic was raging because up in the back row Maurice had turned round so only the back of his head was visible. When questioned about this it emerged that Maurice was upset with the club photographer because he had charged him for some private snaps. Then on a boat trip to Canada in a pre-season tour, Vic insisted the team did light ball practice on the boat too early in the morning for Maurice's liking. Accidentally on purpose, by the second day, Maurice had smashed every ball that had been brought along for the trip into the ocean.

Alan Ball found it hard to take Terry Neill seriously when Terry was his manager at Arsenal. It was never going to be easy for Terry managing players who not so long before he was playing with or against. All young managers must come up against .

this when they have to deal with the senior pros but Terry did himself no favours when he gathered the players around for a team-talk. From a bag he took a handful of plastic toy cowboys and positioned them on the table.

'This is the other team,' he said and then he dipped his hand back into the bag and pulled out a bunch of plastic Red Indians brandishing tomahawks and bows and arrows and threw them on to the table knocking over most of the cowboys.

'And that is us and that is what we're going to do to them.'

The players didn't know whether Terry was trying to be funny or profound or really thought this was clever, but according to Alan with some of them it just confirmed their worst fears.

Another Alan, Hudson, had similar misgivings about Terry Neill as a manager. He told his Arsenal side they should be ashamed of themselves after their poor performance in the 1978 FA Cup Final, when they lost 1–0 to unfancied Ipswich Town. Hudson spoke for many of them when he retorted, 'We played badly, but there is only one man in this room who needs to be ashamed of himself and that's you.' Needless to say, soon after Alan found himself playing football in Seattle and his team-mates soldiered on.

Even I fell for it for a while. My son Calum was showing some talent as a footballer so I sent him to the Bobby Charlton School of Excellence. The only thing he came back with was wispy hair. Maybe some of the poise and balance they taught him there has helped him in his career as a male model. My advice is that if you come across a boy with natural talent keep him as far away as possible from these people and these schools as they will surely blunt everything he has and fill his head up with shit. Tell him to get down the park and keep playing, playing and playing and he will learn, learn and learn. There is no better way.

FITNESS FIRST

John Robertson at Nottingham Forest was a player whose training attitudes shocked even Brian Clough and Peter Taylor, who thought as players and managers they had seen everything. Robertson's biggest effort in training extended to standing on his right leg and then switching to put all his weight on to his left leg. He was overweight, drank too much, ate the wrong food and smoked. And that was just during training. He would hold the cigarette inward in his fist with the tip almost touching his palm in the way schoolboys do to avoid detection. I guess Cloughie and Taylor changed his habits but I doubt he altered completely. It didn't matter; Robertson went on to help Forest to win two European Cups.

Robertson was taking a risk by not giving his all in training under Brian Clough. He was famously dissatisfied with his player Nigel Jemson once after a reserve team match.

'Have you ever been punched in the stomach?' asked Clough.

'No,' mumbled Jemson.

'Well, you have now,' and the manager delivered a solid blow to the young man's solar plexus making him double up, winded.

When I first heard that story I didn't believe it, but some time after when I saw Cloughie on the pitch at the County Ground clumping boys who had ran on to the park, I realised it was probably true. I've seen some angry and aggressive managers in my time but I cannot imagine any of them behaving like that and getting away with it. Mind you, Cloughie also punched

Roy Keane in the face after a perceived poor performance and got away with it.

Some of the things he did were quite mad. Stuart Pearce tells of a time when Nottingham Forest were playing Millwall and the team coach was crawling up the Old Kent Road to Millwall's then Cold Blow Lane ground. At the time Millwall's following had a significant hooligan element and fans and players alike, whether they admitted it or not, approached this fixture with some trepidation. Everything about the place was intimidating, even the ground's name – The Den – and the name of the road – Cold Blow Lane. The fans were very close to the pitch and abuse and threats of violence dished out there were somehow too real for comfort. I remember, in my time, Norman Burtenshaw, a gentleman referee, was felled by a sharp object. Brian Clough was not a man to be intimidated by this and as the coach edged forward he ordered the players to get off and follow behind him in single file to walk the final mile to the stadium. Clough was at the front swinging his stick like a country gent as he cut a path through the Millwall hordes. The players followed obediently behind praying for a safe journey.

The cruellest thing I heard about him doing was more psychological than physical and concerned a player called David Currie. Brian had signed him from Barnsley and within a month had obviously decided that he had made a mistake. One afternoon in the changing rooms at an away ground Clough addressed Currie in front of his team-mates.

'Hey son, have you got yourself a house yet?'

'No, boss, not yet,' replied the player cheerfully.

'Well, don't bother.'

Currie was gone within weeks.

In another dressing room incident Forest were playing at Watford. After the game the players and managers were relaxing in the bath when Elton John, then Chairman and benefactor at Vicarage Road, popped in to say hello. Clough hadn't seen Elton arrive and one of his staff called over, 'Brian, Elton John wants to see you.'

'What does the fat poof want?' he returned.

I loved training. I really did. Strange really when at the end of my Manchester United career it was for not turning up for training that I became notorious for. But, as I have said before, it was not the training I could not face, it was a club that I despaired for that was the root of the problem. For much of my time at Old Trafford I always finished first in the cross-country run or second to my partner-in-crime, John Fitzpatrick. We had a long run plotted out that finished in the descent of the famous Cliff training ground. Nearby was a small stream, and some of the boys would duck out of the run and hang around there until John, myself and the others came into view. Then they would splash themselves with water from the stream to simulate sweat and fall in behind us. None of these boys, as far as I remember, ever made it big at the club. One of the boys around at that time was Eamonn Dunphy and although he never hit the big time at United he did enjoy a good career at Millwall and played for his country. However, I expect he has earned far more from journalism and co-writing such books as Roy Keane's autobiography than he did from playing, so perhaps he knew something we didn't.

Although I was ultra-competitive in training I could not see any validity in getting injured or anyone else on our side getting injured, but not everyone saw it that way. Chopper Harris (who else?) took exception to something Keith Weller, his team-mate, said during a training session and put him out of action for a month. Chelsea manager Dave Sexton was furious having just paid £100,000 for the striker. John Hartson, now going great guns at Celtic, once tried to organise the five-a-side when he was training with his club Luton.

'Right, Wales v The Rest,' he challenged.

'But you're the only Welshman here,' someone pointed out.

'Yeah, me against you fucking lot,' foamed Hartson and apparently he meant it.

In the 1970s there was a TV programme called *Superstars*, in which personalities from all sports would pit themselves against each other over a range of events. I never did it in the 70s, but took part in the past masters *Superstars* in 1983 when I had an excuse for being unfit. In the original series Kevin Keegan, I remember, performed well but occasionally it did show up the fitness, or lack of it, of some of football's other star names. Stan Bowles was the most memorable. Stanley was notorious for burning the candle at both ends and in the middle. Gambling, drinking and women were his vices and why he ever agreed to do *Superstars* we will never know. It was clear from the start that he was under the weather when he capsized his canoe in one event because you could see he couldn't be bothered to keep up. He couldn't run, couldn't lift and in a shooting event the gun kept firing even after he had put it down. Stan walked around the whole circuit with a bemused smile on his face. David Hemery, the Olympic runner, won the competition, which was no shame, but Stan was even beaten by James Hunt whose particular form of athleticism entailed sitting for hours in a racing car. To add to the insult it was with James Hunt that Stan had been pissing it up with the previous night.

I saw Stan on TV recently and noted that among the footballing high-living fraternity from the 1970s being featured he seemed to have worn the best. He was still chirpy, with no sense of regret about how his career or life have turned out and made no attempts to blame anyone else as some do. He told the interviewer he had his drinking under control.

'I know these days when to stop,' he said, '... when I've had enough.'

His most famous quote though is his declaration that 'I have spent hundreds of thousands on birds and booze. I thank God I didn't waste it.' The thing is, Stan really means it.

In response to a question about Stan once at an after-dinner event, I made the observation that when we played the All Star charity games (which were four to seven hours drinking and one hour football), Stan was always the first to arrive and the last to leave.

'Well, if you know that, George, you must have been there before him and left after him,' pointed out someone else in the audience. I had no answer for that.

He attended a players' meeting of England players once. The lads were discussing asking for an extra £200 on their fee for playing for the national side. It was all pretty academic for Stan as he hadn't won many caps and was probably not expecting to collect many more.

'As far as I am concerned, I'd play for my country for nothing,' volunteered Emlyn Hughes.

'In that case,' said Stan, 'you have the three lions and I'll have your two hundred quid.'

This will be a laugh, I thought, when I read recently that Tino Asprilla was joining Darlington. But true to form, it never came off. Tino was an unusual player and I saw him play some games for Newcastle United that had me on the edge of my seat. He could do things with his long legs and the ball that sometimes seemed to be more suitable to a circus than a football field. When he arrived in this country much was made of his criminal record and that he had been convicted of firing a handgun. It turned out that he had fired a gun during New Year's Eve celebrations in his home country of Colombia. Out there that was nothing, everyone did it, but the press chose to ignore that.

Nevertheless with Asprilla there was always the feeling that you didn't know what he would do next both playing-wise and temperamentally. Kevin Keegan and Terry McDermott had real problems getting him to fit in with the training regime at St James Park. Training commenced at ten in the morning but most of the players had been around and changed for some time by then. Asprilla would roll up at half past ten all smiles and Kevin and Terry tried very hard to impress on him the need to get to training on time like everyone else. One morning he turned up at twenty past nine and the manager and the players couldn't believe their eyes and thought at last they had got through to the man.

'Well done, Tino,' smiled Kevin and patted him on the back. Asprilla grinned back although there was this faint look of bewilderment in his eye. It was only a couple of days later it dawned on Kevin and Terry that the clocks had gone back. They never mentioned this to Tino.

It was another Newcastle import, Mirandinha the Brazilian striker, who was the opposite to Tino and did everything he could to please. Once as he lay injured on the pitch, the trainer ran on and knelt beside him checking his legs for broken bones.

'How are you feeling?' he asked.

'I'm very well thank you, how are you?' replied the Brazilian.

SUPERSTITION

Footballers are a superstitious bunch. I know many players who would only walk out of the tunnel in a certain order or wear particular gloves and shirts or perform strange rituals before, during and after games. I know of clubs that have called in exorcists and priests to rid themselves of evil spirits and gypsy curses, and of course there was Glenn Hoddle who availed himself of the mystic services of Eileen Drewery which led to a loss of confidence in his judgement by some. The players went along with Glenn's faith in the healing and other powers of this woman, or so it seemed. He was the manager and they really couldn't say no. Privately they couldn't stop giggling and felt they were indulging someone who had lost the plot. It certainly looked like he had when he was quoted as saying that people with afflictions were being punished for their misdemeanours in a previous life. Peter Beardsley must have thought he was King Herod reincarnated. I have behaved myself since then because I fear coming back on this earth as Glenn Hoddle in a future life. Glenn's views could be described as extremist Christian. When I first heard that he had found God I remember first thinking that must have been some pass.

Kevin Keegan, when England manager, consulted Betty Shine, yet another spiritualist. What is it with England managers and spirits? The spirits we dealt with in my day were far more straightforward and came in a bottle.

Over the years there have been a number of cases of seemingly perfectly sane managers hiring hypnotists and their ilk to come in and try to motivate their players or break some jinx or other. Paul McKenna and Uri Geller are two that spring to mind. Geller is now on the board at Exeter City and his powers have yet to show any sign of working, although someone did tell me their plastic spoon bent when they stirred their Bovril on a cold winter's night at a game down in Devon.

Terry Neill, when he was manager of Spurs back in the 1980s, employed a TV hypnotist called Romark to instil positive thinking into his side. This was before his obsession with plastic soldiers. Terry seemed to think it worked and claimed that the team managed to do some levitation on Cyril Knowles, although what benefit that was, I'm not sure. I do not believe in the magical powers of any of these people. Romark was certainly a con man. His real name was Ronald Markham, and Bob Monkhouse, the comedian, made the mistake of going into business with him. The only magic he did for Bob was to make his money disappear before disappearing himself. Some time later he was convicted of stealing money from his own mother's bank accounts. Not quite robbing your own grandmother but very close.

Returning to Kevin Keegan, when he and John Toshack were at the peak of their goal-scoring powers at Liverpool there was much talk that they must have had a telepathic understanding. A TV documentary team decided to put the theory to the scientific test and they assembled five different shapes and five different colours and asked them to pick a colour and a shape and then concentrate on their choice and attempt to transmit it telepathically to the other. Toshack went first and of five attempts he only managed to get Keegan to call correctly once. Highly inconclusive. Yet when Keegan was choosing and Toshack calling, the Welshman identified four out of five correctly. This caused much excitement among the television team and Kevin Keegan himself was visibly shocked at the result. After the programme a still stunned Kevin remarked to Tosh that the telepathy seemed to work only one way. John Toshack burst out laughing and didn't stop for a while.

'What?' insisted Kevin infectiously laughing along. Then his partner told him that he could see the reflection of what Kevin had picked in the camera lens and the only reason he didn't get five out of five was that on one of them Kevin had obscured the shape with his arm.

I suppose Kevin Keegan stepped in to the space I vacated in the early 1970s when he became the game's brightest star. Inevitably, although we were different sorts of player, comparisons were constantly made between us. Kevin certainly handled the fame better than me and demonstrated a superior staying power, but I must admit I did get some satisfaction from the quote from *Daily Mail* writer, John Roberts: 'Kevin Keegan is not fit to lace George Best's drinks.'

ANYONE FOR TENNIS?

Often the practical jokes and teasing within a squad would be directed at the young lads coming through. Eamonn Dunphy, who I mentioned earlier, tells a story about a wind-up when he was at Millwall, but I am sure similar stunts have been pulled at every club throughout the last century.

At the time Millwall were a Second Division club. The lad in question had just been signed from non-League Southall where he had been making waves but had not yet broken into the Millwall first team. Not that that made him in any way unsure of himself. He was cocky and self-confident and the older lads thought he needed taking down a peg or two. The boy made the mistake of telling everyone what a great tennis player he was, as well as being a great footballer. They resolved to wind him up. Bryan King, the goalkeeper, called for him on the hotel telephone (the team were on a pre-season tour in Bournemouth, of all places) pretending he was from the press.

'Hello, I'm from the *Bournemouth Evening Echo*. We'd very much like to interview you. We hear you're not only a young player to watch but you're also a handy tennis player.'

The players could see the young protégé as he puffed up by the hotel counter. They craned their necks so they could hear more clearly.

'How long before you break into the first team?' continued Bryan, the journalist.

'Hard to say. But I think I've done well,' replied Master Modesty.

King was getting into his stride now. 'And what about some of the players? Eamonn Dunphy, for example, he must be getting on now.'

'I suppose he is twenty-eight,' was the lad's considered response.

'Look, we need a photo for the article. Can I send a photographer around tonight? And do you mind dressing up in your tennis gear? That'll make a nice shot.'

The kid couldn't wait to scoot across the room and tell his team-mates about how the press were coming over to interview him.

'I hope you asked him for a fee,' said Bryan King, who of course had only just finished speaking to him on the phone.

'What fee?'

'They have to pay. Charge him £25 at least or they'll expect us all to give interviews for nothing.'

The lad agreed to this and then Bryan calls him again saying he can't make the interview for a couple more hours. 'Naturally we will be giving you a fee,' Bryan finished.

'How much?'

'Ten pounds, is that OK?'

'Fine,' answered the boy nervously.

When the lad returned Bryan said, 'You did remember to tell him it will cost?'

'Oh yes,' said the kid. 'I told him straight, £25 or no interview.'

Somehow and from somewhere the lad is in the lobby a

couple of hours later dressed in a full tennis kit and clutching a racket. The rest of the players, led by Eamon and Bryan no doubt, sat around ostensibly waiting to go out for a drink. They started to wind the boy up further.

'We don't believe you're a tennis player.'

'I'm not bullshitting,' he protested. 'I played for Essex.'

'Show us your serve then.'

He was a bit doubtful but eventually demonstrated his serve with an invisible tennis ball. They persisted and then dared him to play Harry Cripps, their tough full back, in a game without balls using the settees in the foyer as nets. Harry was in on the joke but the kid was trying to win! Eamonn was calling the scores: 'Thirty-love, forty-love, out, game.'

'That was never out,' cried the kid.

This was the kind of mild cruelty dealt out day after day. The kid, by the way, was Gordon Hill, later of Manchester United and England.

Allan Clarke, most famously of Leeds United and England, had a shocking self-belief and youthful arrogance when he was breaking through, according to Bobby Robson. Bobby, at thirty-two years of age, was winding down his career at Fulham for the second time and Allan was nineteen and had just been picked up from Walsall. Ironically they were playing Leeds at Craven Cottage and it was Allan's debut for the first team. Fulham were awarded a penalty and Bobby, being the club's penalty-taker, placed the ball on the spot and walked backwards to take the shot. Before he started his run,

Clarkey walked over to him. 'Very important, this one son. Take your time.'

Referees were not without humour. In one game Brian Labone, the Everton and England centre half, complained to Jack Taylor about a goal that he had just awarded.

'That was never a goal, Jack,' he protested as he tried to waylay him on his trot back to the centre spot.

'Yes it was, son. You check the *Sunday Express* tomorrow,' replied Taylor.

In that side with Brian was Howard Kendall, who became at the time the youngest player in an FA Cup Final when West Ham beat Preston North End in 1964. West Ham beat us (United) in the semi-final; if we had prevailed I would have been the youngest player to appear in a FA Cup Final. I was born on the same day as Howard but a few hours earlier. Little did I know then that not only was I not going to be the youngest player to play in a FA Cup Final but also I was not to play in a FA Cup Final, full stop.

Pat Partridge, another of the character referees from my era, had cause to book Nobby Stiles once after he had brought down Andy Lockhead, the balding Burnley centre forward. Pat had Nobby bang to rights but he still protested. 'It's my contact lenses, Pat, the glare from the floodlights hits them and I can't see what I'm doing.'

Pat ignored Nobby and wrote his name into his book. Nobby leant forward and pointed to his surname on the page. 'You spell it with an "i" not a "y".'

Brian Moore asked Ron Atkinson, in his role as a television pundit, what he thought about a particular referee's decision. Ron, who was either still in the management game at the time or was hoping to get back into it, considered a little before making his reply. He had been picked up by the media for making a series of foot-in-the-mouth remarks and was determined not to get caught out again.

'I never comment on referees, Brian,' he said firmly, 'and I'm not going to break a habit of a lifetime for that prat.'

2
BOSSES

KICK-OFF

Bill Shankly, while fiercely defensive and proud of his own players, wasn't beyond letting them feel the sharp end of his acerbic tongue. In the 1960s their goalkeeper was a Scottish chap called Tommy Lawrence and, excuse my directness, he was a bit on the fat side. He was known in the game affectionately as the Flying Pig although that has no bearing on this anecdote. Tommy had a particularly bad game one Saturday, which was capped when the opposing team's centre forward managed to slip a ball straight between his legs and into the goal. Back in the dressing room after the defeat, Tommy attempted to pre-empt the inevitable attack from his manager.

'I know, boss,' he pleaded, 'I should have kept my legs shut.'

'Nay lad,' snapped Shanks, 'your mother should have kept *her* legs shut.'

IN THE CHAIR

By definition many chairmen are larger than life. They have achieved status and riches and in many cases have acquired football clubs as very visible symbols of their success. Very often they know nothing about football but like the sound of their own voices and often pontificate at length about the game. Because they are self-made men, used to running the show, they find it difficult not to become involved in the footballing side of the business too. This can be a recipe for trouble. I think it was the late Matthew Harding who, when asked to comment on a campaign to get fan representation on the boards of football clubs, said, 'What is anyone doing on the board of a football club if they are not a fan anyway?'

Every manager now knows that the chairman's or directors' vote of confidence is as good as the bullet. When a chairman declares that the board is fully behind their manager, you can rest assured that before the month is out that manager will be joining the end of the local dole queue.

Alan Ball senior had plenty of experience of all this as a manager. When he was appointed boss at Preston North End the chairman posed with him for photos on the pitch.

'We sink or swim together,' said the chairman as he clasped Alan's shoulder.

Two and a half years later when the chairman was sacking him, Alan remarked, 'Thought you were sinking with me?'

Not all chairmen and board directors were problematical to

managers. Up at Ipswich Town the Tolly Cobbold brewing dynasty has been in control for decades. John Cobbold, known as Mr John, was the main man during the 1960s and 1970s and he was unusually relaxed and pragmatic about the club's fortunes. Mind you, they were lucky enough to stumble on Alf Ramsey and then Bobby Robson to propel their club to heights they could never have dreamt of in both decades. But when things went wrong and Ipswich found themselves tumbling down a division they were always prepared to stick with their managers. When the press asked him at one of these times about the crisis at the club, he said, 'Crisis? What crisis? The only crisis we have ever had at this club was when the Pinot Grigiot served in the boardroom was not sufficiently chilled.'

CAPTAINS OF INDUSTRY

Ken Bates is one of the more outspoken figures in current football. He famously bought Chelsea for a pound although he assumed their substantial debts at the time and, of course, turned the team around and made the ground into a complex of hotels and restaurants (and a football pitch). He is fiercely defensive of Chelsea and has a strained relationship with some quarters of the media. Recently there was a small war between him and former players fought in the columns of the tabloid press. Ken contended that too many people focus on the achievements of the 1970s FA Cup and European Cup Winners' Cup Chelsea sides and not enough credit is given to the teams of the last five years, who have brought far more trophies home. He underlined his stance on this by letting former stars Ron 'Chopper' Harris and Peter Osgood go from their corporate hospitality roles at the club to make way for former members of more recent teams. This is his prerogative and Ken justified his dismissal of Osgood in his own programme notes in September 2002: *'I just feel sorry for you [Osgood] and the fact that you seem to think the world owes you a living. Perhaps you should get on you with life.'*

It is also the chairman's prerogative to change his mind it seems, for only a year earlier he declared in his column in the club programme: *'Peter Osgood was one of greatest players ever and unlike some so-called former legends, he has not believed the world owes him a living and he has got on with his life.'*

Some chairmen buy football clubs, any club, because they are a rich man's plaything, others buy the club they love. Robert

Maxwell is an example of a man who bought a club as a rich man's plaything, and Jack Walker is an example of a fan buying the club he loves. Both men are now dead. One is sadly missed. Nothing turned the stomachs of football fans more than Maxwell turning up at Oxford United with his rattle, wearing his scarf and 'funny' hat with a hammer on it, after he had bought the club and expecting the crowd to embrace him. He had probably never set foot in the place before and if you had asked him about Gordon Banks he'd have thought they were a chain of American financial institutions he might own. Jack Walker, on the other hand, was a local boy made good who put something back into the town he loved. He bought Blackburn Rovers and installed Kenny Dalglish as manager, at the same time providing the money to purchase players such as Alan Shearer. Blackburn rose from the depths of the old Second Division to win the championship and a whole region was reinvigorated. And you never saw Jack parading around in silly hats.

Maxwell was a complete megalomaniac. He tried to buy Brighton & Hove Albion because he thought it was two clubs. When he was running the *Daily Mirror* he used to arrive by helicopter on to the roof of the building in Holborn, London and spend the rest of the day terrorising his employees, from managers down to cleaners. One time he was marching down the corridor near his top-floor office when a young man in a suit was walking towards him holding a cigarette.

'Put that out this minute,' boomed Maxwell as the young man nearly jumped out of his skin. 'What is your name?' demanded the great man.

'John,' whispered the man in reply.

'John? John, what?'

'John Roberts.'

'Well, Roberts, you're fired. You can go to personnel now and collect your cards.'

John Roberts could not look Maxwell in the eye and kept his eyes looking firmly downwards.

'Roberts, did you hear me? You're sacked. What department do you work in?'

'No department Mr Maxwell.'

'What do you mean no department?'

'I'm a photocopier salesman.'

DIVIDED LOYALTIES?

I would have always put Bill Kenwright, Deputy Chairman of Everton, more in the same mould as Jack Walker. This former actor and now theatre impresario was part of a consortium that bought the Merseyside club from Peter Johnson, a businessman who had lost the support of the fans. As far as I remember, Bill's ticket (besides plenty of the folding stuff) was his lifelong love of Everton. Therefore imagine my surprise while thumbing through an old book about the making of a famous 1960s play called *Zigger Zagger* when my eyes fell on the following passage:

> *three days before the opening Bill Kenwright, a former National Youth Theatre member and avid Liverpool fan, walked in and declared in hurt disbelief – You have not used the song of the Kop – You'll Never Walk Alone.*

Was there another young actor walking around the North-West in the mid-1960s by the name of Bill Kenwright? Had the author got it wrong? Who knows?

GOOD LORD

Sometimes at Manchester United when my fame was becoming claustrophobic I used to take my car and drive out of town and pass the time of day going nowhere in particular. One such time was a Sunday morning when I was living in my state-of-the-art but frankly very stupid newly purchased house. The house was like nothing else, having been designed for the space age by a hugely fashionable architect. It had every mod con available at the touch of a button and that became a problem. I would be lying in bed at night, turn over, and suddenly curtains would open, lights would go on and off and the stereo would play as somehow I had tripped a switch or a sensor had been triggered. It was ridiculous and sort of summed up how mad my life was becoming. Worse still it had become public property and fans and assorted loonies would turn up at any time of the day and night and just knock on the door. I knew it was time to go when a local tourist company including a drive past in their coaches as part of their itinerary.

This morning I steered the car out of the city and found myself out Burnley way before I knew it. I came across a park where an enthusiastic game of football was taking place between hordes of local kids. There must have been at least twenty a side. You don't see it nowadays. That's why there are not too many Ryan Giggses, David Beckhams and Wayne Rooneys. I pulled the car up, bumped up the path, switched the engine off and wandered over close to the pitch. I kept my distance because I didn't want to be recognised and disrupt their game or my tranquillity. A few yards away stood an elderly but upright and well-dressed man. He looked sort of familiar and after a while, when he passed me to walk back to his car, a Rolls-Royce I noted, I could see it was Bob Lord, Chairman of Burnley Football Club and millionaire butcher. Bob was a so-called self-made man and was known as Mr Burnley. He was also active in the higher echelons of the Football Association. He nodded over at the boys playing their little hearts out.

'This is what it's all about, eh lad?'

I agreed, expecting he was about to acknowledge who I was, but even though I spoke back to him in my Belfast accent he showed no signs of having the faintest recognition. I decided then not to acknowledge that I knew who he was. I tried to have a conversation with him but it was difficult to get a word in edgeways. He talked about hardship and poverty and rising above it and how genuine the Lancastrian people were. Finally, he said he must go, as if it was I who had delayed him.

'Nice to have talked to you, son.'

'Likewise,' I said and as he walked away added 'Prat,' under my breath and turned back to the kids' match.

A couple of seasons later after a United game at Turf Moor I was formally introduced to Bob Lord in the players' bar. He was utterly charming in his bluff, north of England way. 'You played a great game out there, lad. Keep a head on your shoulders and there is nothing you cannot achieve.'

'Thanks Mr Lord.' He obviously had no recollection of our earlier meeting and as there was nothing else to say I walked away to the rejoin my team-mates and some of the Burnley lads at the bar. Then I heard his voice following me.

'And, George, by the way, in future if you want to call someone a prat make sure they're out of earshot first.'

HIBS NIBS

Playing for Hibernian was a period of my playing career I really enjoyed. I went there on my return from America and was persuaded to join by their charismatic chairman Tom Hart. The Edinburgh side were in danger of relegation and Tom hoped that I could help turn things around. I'm proud to say that in that respect I think I did a reasonable job. Not long after my arrival we beat Glasgow Rangers and I laid on both our goals, we drew with Celtic and I scored, and we drew at Aberdeen. We even reached the semi-final of the Scottish Cup. Crowds were up and everyone was happy. It didn't last for ever but it was good for a while for both sides.

Tom was a real character, he only had one leg, which as he pointed out was one more than David Murray, chairman at Glasgow Rangers, and he loved a drink. In my first season I would fly up from London on the Thursday night, train with the lads on the Friday and play on the Saturday. The idea was to fly back on the Saturday evening. But with Tom that proved impossible. He insisted on a drink after the game and was not too fussed if we had won, drawn or lost. Tom was a social animal first and foremost. I would look at my watch and say, 'Anyway Tom I must go. I'll miss my plane.'

'Vodka and orange.' This was an order not a question. Tom was paying me five grand a week, which in those days was a tremendous amount of money (these days it is a tremendous amount of money!) and I felt very rude and mercenary if I left and refused the hospitality. Therefore I normally went home on the Sunday after a skinful. The following season I gave up trying to fight Tom and I rented a flat in the city and lived up there. Edinburgh was a fantastic place with fantastic people. They took to me as their own and as I had Scottish grandparents I liked to think I was part-Scot anyway.

I was very sad when I heard some years later that Tom Hart had died. I think the drink did for him in the end as it did my old chairman at Fort Lauderdale, Joe Robbie. Possibly it was our mutual interest in alcohol that attracted those men to me, and me to them in the first place. On reflection, I am worried to say that chairmen who got involved with me often seemed to meet premature deaths. Besides Tom and Joe, there was Eric Miller at Fulham, the carpet millionaire, who shot himself, and Brian Tiler who took me to Bournemouth who tragically died in the road accident that Harry Redknapp was also seriously injured in. As I write Milan Mandaric, who is now chairman at Portsmouth is inviting me to get involved with him and his manager Harry Redknapp down at Fratton Park. I think it is only fair to tell him about my worrying history.

Eric Miller was an interfering chairman if ever there was one. When Bobby Robson was manager at Fulham, the chairman approached him and said, 'Ever thought about buying Eddie Bovington from West Ham?'

'No, not really,' Bobby replied honestly.

'I think you should have a look at him.'

'I don't need to, Eric. I know him. I've played against him and I've seen him. He's not for us.'

A few days later Miller raised the subject of Bovington again and insisted that Bobby accompany him to a reserve game against Chelsea that was being played that week in the evening. Reluctantly Bobby agreed and they sat in the stands and watched Barry Lloyd run rings around Eddie who was supposed to be marking him. It was a 3–3 draw but Lloyd scored all three goals, which says something about Eddie's performance that night.

Travelling home in Eric's black taxi (he had purchased his own cab after waiting too long to find one once in London), Miller turned to Bobby and said, 'I thought Bovington played well.'

'Eric, you must be joking, surely?'

You could have cut the silence with a knife until Eric spotted Dave Sexton, the Chelsea manager, outside the underground entrance heading for Victoria station to catch his train home to Brighton. Miller's driver pulled over and offered Dave a lift. Bobby tried to suppress a smile when during a conversation about the game Dave volunteered, 'That poor fella Bovington, our boy Barry Lloyd made a real monkey out of him.' Eric didn't reply but his face tightened. When Dave hopped out at Victoria station, he turned to Bobby and accused, 'You put him up to that.'

Bobby discovered later that Eric Miller was a good friend of the West Ham and England skipper Bobby Moore, who had persuaded Eric that Fulham should buy Bovington. Eddie was Bobby's pal but was not getting first team football. Bobby as ever was trying to do a friend a favour.

When Brian Tiler wanted me down at Bournemouth he was very determined to get me. There was no pretence on either side. I was drinking heavily and past my best. Therefore my contribution on the field was not going to make a huge difference but my contribution on the gate money was. And gate money, in those days, could help struggling clubs survive a little longer. However, even though all I had to do was turn up on a Saturday, it was a responsibility that I didn't really want. I liked Brian and didn't want to let him down and deep down I knew I would. The other thing I didn't like doing was saying no to people so I did what I often did in these situations and made myself scarce. I knew Brian was in London looking for me to sign a contract so I spirited myself off to the Inn on the Park Hotel that I used at times like this. The staff were always discreet and I always went there alone. No one knew this place was one of my watering holes so I couldn't believe my eyes when I saw a beaming Brian walking up the marble stairs and entering the bar.

'I've got to hand it to you, Brian,' I said. 'You don't give up, do you? How on earth did you find me here?'

Brian smiled and tapped the side of his nose.

'Well, this deserves a bottle of champagne, I reckon.' I ordered a bottle of Dom Perignon and two glasses. Looking over at Brian, I could see him relaxing in his chair and folding out some paper on the table and taking a pen from his breast pocket. I asked Pete, the barman, to top our glasses up and excused myself to go to the bathroom. I didn't come back. Sorry Brian, if you're reading this up there.

MONEY, MONEY, MONEY

Some people may be under the impression that the parlous financial state that English football finds itself in is something new. It is not. The figures are larger now and the red ink thicker but football clubs have been walking a financial tightrope ever since I can remember. For every club that was prosperous there were ten that could barely pay the players' wages. For every big transfer you heard about, the next couple of years were spent trying to repair the dent in the club's cash flow. The game has survived for decades on borrowed money and the hard-earned fortunes of indulgent and often starstruck chairmen. In the same way that pubs, restaurants and small retail shops have sucked up the money of the ordinary man's redundancy cheques over the years, the football clubs have trousered the cash of those who have made their millions in industry.

And like most of those pubs, restaurants and shops where the redundancy money has been lost and only the empty premises await the next smiling person with a dream and a cheque, only a few chairmen have actually increased their fortunes by becoming involved with a football club. Alan Sugar struggled for a few years, when chairman of Tottenham Hotspur, trying to get the fans to understand economic realities. But no one was listening. They wanted him to spend large sums of money on players. His money. But Sugar was too cute to drain away his hard-earned Amstrad fortune on a football club, even though he did support them. The arrival of satellite television money to the game in the

1980s and 1990s was similar to the discovery of North Sea Oil to Britain in the 1970s. It was a welcome boost to the economy and even transformed things for a while but it does not alter the basic economic fact – the core product has to bring in more money than goes out the door to survive and flourish.

The old joke about the man who rings up his local team – it could be Carlisle, Torquay or Swansea or anyone else you fancy – and asks what time is kick-off today and meets the reply 'What time can you make it, sir?' is not as far off the mark as one may imagine. Kevin Keegan says he got the jitters when he was at Southampton when he was asked if he could help out financially with the signing of England goalkeeper Peter Shilton. That was in the 1980s when a top flight club was having to ask one of their players (a rich one, I grant you) to chip in to make a signing. In the 1980s also when Bruce Rioch was manager at Middlesbrough and the club was teetering on the edge of bankruptcy, he would park his car over the main drain so the water board could not cut off the water supply.

It stands to reason that a massive correction will take place in the game. It has already started. Wages will plummet. Many players will become part-time as clubs adjust their overheads to become covered by their income. They will have to because banks will call in loans and the monied benefactors will become thin on the ground. Clubs will need to find players again from their local area. The percentage of foreign players in the League will diminish. All this may not be a bad thing as the game returns to its roots to survive.

Much has also been said about underhand financial practices

that were, some say are, prevalent in the game. Even my old colleague and hero Harry Gregg alleged that there were attempts at
match fixing at Manchester United during his time there. He has
never mentioned this to me before and certainly didn't mention
it when he asked me to write a foreword to his recent autobiography. I can honestly say I never came across bribery, bungs and
corruption personally in all my years in the game. There was the
sad case of Peter Swan and David 'Bronco' Layne who got into
trouble for betting on results of games they were playing in
during the early 1960s. They were good footballers, young men
not hardened criminals, and going to prison and having their
careers and possibly lives ruined was a ridiculous but pre-
dictable over-reaction by the powers-that-were. More recently
there have been various high-profile allegations about managers
involved with 'bungs' and the case against George Graham
which saw him sacked as Arsenal manager, but as I say if it was
going on in my day I never noticed. Honest, Guv.

Mind you I can sympathise with Brian Clough who, when
playing for Middlesbrough, despaired when he kept rattling in
the goals at one end only to see his defence make the most
stupid errors and let as many in (and more) at the other. He
recalls particularly one game against Charlton that ended in a
6–6 draw! One season the team scored eighty goals but still
failed to win promotion from the Second Division. Cloughie
became suspicious and went to see his manager who would not
entertain such thoughts of corruption. He then went to see his
chairman who listened sympathetically but could not compre-
hend the thought. Indeed they believed Brian might be loopy

and he was eased out of the club. One of the players leading a rebellion against him was one the defenders Brian had begun to suspect was throwing games. His name was Brian Phillips and in the same scandal that engulfed Peter Swan and Bronco Layne a few years later he was imprisoned and banned from the professional game for life.

The following story is true but for obvious reasons I have to keep the individuals anonymous. It relates to a period long after my retirement. I think it probably says more about the naiveté of some of the people in the game rather than pointing to wholesale corruption. A few years ago the papers got a whiff of a bungs scandal. It was claimed that money was changing hands to oil the wheels of transfer deals and that a group of prominent ex-players were the lucky or unlucky ones benefiting from these backhanders. One of these ex-players was a thoroughly nice man and enjoyed good relations with the men from the press. During a long career he had won almost every honour that English and international football had to offer. However, he was not noted in the game for his intellectual prowess. One morning one of the Sunday tabloids called him.

'Bob [not his real name], is there any truth in the rumour that you accepted a £10,000 backhander in the transfer of Fred Bloggs [not his real name] from Melchester Rovers [not a real club] to [un]Real Madrid?' asked the reporter.

'Absolutely not!' answered Bob defiantly. 'It was only £5,000.'

Sometimes I think about the money that has passed through my hands, and the money I didn't earn. Sometimes, but not often. It is a common cry that footballers in my day did not earn enough and that footballers these days are grossly overpaid. Players in my time *were* underpaid but I would go as far to say that maybe footballers these days (some of them at least) are underpaid. When I was playing, the football grounds of the top clubs were full, week in, week out, yet the revenues generated were not being ploughed back into the grounds for sure. Players' wages did not account for too much of that revenue so one wonders where the money went. Players of the top calibre were still catching buses and trains to games. Johnny Haynes, Jimmy Hill and George Eastham, all peers of mine, campaigned to abolish the maximum wage. Haynes became the first footballer to earn £100 a week. Francis Lee, at the start of his career with Bolton Wanderers, had the temerity to ask his manager Bill Ridding for a wage rise. Francis wanted to go up to £25 a week, the same as most of the more senior players. Ridding told him no and that if he didn't like it he could lump it. 'What else can you do? Labouring is all you are fit for.'

Young he may have been but Franny was the club's top scorer at the time and this was the attitude by many managements towards their players. Yet without the players there would be no football. We had and have the power to transform a club's finances and it seems only right to me that players too should have the power to transform their own finances. Franny went on to prove his manager wrong not only by becoming one of the best forwards of his generation but by making millions from his post-playing business of making toilet rolls.

TAXING QUESTIONS

Mind you, I didn't concern myself with any of these questions of finance at the time because I had so much money coming through the coffers, I couldn't count it. In addition to my wages from Manchester United, I had income from my boutiques, floods of cash being passed over the counters of my clubs, and countless cheques arriving from endorsements, personal appearances and advertising. The only limiting factor on my earning power was me. I kept insisting on time to spend it. Looking back, I can't believe I spent it all and neither did the taxman who caught up with me in the end and made me bankrupt in 1982. It was for a relatively paltry sum of £22,000 but they would not believe I could not lay my hands on that sort of money. Nearly ten years later the Inland Revenue had turned this into £100,000 with accrued interest but a solicitor by the name of Bryan Fugler persuaded them to be pragmatic and they accepted a cheque for £32,500 to discharge my bankruptcy. I remember when I was arguing the toss with the Revenue over some money I had in a trust fund for my son Calum that they would have liked to have got their hands on. The trust gave it full legal protection from the tax man and me come to that.

'What is more important to you, Mr Best, your son or your debt to the state?'

Silly question.

DOC'S ORDERS

I was only ever asked to manage one club. That was Tramps, but I'm sure the owner Johnny Gold was pissed at the time. I didn't really play under many managers. Sir Matt Busby spoiled me. He was a good manager and a good man. One of the all-time greats and for me anyone else was never going to compare to him. I played under Wilf McGuinness, Frank O'Farrell, Bobby Campbell and Billy Bingham, but besides Sir Matt only one other made an impact on me and that was Tommy Docherty. For me, he was as bad as Matt was good.

Much water has passed under the bridge since I fell out with Tommy Docherty and finally stopped playing for Manchester United. Neither of our careers in football ever resumed in the mainstream of the game. I was upset with him and suppose I still am for giving the wrong impression about my final days at Old Trafford. He claimed, at the time, that I had arrived for a game drunk once and another time with a woman in tow. I never drank immediately before a match. Ever. I also never brought a lady to a game I was playing in or into the changing rooms. Why he would say these things I can only speculate. Perhaps he was feeling the pressure so much as the most famous League team in history crumbled under him. He had asked me to return to playing and had said he would be laid-back about my training while I got myself together. I felt he then went back on all of this and made up blatant lies.

I finished with United because I couldn't cope with moving

from playing with ten other superstars to being part of a team that smacked of mediocrity. Mind you, I ended up becoming quite philosophical about our run of form – you draw some, you lose some. Players and fans alike were baffled by some of the signings made by the Doc at first. Even some of the new sign-ings themselves must have thought, 'Surely some mistake.' Sir Matt, who had moved upstairs, was close to signing Alan Ball and Mike England at one point and if those two had joined I would have stayed and things would have been different. But it was not to be.

One player Tommy did sign shortly before my final depar-ture who was worth his weight in gold was big Jim Holton. We played seven league games together. Docherty picked him up from Shrewsbury Town in the lower divisions for £80,000. He was a massive rugged centre half who had the looks of a doorman at one of Bernard Manning's nightclubs but turned out to be the rock of United's defence for three or four seasons. His career was cut short by broken legs and tragically he died at a terribly young forty-two years of age. He was generally perceived to be a dirty player but I never saw it that way. I thought in his own way he was graceful and talented as well as hard. My favourite tale about Jim is the one where his mother is chatting over the garden fence to a neighbour. Jim has just broken through at United and there is a lot of publicity about his highly committed style of play.

'I'm worried that he is going to come home one day with a broken leg,' says Mrs Holton.

'Don't worry,' replies the lady from next door, 'it won't be his.'

Pity Tommy's judgement wasn't always as sharp his wit. He famously remarked, 'The thing about George Best is that he could pass a ball beautifully but he couldn't pass a pub.' Another of his often-used one-liners is his contention that I mixed my vodka with Windolene – 'He still gets pissed but his eyes are clear in the morning.' I was reminded of him recently (and couldn't suppress a smile) when I read he had a narrow escape in a local car wash when, somehow, he became entangled in the machinery. He never really understood how things worked.

My pals took a dislike to him almost as soon as he took over at Manchester United. One night I had to restrain Waggy from punching him on the nose. Waggy ran his own little football team for fun and Paddy Crerand used to train them. It was all a bit of a laugh and every year they would have a big dinner. This particular time Paddy brought Tommy, who had just been installed as manager. Waggy was escorting a very beautiful girl this night whose name I cannot remember. The Doc could not disguise his interest as he sat next to her at the top table leering and then he leant forward to address Waggy, a man he had never met until this day, and grunted, 'I'd love to shag your bird, son.'

However, let us not forget how important he is. For in his autobiography Tommy reminds us: 'I'm as big in the game as Cloughie – if not bigger.' For me, Tommy's book is one of those that when you put it down you can't pick it up again. When he was appointed manager at Second Division Rotherham United he promised them: 'I will take you out of the Second Division.' Tommy kept his word – six months later they were in the Third.

He also took over at Queens Park Rangers for a staggering twenty-nine days where he managed to lose almost every game before falling out with his equally outspoken chairman, Jim Gregory. The chairman called Tommy into the office and opened up ominously with, 'Things are not going well around here, Tommy, there will have to be changes.'

'You can't walk away now, Jim. You're doing a great job!' quipped Docherty.

I never played under or against Sir Alex Ferguson. His management record is beyond dispute. He is without doubt the most successful manager of an English League club ever. He has overtaken Shankly, Paisley, Clough, Chapman and all the others. If another manager will ever surpass his achievements it could only happen if the Premiership develops into a league like the Scottish one where only two clubs really matter. I do not think that will ever happen in England. Arsene Wenger, manager of arch-rivals Arsenal, once said that Alex's only weakness is that he believes he has none. Perhaps this is true. But perhaps Alex is right. It must have been tempting for him to retire in 1999 after winning the treble with United. How can you top that? Retiring at the point would have ensured there would never have been a downside to his career. I bet Brian Clough wishes he had retired at the top rather than suffering the indignity and agony of presiding over Nottingham Forest's relegation in his final season as a manager. Alex has always been friendly and helpful to me and made me welcome at Old Trafford. We have had many a long conversation about football – past, present and future. He recently asked me who I thought would win in a match between the 1999 all-conquering Manchester United side featuring Beckham, Scholes, Giggs, etc. and the side I played in alongside Bobby Charlton, Denis Law et al.

I thought carefully a while and then replied, 'Alex, on balance, I have to say I think the late 1960s side would win, close match though. Maybe 1–0.'

Alex grinned and said with just a hint of sarcasm 'Only 1–0?'

'Well, one of us is dead and the rest are in their fifties and sixties.'

He liked that one.

Herbert Chapman must have been some manager. He won the championship for three successive seasons with Huddersfield Town in the 1920s and then produced the Arsenal team that did it again more memorably in the 1930s before dying prematurely. He was years ahead of his time and obviously knew a thing or two about marketing his club as well as getting them to deliver on the field. In 1939, although after Chapman's death, they made a film called *The Arsenal Stadium Mystery*, starring Leslie Banks, which was a box office smash and probably one of the most ingenious examples of product placement ever. Also Chapman somehow persuaded London Underground to rename their tube station in Highbury after his club. I cannot imagine that even Sir Alex Ferguson would be able to cut through red tape so dramatically and permanently these days.

KING OF THE KOP

Bill Shankly stories are legion, most centring around his dry sense of humour and acerbic comments. Some of his quotations have achieved immortality, such as 'Football is not a matter of life and death ... it is much more important than that.' The fund of anecdotes is enormous and most have found their way into books, magazines and the after-dinner patter of people such as myself, but the strength of the man is that even now, years after his death, you still hear new ones.

In the 1960s, when Tommy Docherty was manager of Chelsea, he signed the prolific goal-scoring centre forward Tony Hateley. Tony was the next big thing at the time and much was expected of him. However, he never really seemed to be able to set Stamford Bridge and the Chelsea team on fire, privately Tommy was regretting his decision but publicly he was sticking with his man. One afternoon the phone rang and the Doc could not mistake Shank's dour Scottish tones crackling at the other end of the line.

'Tom? Bill Shankly here. Your boy, the lad Hateley. I hear he may be a wee bit unsettled.'

Docherty, forever the businessman, sensed that here could be the answer to this niggling situation but could not help going straight into negotiating mode.

'Bill, before we go any further, I have to tell you that hundreds of thousands wouldn't buy the lad.'

Momentarily the line went quiet until Shanks growled before slamming the phone down, 'Aye, and I'm one of them!'

As I remember, Tony Hateley did eventually sign for Liverpool but not before another conversation between the Doc and Shankly when Tommy said to Bill, 'You must admit the boy is fantastic in the air.'

'Aye,' conceded Shanks, 'but so was Douglas Bader and he had two wooden legs.'

Hateley was never considered one of Shankly's best signings and like Tommy Docherty before him he was loath to admit it. In one match Bill and his right-hand man at the time, Bob Paisley, sat on the bench and watched Tony have a nightmare of a game. Paisley kept asking Shanks's permission to bring off the struggling centre forward but Bill would have none of it. Finally Hateley was toppled over by the opposing centre half and before he could get back on his feet Bob Paisley was on the pitch beside Tony calling for a stretcher.

'What's up?' asked a confused Hateley.

'Don't worry, son. You're fine. We'll look after you.'

'I know I'm fine,' said Hateley as he looked down worriedly at Bob taping his legs together and lifting him on to a stretcher.

The substitute was rushed on and Bob sat back down next to Bill in the dug-out. 'How's the boy?' enquired Bill.

'He's fine,' replied Bob, 'I'm just making sure now we've got him off the park you can't put him back on.'

Another time Shankly was frustrated by the progress of one of his youngsters who was on the verge of breaking into the first team. 'The trouble with you, son, is that your brains are all in your head,' he told him.

When an enthusiastic scout had brought another young protégé for Shanks to take a look at, he shook his head at the scout.

'But the boy has football in his blood,' protested the man.

'Well, it hasn't reached his legs yet.'

He was also very adept at psyching his players into believing the opposition in big matches were not what they were cracked up to be. One team talk he gave was before a game against our own Manchester United and he proceeded to take our team apart one by one.

'The goalkeeper Stepney, he's no good in the air and he's not much better on the ground. In fact what's the difference between Stepney and Jesus Christ? Jesus saves. And the full backs, Brennan and Dunne, a couple of clapped-out Paddies, that's what they are, should have been sent out to grass years ago. Nobby Stiles, blind as a bat, runs around the field like a headless chicken, not worth talking about that lad, Foulkes is ancient and wasn't any good when he was young – before the war that was, Sadler needs watching but none of the others ever pass to him so no problems there, the boy Morgan can run a bit but he can't beat an egg and the other lad Kidd can't hold the ball. Big lady's blouse. You see this team really is a shambles. You will take them apart!'

Emlyn Hughes, the captain, put his hand up at the end of the outburst. 'Boss, you haven't mentioned Best, Law or Charlton,' he squeaked.

Shankly fixed his eye on his captain. 'Christ, Emlyn, you're worried you can't beat a team with just three players?' he spat.

He hated losing, everyone does, but Shankly took it to extremes. One season Everton beat Liverpool 2–0 at Anfield which was great revenge as earlier in the season Liverpool had done Everton 3–0 at Goodison Park. After the Anfield game the Everton players were celebrating in the bath and dressing room when Shankly burst in. Some who were there swore that steam was emanating from his ears and his eyes were bulging with rage. 'I just want you lot to know you haven't won bugger all. We beat you 3–0 at Goodison ... so the aggregate score is 3–2 to us.'

He endeared himself to the Liverpool fans very early in his tenure at Anfield by declaring that if Everton were playing at the bottom of his garden he would draw the curtains. He didn't like losing out on players either. Back in the early 1970s he was very keen to sign Lou Macari from Celtic. But the club was keen to hang on to Lou and would not accept a series of increased offers from Bill. When Shanks realised in 1973 that United had beaten him to Macari's signature he announced to the press, 'I only wanted him for the reserves anyway.'

He was delighted though when he signed the big Scottish centre half Ron Yeats early in his Liverpool career. He told a bemused journalist, 'With him at centre half I could play Arthur Askey in goal.' (For readers under eighty years of age Arthur Askey was a bespectacled, bald, music-hall comedian who stood five foot nothing in his socks.) He was so thrilled at Ron's arrival he invited the press to come down to Anfield, 'and take a walk around my new centre half'.

Bill wasn't above having a dig at his peers. When Don Revie

was reported to be ill and missed attending a couple of games when manager of Leeds United, Bill commented, 'I know what's wrong with him – he's got a bad side.'

Another time when Leeds were having a rare bad run Bill was asked for his view.

'To be fair to Don,' he started, 'he has had problems with injuries. His players keep recovering.'

By all accounts he harboured a deep mistrust of some foreign regimes. John Keith, a journalist, who developed a good friendship with Bill, tells of a time when they were in an Eastern bloc country before the fall of communism. It was at the height of the Cold War and a boom time for spy films. Harry Palmer (played by Michael Caine) not Harry Potter was all the rage. Shankly hadn't shown for breakfast and a couple of club officials went to Bill's room to see what was up. When they got there they were amazed to find their manager standing on a chair peering into the light socket and shouting, 'I know you're there. Come out you cowards.'

His own favourite story, which I have to assume was more wishful thinking and most probably made up by himself, concerns the 1966 FA Cup Final when Everton played Sheffield Wednesday. He claims that when Princess Margaret was introduced to the captains before the kick-off she said to the Everton skipper Brian Labone, 'I'm sorry to appear ignorant but exactly where is Everton?'

'It's in Liverpool, ma'am.'

'Oh of course, we had your first team here last year.'

Bill's sharp sense of humour rubbed off on his fans or vice versa. I can remember the team coach passing a church as we drove the last few streets to the ground for one match in the 1960s. A billboard was outside screaming, 'What will you do when Jesus returns?' Underneath someone had scrawled 'Move St John to inside left.'

One season we went to Anfield and the press had been speculating that Denis Law was too old and really should think about retiring. This went on for ages. As Denis ran out on to the pitch the entire Kop burst into the Beatles song 'When I'm Sixty-Four'. I also remember going to a United versus Liverpool fixture in 1991 and it was around the time that Terry Waite, the Archbishop of Canterbury's envoy, had finally been released after being held hostage in the Lebanon for five years. Liverpool fans were arriving at the match wearing T-shirts showing Terry Waite with a bubble coming from his mouth saying, 'What? Manchester United still haven't won the League.'

Twenty years on, to borrow a pearl of wisdom from Ron Atkinson, the joke is on the other foot.

MAINE MEN

One of Bill's main managerial contemporaries was Joe Mercer, who was a wonderful character and a nice man, a great England player in his time and a formidable manager. He forged a partnership with Malcolm Allison at Manchester City that for a period, at least, gave City the supremacy in Manchester. He also caretaker-managed the England team between Sir Alf Ramsey and Don Revie and had respectable results. Malcolm was the coaching and tactical man and Joe was the father figure nice guy. My friends at City told me he was hilarious because he couldn't remember names or at least he thought he could but invariably got them wrong. In team-talks he warned them to beware of Derby's centre half Roy McParland, to watch Sunderland's Mike Pigswill and on one occasion before a friendly with Ajax said they had only one decent player – Johann Strauss. If he were alive today trying to deal with the majority of foreign players in the Premiership he'd be finished.

Joe's good nature resulted in him being the victim of some of the players' practical jokes. On a trip to Australia they flew via Bahrain and Bangkok. At Manama, the Bahraini capital, an Arab gentleman in full Arab dress boarded the plane and took the seat next to Joe. He wasn't very communicative and just sat with a briefcase on his lap looking blankly forward. Francis Lee seized the opportunity for a wind-up. He wrote a note:

Dear Mr Mercer,

We do not wish to cause alarm but we have reason to believe that the gentleman sitting next to you is a hijacker. Please remain absolutely still and quiet until we have over-powered this person.

Francis then folded the note in half, attracted the attention of a hostess and asked if she could pass it to Joe, pointing to him. They watched out of the corners of their eyes as Joe unfolded the note, read it and then carefully folded it in half and placed it in his pocket. He then stared motionless ahead. Only when the beads of sweat began to roll down his forehead did they all relent and collapse laughing around him.

Poor Joe. These players loved playing a practical joke on their easy-going boss. Another time Francis, Mike and Neil Young carefully positioned their car into a ditch, sprung the bonnet open and then staggered around as if concussed. Francis I think lay on the grass. They did this at a point where they knew Joe would pass in his car any minute. As the manager saw them he nearly crashed his own vehicle as he took in the situation. His entire forward line nearly wiped out in a car crash. When he got out they all ran up to him laughing and shouting.

Franny Lee was so famous for taking penalties that he was fondly known by some writers as that famous Chinese striker Lee Won Pen. He had a memorable ritual of taking a very long run-up before striking the ball and normally scoring. One of his colleagues was a good footballer called Tony Coleman, and Tony was a man who never took himself or the game too seriously.

One match when Franny was walking purposefully backwards before his famous run-up, Tony nipped forward and took the penalty. He probably had his eye on a piece of glory but more likely he fancied winding Francis up. It was a trick he knew he would never attempt again as he watched his shot sail hopelessly over the bar.

Joe and Malcolm had a great relationship with their players and some of them never really recovered when their partnership broke up and they both moved on to pastures new. Ron Saunders was one of the managers who had the unenviable task of trying to follow this particular double act. It is always going to be difficult for a manager coming in to a club where there is a nucleus of players who have been there for a long time, have achieved much and are local folk heroes but are approaching the end of their careers. However, there are ways and means of dealing with these situations and Ron got off on the wrong foot, I fear, when he immediately began to refer to Denis Law as 'the old man' and Francis Lee as 'Fatty'. The players were also accustomed to having a good meal on the Friday night before away games and were dismayed when the manager issued an edict that they could no longer have the prawn cocktail starter they all enjoyed. Back in the 1970s prawn cocktails were a luxury to men raised on fish and chips, meat pies and Tizer. Mike Doyle thought bollocks to all that and ordered escargot instead. Ron leant over Mike's shoulder and whispered, 'Are you trying to undermine me?'

'What?' returned Mike, his face a picture of innocence.

'I said no prawns.'

'Snails aren't prawns.'

'Yes, they are, they are a type of prawn,' insisted the manager, who hopefully didn't go on to manage Grimsby.

Saunders should have secured his power base before going in all guns blazing because soon after, in a classic case of player power, the team persuaded the chairman to fire Ron and install one of their own – Tony Book who managed City for the next five years.

ALLISON WONDERLAND

Malcolm Allison was one of the game's most flamboyant characters ever. Famous for stormy relationships with bunny girls, fedora hats and large cigars that would make Monica Lewinsky wince, he loved his champagne. One night he was steering his car home after a night in a club when a police vehicle spotted him driving his motor the wrong way down a one-way street. He was pulled over.

'Excuse me, sir, are you aware this is a one-way street?' asked the officer sternly as Big Mal rolled down his window.

'I'm only going one way,' smiled Allison.

Once he kidded me he had written a book called *How to Beat the Breathalyser* and I fell for it. 'I've just published the sequel,' he continued, *'Refreshing Walks in the Lancashire Countryside.'*

He always had a quick answer, often laced with biting sarcasm. When Manchester City had gained promotion from the Second Division at the start of their amazing revival the then chairman, Albert Alexander, called Mal into his office.

'We've had a great season, Malcolm. The board wishes to express its gratitude. Therefore we have decided to issue you with a bonus of £400, Walter Griffith, the club secretary, is getting the same amount and Joe Mercer is getting £600.'

Mal was stung by what he felt was an inequity and replied, 'Yes, I thought the secretary did well. He booked us into some very nice hotels.'

When City won the championship there was no stopping Malcolm. 'There is no limit to what this team can achieve,' he declared. 'We will win the European Cup. European football is full of cowards and we will terrorise them with our power and attacking football.' Weeks later little known Fenerbache of Turkey dumped City out in the first round.

He knew his own mind even as a young player and afforded no one automatic respect just because they were a big name in the game. When he was breaking through at Charlton Athletic his manager was Jimmy Seed, who had been a top player with Sunderland, Spurs and England in his day. After five years at the Valley, Charlton transferred Malcolm to West Ham United where he was to make his name before illness cut his promising playing career short. Jimmy Seed only ever spoke to Mal twice. Once when he joined and then again when he left.

'I hope you have learnt something in your time with me,' smiled Seed as he saw Mal on his way.

'Yes,' said Mal, 'the art of communication.'

Malcolm didn't have any problem though with communicating with the ladies. He hit the headlines over the years for becoming involved with bunny girls and beauty queens. He explained his penchant for the former in this way. 'They share some interesting characteristics with the rabbit family.' For a while he did settle down with Chief Bunny Serena Williams who my first wife Angela worked with when she too became a bunny for a short time. He also attracted much flak when he had a fling with the world's most famous call girl, Christine Keeler. Christine almost single-handedly brought down the Harold

Macmillan government a few years before when she embarked on an affair with a cabinet minister, John Profumo. The problem wasn't only that Profumo was married to the actress Valerie Hobson but Christine was sleeping with a Russian man who was believed to be a spy. The newspapers called her a call girl because they couldn't bring themselves to say that a government minister had been sleeping with a prostitute.

Sailing close to the wind was Mal's preferred form of transport through the seas of life. For a couple of years between retiring from football with tuberculosis and taking on his first management roles he had made a living as a professional gambler and was a well-known figure on the dog and horse tracks all over the country. He never quite cut the ties he made during that time. A scandal developed when it emerged that Malcolm had been placing large bets on the dogs on behalf of a chap called Joe Lowery. This man was convicted of doping the dogs and, although Malcolm was never alleged to have been involved in the doping and innocently believed he was putting money on for a friend, it left a nasty stain. It didn't help his standing in the game that one of the dogs that had been drugged was a pretty hot greyhound belonging to Alf Ramsey. Mal always liked to stick two fingers up at the establishment and when Lowery was released from prison a few years later, he attended Manchester City's FA Cup winning banquet as the coach's special guest.

However, it was his bit of fun with a model who had adorned the glossy pages of *Men Only* that cost him his job at Crystal Palace Football Club. Somehow, somewhere Mal had met up with Fiona Richmond and he arrived with her at Palace's training ground one day in 1976. Within minutes Fiona was stripped off and rolling around in the mud with the delighted Palace players. To top this she later jumped into the bath, completely naked, with the boys. At the time no one was too alarmed that Hy Money, Palace's female in-house photographer, was also in the changing rooms snapping away. A couple of the boys in the bath faced the wrath of their wives and girlfriends when the pictures appeared in the *News of the World* the following weekend. Some others were relieved that holding their breath underwater had saved them from the same fate but the FA were extremely unhappy. Pressure was put on Palace chairman Ray Bloye to get rid of Malcolm and eventually he did.

Big Mal is probably the only manager I have come across who drank more than his players. Combined. Sadly this did take a toll on his career and not long after his flamboyant revival of Crystal Palace he drifted into a sequence of ever more obscure managerial and coaching posts. Rodney Marsh tried to help him in later years by putting him in the frame for the post of US national team coach. Mal arrived for his interview with the international team committee but had unwisely consumed plenty of Dom Perignon beforehand. He was asked what his strategy for American soccer would be if he were successful in his application.

'Well, you have so many tall people here in America, I would only pick people who are over six feet to play in the side and then we would develop an aerial game that would confuse the rest of the world ...'

He certainly confused the panel as he continued his ramblings and strangely he didn't get the job.

THE LIFE OF BRIAN

Brian Clough arrived on the football management scene like a whirlwind. Up until then managers wore suits, said little publicly and generally avoided the limelight. Some even still wore their army titles with pride – Captain this and Major that. Docherty could be a bit outspoken and Shankly had these endearing turns of phrase but Clough was the first management media superstar. His distinctive monotone way of speaking and his shocking self-confidence and belief transfixed the nation when he burst on to our television screens at the beginning of the 1970s. There was a joke at the time that summed up his impact: Clough, Revie and Shankly have all died and have each sought an audience with God to be allowed entrance into Heaven.

'Who are you?' God asks.

'I am Bill Shankly. I took Liverpool from the Second Division to being the best side in Europe.'

'Okay, Mr Shankly. Come in. And you?'

'I am Don Revie. I too took my side Leeds from the Second Division and they have been the best side in England.'

'Fair enough, Mr Revie, please come in. And you?'

'I am Brian Clough and get out of my bloody chair.'

He caught the breath of the TV audiences when an interviewer asked if he thought his £15,000 salary as manager of Derby County was excessive.

'It's too low,' replied Brian predictably.

'But it's double what the Archbishop of Canterbury earns.'

'Maybe, young man, but the churches are empty and the Baseball Ground is full.'

When he joined Derby County, then a lowly Second Division side, he was determined to shake them up from top to bottom. He decided that from the start all the ground staff should know who was boss. On his first day he called through to the office on his telephone.

'Get me a cup of tea, please,' he ordered of the male voice that answered the call.

'Get your own bleedin' tea,' was the reply.

'Do you know who I am? I am Brian Clough the new manager around these parts.'

'Do you know who *I* am?' countered the voice at the other end of the line.

'No, I don't,' snapped Clough testily.

'Good, you can fuck off then.'

I remember seeing him once presenting some awards on television. Trevor Francis was voted Young Footballer of the Year and as he approached the stage to collect his trophy Cloughie just stared at him and for a minute or two there was an uneasy silence. 'You'll get nothing here, son, until you take your hands out of your pockets.'

Trevor can't have been too traumatised by the incident because a while later he signed for the man himself at Nottingham Forest in the first £1m transfer.

Cloughie was a drinker too, although in those days the

imbibing habits of managers didn't come under media scrutiny in the same way as the players' habits did. I suppose being that little bit older than the players they were less likely to be captured under the weather in a nightclub or a bar. One old First Division manager I know, used to call Clough and his co-manager Peter Taylor the Exorcists because whenever they visited his ground the spirits would always vanish. I don't know if it was his drinking that made him late for training on occasion but apparently he would sometimes roll up late and then say nonchalantly to his waiting players, 'Oh, there you are,' as if it were they who were in the wrong place at the wrong time.

As with me, it all caught up with Brian in a physical way and at the beginning of 2003 he also underwent a liver transplant. The papers couldn't resist a joke – they said the good news was that Brian was to get a new liver; the bad news was that I was the donor. I wish him all the best in his recovery.

ENGLAND EXPECTS

The thing about managers is that they tend to be judged only on their last management stint rather than on their record as a whole. Take Graham Taylor, at the end of his reign as England manager he vied with Peter Sutcliffe as the most reviled man in England. He was painted by the media as an incompetent idiot and there was little more than a murmur of disagreement from the population as a whole. Not long before, he had been the modest but determined quiet man who had taken Watford from the Third Division to the top flight. After his sacking from the England job and the *Sun* picturing him as a turnip, it was hard to imagine Graham Taylor living out his life safely let alone returning to the game as a club manager. But time and more international failure under subsequent managers improved his standing and the historical perspective on his reign. When eventually he did return to club management at Watford and Aston Villa he was being hailed as a saviour.

Rodney Marsh claims that Graham Taylor once said to him, 'I remember playing against you when I was a full back at Lincoln City and you were at QPR. I was thrilled because I had a good game and you only got two goals. Do you remember that?'

'No,' said Rodney. 'I had no idea you used to be a footballer.'

People sometimes forget that Bobby Robson had a period too when he was pilloried as England manager and his abilities were held up to question. Again his stock rose and he ended up gaining a knighthood and reviving Newcastle in spectacular fashion. These days he has even replaced the Queen in presenting the FA Cup to the victorious team captain. It is impossible for all of the managers to be successful all of the time. We don't expect it of players so why do we expect it of managers? I couldn't do their job, I know that. I would not be able to deal with ignorant but powerful chairmen who couldn't see beyond the following Saturday and as soon as things start to go badly treat you like shit. Bobby Robson himself tells of when he was manager of Fulham in his early days way back in 1968. Things were not going well and Bobby realised there was some frostiness towards him from the boardroom but was not unduly alarmed. In those days managers tended to be given far more time than they are nowadays. One afternoon after a meeting with the directors he steered his car out of Craven Cottage and on to Putney Bridge. As the car edged forward he saw an *Evening News* sports billboard proclaiming ROBSON SACKED. What Robson is that? he wondered. Bryan 'Pop' Robson a prolific goalscorer with Newcastle United flicked into his mind but he might get transferred, not sacked and a Geordie club matter would hardly be headlines in the London evening papers. He didn't think much more about it until he was halfway down Putney High Street. It was him!

BIGGER THAN
THE CLUB?

Malcolm Macdonald was a young centre forward with Fulham at this time and he could probably have told Bobby that the writing was on the wall. Malcolm said that the club had become fixated on their ageing England hero Johnny Haynes. He claimed that the team was split into two camps – Johnny's chosen few and the rest. Malcolm's perception was that the Haynes camp would not even pass to the younger players and they did not talk to each other outside their groups. Malcolm says that Bobby attempted to break up this unofficial structure but Johnny Haynes' group's influence was too strong. Johnny was a world-class player at a back-street club and even though he had fought for his £100 a week he remained loyal to Fulham and never moved on despite ample opportunity. Therefore it was inevitable that his power base at Fulham would be virtually unassailable. Johnny Haynes succeeded Bobby Robson as player-manager and promptly told Malcolm Macdonald there was no room for 'his type of player' at Craven Cottage. Malcolm went to see the chairman, the comedian and presenter of *Sunday Night at the London Paladium* on TV, Tommy Trinder. Even Trinder's permanent smile lapsed when Malcolm said if he had to leave Fulham the last thing he would do before departing was smash Johnny Haynes's face in.

A member of that Fulham team was one of football's biggest characters. Tosh Chamberlain was a local lad who played on the left wing. This position was handy for chatting to the fans on the terraces, something he often did. Sometimes he would be passed a cigarette to puff on while he waited for Johnny Haynes to pass the ball. One time Johnny did and Tosh wasn't there to collect it. He had wandered down the tunnel for a quick slash. How Johnny and Jimmy Hill, another player who took his game very seriously, took that I cannot imagine.

On a similar theme Michael Parkinson, who is a man not given to bullshit, will tell you about a goalkeeper at his beloved Barnsley Football Club in the 1940s named Pat Kelly. Pat also had a verbal rapport with the crowd behind the goal and with only a little encouragement was prone to walking up and down his eighteen-yard line on his hands for their amusement. Spotting this once an opposing forward attempted to lob the upside-down goalkeeper and Pat unbelievably managed to run back-wards on his hands and catch the ball with his knees. If this had been caught on film it would certainly rank as one of the great-est goalkeeping saves ever. Sadly in 1940s Barnsley there was no food let alone cameras.

Parky also witnessed another classic goalkeeping incident when his team were playing the now defunct Bradford Park Avenue. Derby's great goalscorer Kevin Hector had started his career there. Their keeper was another eccentric by the name of Chick Farr. Chick had a habit of leaning up against his post and chatting away to the crowd. He would feign almost complete disinterest in the game being played in front of him and once when Barnsley's winger Johnny Kelly let rip with a thundering shot, Farr merely reached upward and pulled the wooden crossbar down so the ball shot harmlessly over the bowed bar. Besides a telling-off from the referee, Farr got away with it. I have never known Michael Parkinson to take drugs.

Alan Ball talks of a similar situation to the Haynes one when he joined Blackpool as an apprentice. The great Stanley Matthews was still at the club and Alan found him very aloof. It was a practice for senior players to tip the boys a shilling or so when they had cleaned their boots but Sir Stanley never saw fit to do this or not at least to Alan. When Alan broke into the first team and played alongside Matthews in a practice match he passed what he thought was a great ball into his path but Stanley made no effort to collect it. A little later in the game he rebuked him. 'When you pass to me in future, son, I expect the ball at my feet.' Alan knew Matthews was getting on but said he didn't realise his legs had packed up all together.

Alan Ball's father, as we know, was a manager for some years plying his trade in the lower divisions. When he took his young son for trials with League clubs as a teenager he introduced him as Alan James, so that the boy didn't get prejudged in any way. He pushed young Alan more than any other footballing father I have heard about, to the extent that when Alan started courting Lesley, who would later become his wife, he built up a dossier on all the reasons why he shouldn't get involved with her and presented it to his son. Fortunately, Alan had enough courage this time to go against the old man.

THE DON

I never played for England. I do not bear a grudge about this. I like to think it was because I am Irish. However, many of my peers did and I have to say almost without exception they had a great admiration for Sir Alf Ramsey as their manager and an almost equal lack of admiration for his successor, Don Revie. Unless they played for Leeds United. I never had a great deal of contact with either man, certainly never played under them, and therefore I only ever got other people's opinions. Don Revie fell out with Alan Ball and Malcolm Macdonald big time when he ended their international careers with letters signed in his absence, which was certainly insensitive. Even more so when you consider the press knew before they opened their envelopes that had arrived in the post. They never really established why they got the chop when they did, as they were both on sizzling form. Alan suspects it was because they visited Bernie Winters's house before an international match. Don perhaps didn't feel it was appropriate behaviour for footballers to mix with television celebrities – or maybe Don was a mad Morecambe and Wise fan?

Bally has also recounted a time when Revie was attempting to sign him for Leeds United from Blackpool. Alan was in dispute with the club by this time. Revie paid him in cash to continue his argument with Blackpool in the hope that Blackpool's management would despair and accept his offer. The two would drive weekly to a meeting point on the moors when Revie handed over a wad of notes adding up to £100. This happened at least three

Me as a model young professional who still only dreamt of scoring *on* the field.

A young Paddy Crerand, who became my
minder on the pitch, takes a post match bath.

An equally young Shay Brennan –
the friend who made me laugh so much off the pitch.

Shay still claiming, several decades later, to have set up my goal in the European Cup Final. He'd actually passed back to Alex Stepney before the big keeper launched it up field to me. An assist of sorts I suppose.

I tried to convince Billy Bingham that I was Northern Ireland's best option in almost any position as this training ground picture testifies.

Showing some youngsters how it's done. You'll notice I opted to score with my head so as not to scuff my Chelsea boots.

A quick kick about in my bar Bestie's in Marylebone, 1990. The only action my foot was seeing by then, apart from kicking punters out at last orders.

© HULTON ARCHIVE

(opposite top) Flying high – me in the cockpit on the way out to Poland
for the game with Gornik on our way to European victory in 1968.

(opposite bottom) Sir Matt offers words of encouragement as
we rest and contemplate extra time against Benfica.

That magical night at Wembley. David Sadler and
I can't suppress the smiles despite our exhaustion.

Taking on Everton's Alan Ball in a 1969 FA Cup game,
a great friend on and off the field.

Skinning Mike Summerbee down the wing
again in the 1970 derby at Old Trafford.

In full flight for Fulham in December 1976 against Oldham.

The old enemy Leeds – Jack Charlton, Peter Lorimer and Paul Reaney.
Our games were always hard-fought, brutal encounters.

Not quite as brutal as this man: Ron 'Chopper' Harris –
already looking for me as he leads out Chelsea.

Tony Dunne and Bobby Charlton restrain me after being sent off for swearing (allegedly at the referee, but it had actually been directed at Willie Morgan) against Chelsea at the Bridge in 1971.

Another lecture from a frustrated Sir Matt shortly before I went before the FA Disciplinary Committee in 1971. After three sendings off in one season I receive a record £250 fine and six-week ban.

Big Malcolm Allison – as flamboyant as English
management ever got. And almost as renowned
for the birds and the bubbly as yours truly.

(*opposite*) Brian Clough and Bill Shankly – surely the two most
quotable men the game has ever known – lead out Leeds and
Liverpool at Wembley in 1974 for the Charity Shield.

A few teams you probably won't have seen me playing for:

Cregagh Youth Club – the first team I turned out for on the Belfast estate where I grew up. You can just make me out in the middle of the front row without a shirt.

Barry Fry's Dunstable for a 3-2 win against Manchester United reserves when my team mates included an accountant and a paint-sprayer.

And Walford Boys aka the EastEnders team circa 1990,
which then included Tom Watt, Nick Berry and Sid Owen

Despite what they say I always loved training. Here I am slowing up Denis with a bad joke at The Cliff in 1970.

On holiday in Portugal with Denis – breaking the news to him that he's paying for dinner.

times but Revie wasted his (or Leeds' money) because Alan eventually signed for Everton. Years later there were allegations that Revie attempted to bribe Wolverhampton players not to try too hard against Leeds in a crucial League game.

However, the thing that really made me laugh about what they told me about Revie was how seriously he took everything. Before an England game he would assemble all the players and drone on for hours about the opposing team and the tactics that should be adopted. He would hand them all a thick file and tell them to retire to their beds and read it thoroughly. These files contained ridiculous details of all the opposing players, from their dates of birth to their playing records and Revie's observations and diagrams. It was full of stuff like when 3 moves to the right, 5 will play deep and 6 could close in but 4 is likely to be substituted, etc. Apparently it was total gobbledegook and often half the players he had dissected were not even in the named team the following day. He even did this against Cyprus which was then akin to Manchester United players being made to study dossiers for hours on the Barnet FC team before a third round cup tie. One England player told me that as he walked along the hotel corridor of the players' rooms all you could hear was the plonk of the files landing in the plastic waste-bins and the chink of the mini-bars rattling as they were being raided.

Alan Hudson maintains that Don Revie never wanted to pick him for the England team and that it was only because the press were demanding it that he finally gave in and selected him. Alan had a reputation, for drinking and for speaking his mind. These qualities were no-nos with Mr Revie, regardless of talent or form. This was 1975 and Alan Hudson was setting the First Division alight with Stoke City, and his mercurial presence in the team was driving this unfashionable and normally lowly club to challenge for honours. The press wanted him in. So Revie waited until England were playing West Germany before he put Hudson in the side. West Germany were at the peak of their powers and Alan believes that Revie believed that Beckenbauer and company would snuff Alan out the game and the need to pick him again would be averted. As it transpired Hudson is generally considered to have had the best international debut ever. Franz Beckenbauer hailed him as one of the greatest players in the world. However, Revie had the last laugh. He played Hudson in the 5–0 demolition of Cyprus and then never again.

Jimmy Armfield was one of the people who followed Don Revie into the Leeds United hot seat. Unlike Revie he had no enemies in the game. He had played quietly but diligently for years for Blackpool and England and everyone wished him well when he turned his hand to management. He didn't really last at it and is now a respected and I suspect very happy radio journalist. He wasn't without a sense of humour, as this anecdote reveals. Jimmy was addressing Duncan McKenzie, Leeds's talented striker who was perceived to be inconsistent, before one game.

'Duncan, I don't want you to play your normal role today … try to play well.'

Sir Alf Ramsey is generally thought to have had a raw deal from English football and I agree that he did. It is a scandal that the captain (Bobby Moore) and manager of the World Cup winning team saw out their final years in the footballing wilderness. Walter Winterbottom, Alf's predecessor, had a bit of a raw deal too. The achievements or lack of them of the pre-1966 England team are firmly put on poor old Walter's shoulders yet he wasn't even allowed to pick the bloody side! Unbelievably, but up until Sir Alf, England teams were picked by a committee of FA bods. And anyone who was ever hauled up before the FA will tell you how much some of these dozy old fools knew about football. Walter died only recently but such is the obscurity he found himself post-1966 that his death was barely reported and when you mentioned it to people, even in football, they looked at you puzzled and said, 'I thought he died years ago.'

I got hauled up in front of these old codgers at the FA a few times and they would ban me from playing for a few games. Sir Matt would come with me and we would dress up in our suits and stand there while I was told off like a naughty schoolboy. I found them hard to take seriously. These old men who had never played football. They reminded me of old Mr Grace out of *Are You Being Served*. They'd mumble something, cough and a body part would fall off. They banned me from playing for knocking the ball out of the referee's hands once. It might have done me some good though because on my return I managed to put six goals past Tony Book's goalkeeping brother in an 8–2 trouncing of Northampton Town.

I never got to know Alf Ramsey well but he always struck me as a little strange. There was the curious case of his accent for a start. He spoke in a strangled attempted upper-class accent that obviously was not his natural tongue. When interviewed he had a habit of using the phrase 'most certainly' rather a lot. I even thought he might have had a bet with someone to see how many times he could insert the phrase into a brief television interview. He was the only man in Britain to call Bobby Moore, Robert. His ability as a manager though was beyond question. He had moulded a mediocre Ipswich Town side from a lowly Third Division outfit to League champions in just five years. He spent almost no money and there were no stars in that side. Even football aficionados will struggle to name any of that team's players unless of course they come from Ipswich. Their goalkeeper though was Roy Bailey, who was the father of United's own Gary Bailey.

Alf did possess a dry sense of humour. After the World Cup in Mexico in 1970 when England failed to retain the trophy, the squad was travelling home on the aeroplane. They were a dejected bunch, coming to terms with their failure. Jack Charlton stood up and moved to the front of the plane where there was an empty seat next to his manager.

'Alf,' he started, 'I've been thinking. Well I'm in my thirties now. I'll be forever grateful for what you have done for me. I never dreamt that I would play for England or win a World Cup. But I'm not as fast as I was. Well, Alf, to get to the point, I think I should retire from international football. It's time to give the young'uns a chance.'

Alf's expression did not change throughout and he just stared ahead. When Jack finished he did not turn to him but said, almost without moving his lips, only 'Quite.'

Ron Atkinson may not have enjoyed quite the managerial

success of the Revies, the Shanklys or the Fergusons, but his personality is etched into the public consciousness as much as any of those men. Indeed 99 per cent of all parodies and comic interpretations of managers are based on Big Ron. When he first came along there was no one quite like him. Imagine if Don Revie had turned up on *Match of the Day* wearing a chunky gold identity bracelet. Picture Bill Shankly growing what hair he had left long and then one day walking out on the pitch of Anfield with it swept over and stuck down across his head to make it look as if he was well thatched. Exactly. He was so unlike what had gone before. Ron had more in common with Frank Butcher, the second-hand car dealer of *EastEnders*, than Frank O'Farrell, one of his predecessors in the Manchester United hot seat.

But Ron was a good manager and he knew it. He did more for United than Docherty ever did and when he asked me to play for United again I knew he wouldn't stitch me up. Unfortunately by that time I was thirty-five. If only he had come along earlier. When he was boss at Atletico Madrid in 1988 he declared, 'I believe there are only a select few managers who can handle the real giant clubs of the world. I happen to be one of them.' A month later Ron was sacked. Not that it would have got him down. It is his ability not to allow the ups and downs of the football manager's life to destroy him that the British public admires. Ron has always been pretty clear on where his priorities are. When he was asked what the highlight was for him of the 1994 World Cup in the USA he said, in all seriousness, that it had been bumping into Frank Sinatra.

Ron is not all double-breasted suits, dripping jewellery and one-liners. He takes his football very seriously. When manager of Sheffield Wednesday in the late 1990s things weren't going too well and after one defeat he lambasted the team in the changing rooms. He turned on Paolo Di Canio, 'You are a fucking prick! Next time you go to collect your wages, take a long hard look at yourself in the mirror. You ought to be ashamed of yourself.'

Di Canio and some of the other lads were of the opinion that Ron probably spent a touch too much time looking in the mirror himself and other non-Wednesday activities such as television appearances and opening fetes. They didn't mind this too much. Ron and the players got on well but Di Canio particularly felt this was a classic case of the pot calling the kettle black.

'Who the fuck do you think you are talking to,' raged the Italian. 'You are the one who should be ashamed of yourself. You turn up for training once a week!'

Both men became more and more heated until someone threw the first punch and they were engaged in a full blown tear-up. It took almost every other man in the changing rooms to pull them apart. Three weeks later Ron Atkinson appointed Di Canio team captain.

3

OVER LAND AND SEA

KICK-OFF

When I first arrived in America, in an effort to drum up enthusiasm, I was billed by the media as 'the White Pele'. The Brazilian had already caught the nation's imagination playing for New York Cosmos. I decided to put everyone right, though, at my first press conference when I told the assembled media that I was not the White Pele and that Pele was in fact the 'Black George Best'.

ASYLUM SEEKERS

Through football I have been lucky enough to travel the world. Some countries I have visited many times, some I have even lived in. I reckon I have been to most of the places worth going to in this world now but until I came to Manchester from Belfast I had never been abroad. Funnily enough one of the first places I visited made working-class 1950s Belfast seem positively luxurious.

In 1965 Northern Ireland played Albania in a World Cup qualifier and I was selected despite my tender years. We stayed for three days in the Albania capital Tirana and I was shocked by the poverty and the air of oppression in the then communist country. I can remember walking through a market where traders were selling very unappealing-looking meat and chicken. Locals were coming along and picking up the meat, handling and squeezing the goods before deciding not to buy and putting it back on the stall for the next person. There was hardly a car on the road yet there appeared to be a traffic policeman on each corner and in each square. The few cars that we did see were all the same colour, the same make and looked as if they were held together by string.

Still, never fear, our Albanian hosts had plans for us and on the first day we were loaded on to a coach and taken on a magical mystery tour. The coach driver got lost a few times and kept stopping to ask local people directions. Finally when we arrived it dawned on us all that the tourist attraction we had been brought to admire was in fact a mental institution. Haunted-looking people shuffled around the grounds in loose-fitting dirty smocks, staring vacantly or muttering to themselves. They seemed unaware of this bunch of foreigners in a coach watching them. Maybe this was a regular occurrence. Was this Albania's only tourist attraction? It reminded me of Longleat and the other safari parks that had been opening up at home. In these parks families drove into a fenced-off area of the English countryside and watched lions and tigers from the safety of their locked vehicles. Here we were watching the cast of *One Flew Over the Cuckoo's Nest*. It got better, but only slightly. In the evening we were taken to the cinema where we were treated to a Russian film with Albanian subtitles.

Strangely, since the collapse of communist Eastern Europe, we have all learnt a bit more about Albania and one of the most interesting facts is that the population idolises the British comedian Norman Wisdom. He is a national hero there and his visits to the country are accorded royal status. They chant Pitkin, after the hapless character in an ill-fitting suit and cap he played in a series of 1950s Ealing comedies. The Manchester United team bumped into Norman himself when we toured the West Coast of the United States in May 1967. While walking through San Francisco with David Sadler we saw his name on a billboard outside a theatre and went in and watched his act. Although we didn't introduce ourselves or go backstage someone told Norman we had been in and the next day he came to our hotel to introduce himself. We were training and Norman had no hesitation in changing into kit and joining in the five-a-side match we were playing. He was a good footballer and extremely fit, giving some of us the runaround. We were all a bit shocked, to be honest. I was shocked again recently when I noticed in the newspaper that it was his birthday and he was ninety-one years of age. I couldn't believe that I played competitive football with a man who is now ninety-one. It certainly made me feel old. I counted backwards and worked out that the day he played with us in America he was already fifty-five years old. I really had no idea.

My finest game for Northern Ireland was in October 1967 when we beat Scotland 1–0. The Scottish side had been fashioned around the Celtic team that had just won the European Cup. The scoreline does not reflect the way our humble Irish team tore them apart. I knew I had played well but many people have kindly said since it was one of the best individual performances they ever saw. Paddy Crerand told me later that during half-time the two full backs Tommy Gemmell of Celtic and Eddie McCreadie of Chelsea exchanged words. 'I'm having trouble with this boy,' said Tommy, 'do you fancy changing sides?'

'Go fuck yourself,' retorted Eddie with his customary directness.

GOODNIGHT VIENNA

I remember playing a game in Austria in 1966 when I was a young Manchester United player. The match was over and with the blessing of the manager a few of us went out for a drink on the understanding we would not be back too late as the coach was leaving at dawn for an early plane back to Manchester. We hit central Vienna and I was fortunate enough to chat up a very pretty young lady who was staying at a nearby hotel. It was soon apparent that we both felt there was a more attractive alternative to staying up all night drinking and we sneaked off from the group back to her hotel room. After some physical exertions we both fell sweetly off to sleep. Luckily, and only because I had not drunk too much and had got off to sleep relatively early, I awoke as the morning light streamed through a gap in the curtains and jumped out of bed and flung my clothes on.

'Sorry darling, I have to dash, my coach will be leaving any minute now. Honest.'

I said 'Honest' because when I said this it was not normally true. She smiled and shrugged, 'Okay, George, have a nice life.'

In those days I really liked those philosophical ladies. Outside I started rushing but soon realised I had no idea where I was. It had been dark when we left the bar for the hotel and we had taken a cab from our hotel to the bar area where we had been drinking. On top of this I couldn't think of the name of the hotel the team were staying in. I knew what it looked like but that was it. There was not a car or pedestrian on the road and for the first time I started to get a bit worried. I walked and walked hoping to recognise a landmark. I passed a couple of early-risers but could hardly ask them the way to my hotel whose name I did not know.

Then by a wonderful stroke of luck I spotted a United director, Mr Gibson, walking in the opposite direction on the other side of the road so I crossed and followed silently behind him. We walked back the way I had come and passed the hotel where I had spent the night; we turned the corner and there, almost next door, was the team's hotel! The team coach was outside and the players were milling about by the doors chatting. Dave Sadler, my roommate, spotted me as I tried to look as if I had been there all along. Looking at my crumpled dress he whispered, 'Don't worry, I've packed your stuff and put it in – just get on the coach. I told Jack you got up real early and went for a walk.' Dave looked really pleased with himself for covering for me. But at that point Jack Crompton, our trainer, approached with a knowing look on his face.

'Morning, George.'

'Hello, Jack, I couldn't sleep so I went out for a stroll,' I volunteered although I hadn't been asked.

'Umm,' said Jack, 'good of you to have made your bed before you went.'

Nice one, Dave.

HOLIDAYS IN THE SUN

Almost as soon as I started earning and had established a network of friends in Manchester, me and a bunch of pals took a foreign holiday and at that time Majorca had just come within reach of the ordinary working man so we decided to go there. When we first arrived there was barely a bar or restaurant on the island and each year when we returned we noticed more and more development. I regret now that we didn't take up the many offers we had of buying some land. We went every summer to that same Spanish island for the next fifteen-odd years and although there was some team changes over the period it was the same core of friends from Manchester and beyond who turned up each time for a week or two of drinking, chasing women and hilarity. As the years went by it was like a personal challenge to turn up. Even as all our lives took different twists and turns, none of us wanted to be the first to drop out and admit we were finally becoming middle-aged.

There was Malcolm Wagner (known as Waggy) and Tony Marsh, who had been a compere and had introduced the Beatles at various concerts not so long before. There was Colin Burn who was already a nightclub owner and serial entrepreneur and there was also a mysterious chap by the name of David Sirocco of whom more later.

Tony Marsh was a real character and always had us in stitches. One year he turned up with a lady who seemed very pleasant. Tony seemed a bit uncertain about her though and kept g the need to assure us of her worth, 'she's good to me you know, she'll do anything for me.' These regular statements were made worse by the fact that the poor girl was sat alongside him when he said this. One morning after a heavy night Tony asked his girlfriend to cook us all a late breakfast and she served up really nice sausage, bacon and eggs.

'Told you she was a good girl,' smiled Tony. 'She'll do anything for me.'

'Anything?' asked one of the other lads with a mischievous grin. Tony whispered in the girl's ear and for the remainder of our meal she was on her knees with her head in Tony's lap giving him a blow job as we all finished our fry-ups. Tony lived life to the full and sadly died a few years ago from a heart attack.

Alex Harley, who had played professional football with Manchester City and Birmingham, came along some years. Although he had recently been an athlete he had developed a raging drink habit and as soon as he hit the island he hit the drink. He was a great fella who had the gift of the gab and could charm the ladies so easily. Unfortunately, though, he loved his drink more and when it was time to go back to the chalet or hotel room he was too pissed to get out of his seat, let alone get his trousers off. This used to upset Waggy and me and Alex himself. He would vow that this night would be the night he would get his nuts and stay sober but three pints later all his resolve had crumbled. One last night Waggy and me decided we would keep him sober. We tried to drink slowly. When it was our round we got him shandy. When he went to the toilet we swigged back most of his drink. Soon he was chatting at a table to a gorgeous-looking girl. This was looking good. As the evening wore on Alex kept buying himself and his girl drinks and we kept swigging his without his knowledge. At one point he looked over at the bar and gave the thumbs-up. In the early hours I decided I would run them back to our villa in the car and threaded my way across the dance floor only to find Alex shaking the girl's shoulders as she sat, head slumped on the table, comatose through alcohol. He didn't get his nuts after all. Alex lived life to the full and died sadly a few years later back in Birmingham.

They didn't come more baffling than David Sirocco. He lived in Majorca. We had no idea where he came from or about his family and background. He operated alone, floating around the beach performing massages on holidaymakers. He dressed all in white and was a tanned, stunningly good-looking man; if you visited Majorca in the 1960s or 1970s you probably came across him. He's the sort of man you don't forget. His massaging finished at 4.30 and then he would conduct yoga classes on the beach. The women absolutely adored him and they fell at his feet but he showed little interest. Indeed he was positively rude to them and took great pleasure in delivering stinging insults and belittling them in public. Looking back on it, perhaps he had some sort of problem in that area.

One year he just wasn't there and although we asked around, no one seemed to have any idea what had happened to him. We thought perhaps that he had ended up in prison as he lived a stylish, mysterious, hand-to-mouth existence and sailed close to the wind but our enquiries yielded nothing. Perhaps he had moved on like so many of these people do when maybe they outstay their welcome or upset the wrong person. Slowly we forgot about Tony. Years later, though, Waggy and I were out in Johannesburg, South Africa, and we had just booked into our hotel when we took the lift to our floor. Staring at us from a poster on the lift doors was David Sirocco's face. There he was, same clothes, same name and he was the hotel's resident fitness, yoga and meditation instructor. Waggy and I had a good laugh, dropped our gear off in our rooms and went back down to reception.

'Can you tell us where we can find David Sirocco?' Waggy enquired.

But Tony had left the hotel for good only the day before. We never heard of Tony again and I must admit that I assumed he was probably dead until Waggy told me he was watching the television the other night and there was some late-night programme about fitness on. It was an American night-time filler and Waggy was paying little attention but sat bolt upright when he recognised the voice of the man on the screen talking about mind and body. Sure enough it was Tony.

Johnny Prescott, the boxer from the Midlands, was another one who came on holiday with us. Johnny was a good heavyweight who fought Henry Cooper for the British Heavyweight title in 1965. Henry knocked him out in the tenth round. He had already beaten the other well-known British heavyweights of the period – Brian London and Billy Walker. His final professional fight was against Joe Bugner in 1970. I remember one year when we couldn't be bothered to chat the girls up to get them back up to the villa, we simply had some cards printed. They just said that there was a party, the time and the address and then whenever we saw a pretty face we handed them a card.

Mike Summerbee, Johnny and I were walking downstairs into a club as a stunning Swedish girl came up them. Mike instinctively handed her a card but failed to notice the aggressive-looking boyfriend climbing the stairs behind her. He looked at the card and didn't like it; so much so, the shoulders went back, the chin out and he started to poke at Mike's chest. Mike wasn't making a good job of explaining himself and the chap clenched his fist. Before he could bring it up on to the Summerbee jaw, Johnny Prescott pushed Mike to one side and cracked the bloke spark out. We did a runner and ended up in another club but Johnny was a gentleman and he was worried about the man he had just dispatched into next week and insisted we return to see how he was. We did and both the man and the club owners were very fair and accepted our apologies, although the next day, while laying on the beach, we saw a group of muscular, blond Swedish men heading towards us. We thought there was going to be another showdown. Fortunately all they wanted was a game of beach football.

Billy Walker was one of the biggest names in English boxing in the 1960s and after having a stab at acting in a couple of British film comedies he was able to retire to Jersey, having managed to hang on to the money he had earned. His brother George Walker was even more adept at accumulating the cash, turning a baked potato franchise into the Brent Walker leisure empire. When he was on the way up he had a pretty secretary by the name of Angie Macdonald and I clapped eyes on her at a fashion show in London. A few years later we met up again when I was in America and she became my first wife. By that time Angie had become a personal trainer to Cher and was living in with the singer in her Los Angeles home.

Talking of British film comedies, two of the lads that formed part of our holiday gang were dead ringers for Sid James and Bernard Bresslaw. This was the London lot led by Laurie Jacobs, a black-cab driver. Laurie was our very own Sid James, not so much in looks, but he had the wicked sense of humour and the laugh. However, his sidekick was in every way a double for Bernard Bresslaw, Sid's foil in the Carry On films, and Laurie used to wind him up similarly. It all sounds pretty childish now but we had hours of amusement from things like Laurie defecating into a shoebox and leaving it under his pal's bed for the night.

AMERICAN DREAM

Before I went to play in America I was offered a job as a player and publicity manager of the North American Football League in Canada. This was when Manchester United were really suffering just towards the end of Frank O'Farrell's short tenure as manager. I was never really going to take the job but went out to have a look. The posters that I saw all over Manchester and London proclaiming DRINK CANADA DRY may have had something to do with it. I didn't stay in Canada very long but did drift down to California and thought, I like this country, I could live here.

When people talk about the British invasion they are normally referring to that short time in the mid-1960s when British pop groups dominated the American music charts. Led by the Beatles and the Stones, a whole host of other beat groups broke through on the other side of the Atlantic. Herman's Hermits from Manchester, for example, were far bigger in the States than they were at home. They even got to make a film like the Beatles did called *Hold Tight*, which is now long forgotten. However, there was another British invasion in the following decade when the USA decided to create a soccer industry from scratch and imported stars from all over the world, but especially Britain, to kick-start the game into action.

I thought it was a great concept and their strategy was the right one. The cream of the world's footballing talent ending their careers in America, where they would not only entertain and galvanise supporters but would also educate and develop the youngsters. This would introduce continuity and America could grow their own talent thereafter, because it would only be at that point that the game would really integrate with their society. The first part worked great; anyone who was anyone was out there from Pele to journeymen from Stockport County and a buzz was created and the crowds came. I spent time with Los Angeles Aztecs, Fort Lauderdale and San Jose Earthquakes in the 1970s and '80s and despite having to embrace such wheezes as entering the arena on the back of a motorbike (as opposed to running out the tunnel at Ayresome Park on a cold winter's night) I took it all very seriously. I wanted the US game to take off and I loved living abroad and experiencing new and different cultures. I remember reading that Paul Rideout, the former Everton striker, was shocked to discover when he moved out to play football in China that television programmes were in the Chinese language rather than English. Also Ian Rush is quoted as saying he couldn't settle in Italy because it was like living in a foreign country. I'm not sure what they expected but we had no such problems adapting to life in America.

PROPER CHARLIE

At Los Angeles Aztecs I was in good company. Bobby McAlinden from Manchester City was one of my greatest friends, Ron Davies, the former Southampton and Wales centre forward (who just came out for a holiday and stayed) and the old Chelsea maestro Charlie Cooke all became my new 'buddies'. When I knew Charlie in England he drank like a fish and was an integral part of that famous drinking academy at Chelsea Football Club in the late 1960s and early 1970s. Charlie could play. Jim Baxter famously said that when Charlie Cooke sold you a dummy you had to pay to get back into the ground.

When we met up again, though, Charlie had changed. No one trained like Charlie and although at that time in his thirties he was fitter than anyone else at the club. He was forever challenging the young boys to races and other tests of fitness. He had become almost evangelical about his body. He had also developed a philosophical streak. 'George your body is a temple. Worship it,' he would say. He had stopped drinking and smoking completely and implored me to do the same. He came out with an ever more bizarre series of homilies and words of wisdom and I became convinced that Charlie was partaking in some mind-altering drug. Of course he wouldn't hear of any such thing. The new, improved Charlie Cooke was pure in mind, body and spirit.

Charlie loved a joke. One day we were staying in a motel the evening before a game. The rooms were arranged in a circular fashion with their doors facing out on to a central swimming pool. We'd arranged to meet in the bar for a drink and maybe a meal but a couple of the young American players who were usually quite up for it said they'd give it a miss and stay in. Our suspicions were immediately aroused. Later that evening Bobby, Charlie and I crept around the back of their room while another bunch of lads went to their front door. Through a small gap in the curtains I could see them clearly stretched full out on their beds both with healthy spliffs between their fingers and blowing large smoke rings upwards. Between them on a small coffee table were the tin, the papers and other paraphernalia for rolling joints.

'LAPD – OPEN THE DOOR,' shouted the boys at the front door and never had I seen them move so fast. Both of them literally jumped into the air and ran towards the French windows to extinguish their joints. As they struggled with the curtain and threw the doors open they were faced only with me, Charlie and Bobby doubled up with laughter.

Charlie really was the king of the mickey-takers. He loved winding people up and most of it was just good fun but he did have a difficult relationship with one of the backroom staff. I didn't like him much either but Charlie hated him and delighted in making him look stupid. During training we had large drums of Gatorade, an energy drink, around the place that we were free to swig as and when we felt the need. Charlie being the hardest trainer of us all normally drank the most. One day this guy approached each of us individually and whispered, 'Don't touch number three', referring to one of the drums of Gatorade.

However, by all accounts he deliberately hadn't mentioned this to Charlie. We found out later that he had laced number three with some sort of hallucinatory drug and poor old Charlie had been knocking back pints of it. Charlie never found out but he complained the next day about these strange apparitions he had seen on his way home. It was mad, looking back on it, Charlie could have killed himself, or others, as he drove home that day, not to mention the psychological damage that could have been inflicted, but at the time we thought little of it.

THRILLER IN MANILA, NEW YORK

Bobby McAlinden is a great pal. We were strangely born on the same date – 22 May, 1946. He had been on the books at Manchester City but had never really scaled the heights in English football. But when I accepted the offer to play for the Aztecs I insisted that he was part of the deal. Neither side regretted it. Bobby's fantastic work-rate and enthusiasm endeared him to his new team-mates, the crowd and the management, and Bobby, well, he still lives in America.

I'm not sure if Bobby was with Manchester City when they did the States in a pre-season tour at the end of the 1960s. Summerbee told me about it. Up to that point none of the squad had been to America before and the whole culture and way of life had come as a bit of a shock. One evening Neil Young and George Heslop returned to their hotel in San Francisco white-faced and barely able to speak. They hadn't even been for a drink. They had merely been to the cinema and then popped into a hamburger bar for a bite to eat before they came back to the hotel. While they ate their food a row developed at the counter between customers which they watched warily. When one man pulled out a gun and shot two others they almost choked.

Bobby and I were inseparable in America. We played together, drank together and opened a bar together. One time the two of us travelled from Los Angeles to New York for a few days. It was the time of the big fight between Muhammad Ali and Joe Frazier, the so-called 'thriller in Manila' being staged in the Philippines. Bobby and I found a bar with a large-screen television and pulled up a couple of seats near the front long before the fight started and the pub began filling up. In order not to lose our seats we only went to the toilet separately and quite a bit of drink was consumed as we waited for the fight to start. A very large and loud American man arrived in the bar and forced his way to the front where we were sitting. He too had probably had a few drinks but unlike us he wasn't keeping himself to himself. He had no idea who we were – my face was not at all recognisable in New York. When he started mouthing off how Frazier was going to whup Ali I couldn't resist having a bet with him. As boxing history tells, Ali won and our corpulent American friend was none too pleased. He wasn't too keen on paying up either and in an effort to welch on his bet he started to get lairy and pretend he was angry with us over something else. Suddenly he was leaning over Bobby and poking him in the chest. 'Come outside,' he kept shouting. It was one of those moments when you start to act but you can't remember making any decision to do so or even understand why you did.

'I'll come outside with you,' I said calmly, shocking myself because the guy towered over me. This man mountain and me walked out on to the street with him shouting and swearing as the crowd parted to let us through.

'Are there any rules to this fight?' I asked as we stood facing each other in the doorway, but before he could reply I kicked him as hard as I could in the balls. He doubled over and then rocked over backwards on to the floor. Fortunately for me a couple of bouncers appeared before he could recover his composure and literally lifted him off his feet and rushed away with him shouting, screaming and swearing. When I walked back into the bar the whole place erupted into applause. It was like *I'd* just won the thriller in Manila. To cap an already bizarre evening a man approached us and put his arm around me. 'Gee, that was great, let me buy you a drink.' I had noticed him earlier in the bar and thought he looked familiar.

'I know you from somewhere,' I said.

I could see he was surprised that we didn't know definitely who he was. We must have been the only people in New York who didn't know him at the time. He told us he was Kevin Dobson and he played Lt Bobby Crocker in the massive TV hit police series *Kojak*.

Hermosa Beach, where I had an apartment while I played for the Los Angeles Aztecs, was the weirdest place. Well, the place was not weird but the people were. The people I fell in with anyway. We all drank in a bar called the Mermaid and the common denominator among us was that we all had money, time on our hands and loved a drink. There was an older guy we called Unc, I presume this was short for Uncle but maybe it was short for Unclear as this is how he ended up every night. He was the resident bookmaker and we would place our bets on sporting events anywhere in the world with him. He was a great drinker and every night, almost as a ritual, one of us less drunken friends would walk him home from the bar. Nevertheless at any time in the evening he could cite you the exact state of play of your betting account with him or calculate to the nearest cent your winnings on any bet. He never wrote anything down yet anyone who thought the drink would cloud his memory and he would forget the odd losing bet had another think coming. Sadly Unc died not long after I returned to England.

When I was at San Jose Earthquakes Malcolm Wagner and an accountant came out to visit. Not many people come out to visit and hand you over fifteen grand but Malcolm did. He had been tidying up our various business interests in the UK and the accountants had calculated that this sum was due to me. I wasn't expecting anything so it was a welcome surprise. It was here that Malcolm first met Angie, who later became my first wife. Years later he told me he went off her rapidly when she was in England and she confided in him, 'I hate Manchester. Everyone's got bad teeth.' Waggy wasted much time thereafter orally examining himself in the shaving mirror.

Many players could not adjust to the razzmatazz of the American game. The Americans viewed it as entertainment first and competitive sport second and that is how they approached the whole scenario. For me, I understood this but it took some getting used to when players you last came across on the mud bath of, say, the Hawthorns were introduced over the speakers as Bobby 'Paleface' Hope or you meet up with old colleagues and discovered they were now known as Jimmy 'Quickdraw' Ryan. Peter Osgood, who spent time with Philadelphia Fury, finally had enough of it all when he played a game where the opposing team arrived on the pitch on horses, wearing Stetsons and firing cap guns. He turned round to Alan Ball and said, 'I'm going fucking home.'

Rodney Marsh loved it though and he lived and made his home out there and still retains business interests to this day. He was always an entertainer first and never lost sight of the fact that people paid money to be entertained. When I say he couldn't take the British game seriously I mean that in the most complimentary way. He had no truck with the boring, negative, win at all costs style of football that competed with flair and entertaining football for supremacy in our era. Of all people it was natural that he should adapt to and embrace the American game more than anyone else.

I enjoyed my time in the States and I admired American attempts to develop the game in such a short space of time. At the time British clubs could have learnt a great deal from them about marketing, presentation and the making of money. Indeed, many of them still could. I am not of the school of thought that the only true fans of football must be working class and have done time standing on cold, windy terraces sipping watereddown Bovril and eating rancid meat pies. We seem almost proud of the spartan, austere and sometimes dangerous conditions we endured in football grounds for decades. Football should be exciting and passionate but it should also be inclusive, fun and comfortable.

PART II

OFF THE PITCH

4

THE DRINK

KICK-OFF

Slim Jim Baxter is a folk hero in Scotland and anyone who saw
him play will tell you why. Jim, who died recently, also had a
lifelong, on–off love affair with alcohol. He was twice as bad as
I was – he had two liver transplants for a start. When he played
at Nottingham Forest, at a time when many of us were drinking
with gay abandon and long before any chickens had come home
to roost, he told me the following story.

He had been on a big weekend bender with his pals and
woke up on the Monday morning with severe back pains.
When they had not gone two days later he decided to see a
doctor. For obvious reasons he went to see his own GP rather
than the club doctor.

'How much would you say you drink a day on average?'
queried the medical man after a brief examination.

Now, at this time Jim was drinking six or seven pints most days after training and on Saturday night and Sundays substantially more but he was embarrassed to tell his doctor the full extent of his alcoholic intake.

'I suppose about two to three pints a day on average, doctor,' he lied hesitantly.

'Two to three pints a day!' exclaimed the medical man. 'Carry on like that and you'll become an alcoholic.'

WHERE DID IT ALL GO WRONG?

No surprises that this section turns out to be one of the bigger sections in the book. But then drink has been the biggest thing in my life. I said biggest not best. Drink contributed to cutting my career short and may prove to cut my life short but I would be lying if I said I regretted it all. It was the petrol that drove my social life and I packed a great deal in from the age of seventeen to fifty years old. The famous 'George, where did it all go wrong?' story sums it up. I'd been to a casino with Mary Stavin, who had won the Miss World contest shortly before. We'd done well in the casino and I had exchanged my chips for plenty of cash. I think it was close on £20,000. Tucking it into my jacket, we walked back to the Holiday Inn in Birmingham where we were staying. In our room I spread the notes across the bed and began counting the cash as Mary slipped into a negligee. Excited by my good fortune I called down to the night porter for a nice bottle of Dom Perignon champagne. It was clear from his accent that he too originally hailed from Belfast. When he arrived in the room he placed the champers and the glasses on the table and then looked over at me and the money spread across the bed. Only a fellow Irishman would have brought three glasses. He then looked over at a partially dressed Miss World brushing her hair like a beautiful mermaid. I opened the champagne and gave him one of the £50 notes as a tip. He was obviously pleased with this, as the money probably represented a week's wages for him. Yet he hesitated as he tucked the note in his pocket. 'Can I ask you something Mr Best?'

'Of course,' I said.

He looked again at Mary, looked at the money on the bed, looked again at me and his face assumed a look of genuine pity. 'Tell me, Mr Best – where did it all go wrong?'

Here I was in a top hotel with the world's most beautiful woman and drowning in cash and champers but Joe Public was shaking his head, bemoaning my decline! Yet I was living out the lifestyle that millions of males, at least, would have given their right arm for. How could I not have got swept up in the sheer headiness of it all? Attitudes to drink and drinking have changed so much over the years too. Now it is more socially acceptable to be a pothead than a pisshead. Back in the 1960s and 1970s while half the country drove home from the pub paralytic, Mick Jagger and Keith Richard of the Rolling Stones were locked up for smoking cannabis. Sir Mick Jagger if you don't mind. There's proof if you need it on how the ground has shifted!

I should have realised I had a problem when I was out drinking and clubbing and would stagger back to my hotel. 'Can I have a wake-up call please?' I would slur to the receptionist.

'Of course, Mr Best. What time?'

'Seven a.m., please.'

The receptionist would then pull a face like she had a mild pain in her back and say, 'Er, it's a quarter past seven now, Mr Best.'

This happened many times. Yet I never saw myself as vastly

different from many of my contemporaries. Now Malcolm Macdonald admits he was drinking a bottle of whisky a day and Rodney Marsh has held his hands up to a serious problem, but at the time the belief among the public was that it was just me.

My friends have told me since that they didn't realise I had a problem, especially in the Manchester days, because basically they were all living the same life too. My great pal Waggy did reflect though that there came a time when we would be partying to two or three in the morning and he would finally turn in but I would refuse to go home with him. Instead I would move on to the more obscure drinking dens, like Philomena Lynott's joint in the front room of a hotel. Places like these catered for gentleman of the night, like croupiers, or musicians who wouldn't start winding down until the early hours. He thinks maybe this was the point where the drink became more important than the going out.

David Sadler tried to sit me down once and talk to me. We had been close since we were boys and had roomed together and at Mrs Fullaway's. 'What are you doing to yourself?' he said. 'Think of your health.'

I took no notice. Not long ago we talked about this. Dave dismissed this with characteristic diplomacy. 'I was only worried about my win bonus, if you didn't play,' he smiled.

It must have crept up on me. When I first got to Manchester and went out with Dave Sadler and the lads, we frequented the snooker halls or bowling alleys and the question of having a drink was never raised. Even when I caught the bug of chasing women and I started to go to pubs and clubs with Mike Summerbee we never really drank a lot. We were both shy and conscious of our accents and I guess we both started drinking a little more to rid ourselves of that particular inhibition. You see, I mumbled into my chest in my broad unintelligible Belfast brogue that was so thick *I* had trouble understanding it, and Mike, being from Wiltshire, spoke like a Wurzel. He found it very difficult to keep the word 'fertiliser' out of his conversation.

One of the saddest stories of footballers and drink is that of Albert Johanneson. He was a talented black South African player with Leeds United in the 1960s. Mistakenly he is often referred to as the first black player to become established in top-flight football. In my memory there was a lad called John Charles at West Ham at the same time and before me the comedian Charlie Williams was playing at Doncaster Rovers. Charlie was certainly the first black stand-up comic I can recall and had the catchphrase "Ello, flower'. In those days he would deal with hecklers by saying 'Shut up, or I'll move in next door to you.' He'd be crucified for that now and so would anyone who laughed at it. Back to poor Albert though. He was part of the Leeds team that was developed under Don Revie and gained promotion to the First Division. Unfortunately he didn't survive in the team as they emerged as the strongest in the League in the late 1960s and he faded into obscurity. Years later that team, now mostly living in comfortable retirement, discovered that Albert was still in the Yorkshire area but had slipped down life's greasy pole and was a penniless alcoholic often sleeping rough on the streets. They organised a benefit dinner for him in Leeds to raise money but what they didn't know was that by the time the dinner was held he had been in rehab and had been off the alcohol successfully for some weeks. His doctors and counsellors were delighted with his progress. The dinner though was all too much for an emotional Albert and he caved in under the temptation, smashing back bottles of champagne and more. By the end of the evening he was a gibbering wreck. Only weeks later he was found dead, through alcohol, in his small flat.

ALEHOUSE BRAWLERS

An early team that had a reputation for enjoying their drink was the Southampton side of the mid-1960s. Bill Shankly famously described them as 'alehouse brawlers' but this is likely to have had more to do with his displeasure at his beloved Liverpool side being beaten once by Southampton than any hard evidence of their social habits. One of the alehouse boys was Jimmy Gabriel, a Scot, who had enjoyed a successful career at Everton before his move to the south coast. One morning he was late for training and when he finally turned up he looked terrible. It hadn't been a drinking night the evening before so the lads were curious. 'What happened to you, Jim?'

'Well,' he explained, 'I was sitting indoors last night watching telly and in the film that was on this cowboy walks into the salon, orders a bottle of whisky and swigs it back in one. I couldn't believe that could be done, so I decided to try it. I managed about three-quarters of the bottle and I couldn't bloody move. I had to throw my shoe up at the ceiling to let the wife know I couldn't get up from the chair.'

In the 1970s Southampton made the FA Cup Final and were to go on to beat Tommy Docherty's Manchester United. After they won their semi-final they were down at Portsmouth for a routine Second Division match. The night before the match Mick Channon arranged a drink up in his hotel room to celebrate their making the Cup Final. Most of the team attended and without the manager's knowledge they drank crates and crates of lager that they had sneaked into the room. The session went on until the sun came up. Lawrie McMenemy, the manager, was no idiot and he knew straight away when a badly hung-over team assembled in the hotel foyer in the morning. He was furious. His mood didn't improve when the team filed in for half-time, hanging on to a 0–0 draw and after playing abominably.

'You should be ashamed of yourselves,' he bellowed. 'There are five thousand Saints fans out there. They've all turned out today to pay tribute to you shower for getting to the Cup Final and this is how you repay them. You should be hanging your heads in shame.' Mike and the boys were hanging their heads but not necessarily with shame. In the second half the hang-overs had begun to clear and the Southampton boys started to put it together and they finally scored. When they filed in at the end of the match the players were jubilant. McMenemy stood and regarded them with his arms folded. He shook his head. 'You lucky, lucky bastards.'

'Boss,' chirped Channon, 'we stopped drinking at five. If the drink hadn't run out and we could have carried on we'd have beaten them by three.'

Stories of players and their antics out on the drink are numerous and in the days before sham political correctness it went largely unreported. One of the reasons for this was, especially during overseas tours and tournaments, the press boys were out on the razzle with us. Part of the traditional journalist's remit was alcohol. I would go as far as to say that many of them were heavier drinkers than we were – the difference was we were athletes and would be up in the morning to attend training; they were not and could not surface before midday to file their copy. When I see the righteous indignation spouted these days I have to laugh.

Naturally, we were given curfews by the managers – a time we had to be back in the hotel by. But half the game was how to get around that, or if you didn't care for the manager just to flout it. In the 1970s the Scottish team had gathered in Scotland for an international get-together and the manager at the time was one Willie Ormond. The lads were allowed out for a drink with Willie's blessing but he told them all they had to be in bed by midnight. At midnight they were still banging the cocktails down. When they returned to the hotel in the wee hours (as they would say) the hotel was all locked up and they knew that if they rang the night bell their escapades would be discovered. One of them spotted a window open a couple of floors up and they all agreed it must be the bedroom of one of the players who had not accompanied them on the session. The Scottish party had occupied the entire second floor of this hotel. Lou Macari at five feet five inches was the smallest of their number and he was dispatched to climb the drainpipe and enter the window and then come back downstairs and let the others in quietly. Lou says he shinned the drainpipe with ease and slipped into the room. As he tiptoed across the carpet, a voice from the bed said calmly, 'Hello, Lou.'

Lou turned around and saw the figure of Willie Ormond, his manager, sitting up in bed. 'Hello, boss,' he replied and then continued tiptoeing to the door.

WHAT DID I DO?

As any serious drinker will tell you, one of the biggest hazards of following this path is memory loss. There is a tired old phrase – 'if you remember the 1960s you weren't there' – well, there is some truth in this. Except in my case most of the blanks occurred during the 1970s, 1980s and even a bit of the 1990s. There are large parts of my life I do not remember although most of these blank spaces are well after the end of my playing career and most events have been reconstructed for me at later times. In the early days of my drinking it was just the previous night's events I could not remember and then as the day wore on those memories would come back to you – and they would normally make you wince. However, later in life whole week-ends or even weeks and months would disappear into an alcohol-sodden black hole and even when you did remember unpleasant episodes, people you had upset, insulted or let down, you didn't care. One day I was in the Phene Arms in Chelsea when the landlord told me there was a call for me.

'George, I've tracked you down at last,' said an Irish voice at the other end of the line.

'Who is this?' I slurred.

'This is Pat Doyle, George. From Patrick Doyle, Classic Cars in Dublin. What do you want to do about your Mercedes?'

'What Mercedes?'

'The one you bought in here for repairs, two years ago.'

That sort of sums up the Chelsea years.

As I said, anyone would think I was the only footballer who drank too much during my career, but although my story is high profile the drinking culture was pretty ingrained among many professional footballers in my day and continues even now. Manchester United themselves would have problems with some players' excessive drinking long after I retired. Bobby Moore, possibly the most famous English player of all time, loved a drink. He only supped halves but seemed to be able to go on twice as long as all of us, so by my calculations that means he was drinking as much as everyone else. He was one of those people who never showed outward signs of drunkenness and probably that was why his drinking passed without comment.

My Northern Ireland colleague Derek Dougan was another who could put them away in his day. Derek was a big chap who had been a rebel in his early footballing days – one time he shaved his head as a protest against footballers' rights or lack of them – this at a time when footballers would think it was the height of daring to roll their socks down. I was with him in Cyprus for a Northern Irish international match where we settled in a little taverna for a drinking session. The bar owners were nice people and kept our drink flowing, they kept tabs on our spending quite informally by chalking up the number of beers we had on the bar. They were doing this by marking five lines and a sixth line striking through it to signify every sixth drink. It was agreed at the end of the night we'd settle up according to the totals. The Doog had other ideas and each time he went to the toilet he licked his fingers and rubbed one of the boxes away. He thought this was hilarious until one of the waiters noticed him and took him to task. Derek was having none of it and denied he had done this, and before we knew it, the excitable little Cypriot and the towering Irishman were rolling around on the floor fighting. Between us, the players and the taverna staff, we managed to break them up, settle the bill and get out before things really turned nasty. Derek is a nice man and true to form he went back there alone some hours later to apologise and ended up having a friendly nightcap with all the staff.

Alan Ball liked to partake. It was often the way that those players who never stopped running on the field and were an example to everyone else in training were among the most enthusiastic imbibers. Alan Hudson is another example. Bally knew when to stop though and sometimes he adopted extreme measures to do so. One evening he walked into a north London pub where his Arsenal team-mates were socialising and he put a wad of notes over the bar to send the message around he was after a real session. However, he announced he was leaving at ten o'clock.

'Even if I try and stay then you must make me go,' he said. 'Even if I say I have changed my mind and refuse to go, punch me on the nose, I mean it.' At ten Alan Ball was showing no signs of leaving the bar.

Indeed he could be heard shouting, 'Who's got the whip?' Bob McNab approached him and reminded him he was supposed to be leaving.

'Shut up, Bob. Have a drink.'

'No, you said you really had to go at ten and we should make you leave,' persisted McNab.

'Bob. I'm staying. Right? I'm fine.'

Bang! Alan's nose exploded with blood everywhere. With friends like Bob McNab who needs enemies?

Of all the high jinks and practical jokes we played on one another, often through drink, nothing can compare to Peter Beagrie's moment of madness when Everton were on a pre-season tour of Spain in 1991. It was after a game with Real Sociedad and Beagrie had become separated from his team-mates during the course of the night's drinking that followed the match. Lost and the worse for wear, he staggered out of a bar into the night and flagged down a local youth on a motorbike. He asked the boy to take him to his hotel. When they arrived at the San Sebastian Hotel it was all locked up and Beagrie's shouts could not locate a night porter. He then commandeered the boy's bike, mounted it, drove around in a circle and then in true Steve McQueen *Great Escape* style bumped up the concrete steps and drove straight through the plate glass doors. Worse than the forty stitches that Peter required perhaps was the fact that he had gone to the wrong hotel.

FRIDAY ON MY MIND

There were players too who were just as bad as any of us in the burning of the candle at both ends stakes but because they were not playing in the top division it passed the outside world by. One was a lad called Robin Friday who had problems with drink and drugs and died tragically young. Charlie Hurley, when manager of Reading, picked him up from non-League Hayes in the 1970s. Charlie had been tipped off about his great talent but was warned he was a bit of a nutter and that he had had spells in borstal. Robin enjoyed a great season at Elm Park where he delighted the fans with his individuality, goal scoring and stunts, such as pulling his opponents' shorts down. He was transferred to Cardiff City where British Transport Police, who had discovered that he had travelled there on a platform ticket, arrested him on arrival. Managers soon learnt that they could not guarantee whether Friday would turn up for a game or not. It all depended on how heavy Friday's Friday night had been. He never achieved his potential and never played in the top division. He was only thirty-eight when he died.

Another live wire was Graham French who played under Alec Stock at Luton a decade earlier in the 1960s. One morning the Luton team were waiting on Luton station to board their special train for their away match at Bury. Graham French was nowhere to be seen and Alec refused to leave without him. Finally French staggered on to the platform in his Friday night suit, shirt hanging out, beer can in hand, still pissed. Somehow the boys crowded around him and got him on the train without Alec examining him and allowed him to sleep all the way to Bury. He resumed sleeping in the Gigg Lane dressing rooms until 2.30 when his team-mates woke him and got him into his kit. He went out on to the pitch and played well, making two of the Luton goals but some way through the first half he received a pass on the halfway line and put his foot on the ball.

'Will you please stop passing to me,' he shouted. 'I'm knackered. I want to go to sleep,' and then he just walked off the pitch.

Mickey Thomas, who was a jinky little winger who played for a number of League clubs including Manchester United and Chelsea, is one of that select band of famous footballers who have tasted porridge. I'm another of them. Thomas played more than fifty times for his country, Wales, and when he arrived at Old Trafford was saddled with the title 'the Welsh George Best'. I suppose in one way he lived up to the name because he soon fell into a pattern of drinking, missing training and overseas jaunts. He had joined from Wrexham in 1978 for £300,000 and despite endearing himself to the Stretford Enders with his exuberant personality and playing style, his relationship with manager Dave Sexton was understandably strained and he moved on. Just about everywhere. During the 1980s if you tuned in to *Match of the Day*, Mickey would be on in a different kit nearly every month. He got himself into serious bother in 1993 when he became embroiled in a dodgy £20 note scam. Basically he was accused of selling counterfeit notes for a fraction of their value had they been genuine. When Mickey arrived in court for sentencing he waved a £20 note at the gathered newsmen. 'Anyone got change for the phone?' he laughed.

When one of the reporters asked him what punishment he thought he might receive, he replied, with some foresight, 'I doubt if I'll get a fine. Because the judge will think I'll just print the money to pay it.'

Mickey Thomas received an eighteen-month custodial sentence.

I think he had a lot of bad luck, did Mickey. When a lady friend of his invited him down a country lane in his car for a spot of back-seat bonking he was not to know he was being set up and soon to be set upon by a jealous husband who stabbed him repeatedly in the arse with a screwdriver. Obviously this was the nearest part of his anatomy to view at the time. His best faux pas though in my opinion was when he was signing for Chelsea. Ken Bates was sitting at the desk next to him as Mickey put pen to paper. An attractive lady walked past the room and, true to form, Mickey's eyes fixed on her like a magnet and followed her down the corridor.

'I wouldn't mind giving her one,' Mickey commented.

'That's my daughter-in-law,' replied Mr Bates.

He had a lovely swansong to his long and eventful career when he had rejoined lowly Wrexham and they had drawn the mighty Arsenal in the 1992 FA Cup. Mickey got the goal that sent the Gunners out of the competition and sent the Welsh club into a frenzy. Before the match Mickey had asked the Arsenal goalkeeper David Seaman for his gloves at the end of the tie. I expect he believed that Wrexham would lose and the gloves would be a nice memento for someone he knew. Of course, at the end of the match, the ecstatic crowd were on the pitch mobbing the team and it took Mickey some fifteen minutes to get back to the changing room. He was touched, therefore, when he found David Seaman in the tunnel waiting for him and proffering his goalkeeping gloves. 'Thanks, Dave,' he said. 'That's really good of you.'

Seaman shrugged and patted Mickey on the back. 'Well, they don't bloody work do they?'

THEY DID LOVE TO BE BESIDE THE SEASIDE

There were two so-called 'Blackpool incidents' which made headlines and caused much righteous indignation at the time. One was with Chelsea in the 1960s and the other with West Ham in the 1970s. Tommy Docherty took his young Chelsea team up to Blackpool on the eve of an important League game against Burnley in 1965. The Blues were still in with a chance of winning the League championship. They stayed overnight in the stylish Norbreck Hotel and the Doc issued firm instructions that his lads were not to go out on the piss.

A young George Graham had different ideas and when they thought the Doc had gone to bed for the night he led almost the entire team down the fire escapes and out into the crisp Blackpool night air. Terry Venables, Eddie McCreadie and Barry Bridges were among the escapees. For some reason the night doorman saw fit to tell Tommy Docherty as he returned to the hotel (what was he doing out at that time of night?) in the early hours of the morning that his players had all only just arrived back and were the worse for wear. Tommy refused to believe this and asked the doorman to accompany him to their rooms with his master keys. They opened the first door and Tom was pleased to see human shapes in beds and hear the gentle snoring and breathing of his players. However, in the next room the smell of Old Spice aftershave was overwhelming and the manager pulled back the covers on George Graham's bed to see the young Scot lying there in his best, but now creased, suit. Doc did not see the funny side and felt the need to assert his authority and, in a classic case of cutting off his nose to spite his face, ordered the eight guilty players on the first morning train home. Although emergency reserves were bussed up from London, Chelsea fielded a poor side for the match against Burnley and lost 2–6. Chelsea's championship hopes were dashed. The incident led to a long-running power struggle between the young Terry Venables and Tommy Docherty that finally ended in the break-up of a promising young side.

The incident with West Ham in 1971 involved Bobby Moore, Brian Dear, Clyde Best and Jimmy Greaves. These four drank first at the Imperial Hotel in Blackpool where they were staying, and, getting the taste, decided to move on to Brian London's nightclub in town. London was famous at the time for being an English heavyweight boxer who got bashed up by a classy Cassius Clay. This was no great shame, all of our heavyweights got beaten by Clay (later to change his name to Muhammed Ali) although Henry Cooper made the best fist of them all. They were back in bed from Brian London's club by 1 a.m. – hardly the crime of the century – but when West Ham crashed 4–0 to the inferior Blackpool in the third round FA Cup tie some people were very unhappy. One 'fan' even went to see Ron Greenwood, the manager, at his Upton Park office on the Monday and at the same time alerted the newspapers. This man had seen Bobby and Jimmy and the others out drinking at Brian London's club. No doubt he had chatted to them and offered to buy them more drinks too. The football writers were disgusted. Down Fleet

Street way ruddy-faced men were choking on their vodka and tonics. West Ham suspended the players for two weeks and fined them a week's wages. (Clyde Best received a lesser punishment because apparently he hadn't drunk as much as the others.) Bobby, who was stripped of the captaincy, was none too pleased about the whole thing. They had not brought shame to the club by getting involved in some unsavoury incident, they had been in bed by 1 a.m. and up at ten so had not deprived themselves of sleep and they only did what players up and down the country did each weekend. He felt that as a loyal servant to Ron Greenwood and West Ham he should have been treated better. But true to the man he was, Bobby kept his opinions to himself and got on with things.

THE MANCHESTER
RAT PACK

There was a bunch of us who all came together at a certain time and for a few years we really did party non-stop. We painted Manchester red. Every bloody night. We weren't known as the Rat Pack at the time but I'm sure we were referred to as the Rat-Arsed Pack more than once. Most of this crowd came from outside the game but we shared other common interests: drinking, women, fun and making a bit of money here and there. It was never a case of George Best and his mates. It was more like 'that lot' of which George Best was one. I may have been the most famous among us but that did not mean I was the key member. At that time, in the places we hung out at you could not move for well-known people. No one was hung up on my celebrity although they would all be the first to acknowledge that it helped to open doors. Especially bedroom doors. It was an exhilarating few years and the friends who came together at that time remain close to this day, although, sadly, some have left to meet their maker along the way.

I encountered Malcolm Mooney first. We chatted at a party and immediately struck a chord with each other. He was a smartly dressed young man who had a background in the rag trade. Mods had exploded on to the scene and suddenly young people up and down the country became obsessed with their appearance. A decade earlier the advent of rock 'n' roll and the emergence of the Teddy boy became the first youth cult. Before then young people remained children until they became adults. There were no teenagers. No in-between. The Teds had a distinctive clothing style consisting of drainpipe trousers, winklepicker shoes and slicked-back hair; the variety of dress was limited. When the Mods came along suddenly young people were spending all their money on clothes and they competed furiously with one another in the fashion stakes. The traditional stores like Marks & Spencer, C&A, John Collier and Burton could not keep up with the rapidly changing tastes and styles, especially when the more colourful, psychedelic designs came in during the mid-1960s. A new type of shop sprung up to fill the gap – the boutique. Soon no self-respecting young person would admit to buying his or her clobber from anywhere else other than a boutique. In the same way young people stopped going to dances – they went to the discotheque. Same place, new name.

Malcolm suggested we went into business together and open up our own boutique to cash in on this boom and to cash in on my alleged position as a young person's role model. By this time I was getting the same sort of adulation that only pop groups like the Beatles and the Rolling Stones enjoyed. Bill Wyman, formerly of the Rolling Stones, said recently that in those days he and the boys would pick up the teen mags to see how well they had been featured only to get a bit vexed to keep seeing my teeth smiling at them from the front pages. I was the first player to attract a female fan base. Before me the very thought of girls screaming at a footballer was ridiculous. If a gaggle of young girls chased Stanley Matthews, Tommy Lawton and Wilf Mannion down the road after an England match they would have stopped in their tracks bewildered. Then they would have likely grabbed them by their ears and dragged them home to their parents' houses.

Edwardia, as our boutique was named, was situated just off Deansgate in Manchester and straight away it became a focal point for the press, sightseers, young girls and occasionally customers. Malcolm had negotiated the exclusive rights to sell Ravel shoes and myself and Mike Summerbee invested £1,000 each. Malcolm managed the business and I just used to turn up in the afternoons after training and hang around. It was great fun for me as there were always beautiful girls knocking about and many a wonderful relationship could have started behind the curtain in the changing rooms of the shop. We had a young boy, Gary, who helped us out in the shop and more than once I dispatched him to follow a bus when I had spotted a very pretty girl looking down from the top deck and our eyes had met. Gary could sprint and would get ahead of the bus, jump on and persuade the bemused female to come back for a chat at the boutique. More often than not though I was pestering Malcolm to close and cash up so we could get on to the pub.

Despite all this and our lack of real commercial experience, the businesses were reasonably successful and ran their course. They were finally taken over by a Stock Exchange quoted company called Lincroft in the early 1970s. By this time I had lost interest and Malcolm wanted to move on and pursue his dream of running a small restaurant with his lovely French wife Dominique. He finally got his dream and opened up a place in Cheshire where he was growing his own vegetables and generally loving his new-found tranquil lifestyle. One night he drove back to his home after locking up his restaurant but was nagged by the doubt that he had not turned off an appliance so he turned his car around and drove back to the restaurant. Somehow on that night-time journey his car collided with an articulated lorry and Malcolm was killed.

I was a pallbearer at his funeral in November 1974. It was a terribly sad time. I remember at the ceremony I met Malcolm's twin brother for the first time and I have never been so freaked out in my entire life. I've met identical twins before but rarely are they truly completely identical. Malcolm's twin was. Besides looking the same, he spoke the same, walked the same and had the same mannerisms. He even coughed the same. I found it hard to look at him let alone talk, such was my shock.

Malcolm was such a good friend. The following story is just one example of how good a friend he was. I was in London on the eve of an Arsenal match against United. I was fond of a restaurant called Alvaro's and used to go there alone early for a plate of spaghetti and a couple of glasses of wine before having an early night in preparation for the game. It was a balmy sunny evening and I sat there chatting to Alvaro himself and together we watched the world go by through the open door. Then a girl breezed past and my stomach somersaulted. She had glanced sideways and for a split second our eyes had locked. I don't think I had ever seen such a beautiful girl in my entire life. Maybe I had been watching too many shampoo adverts but I asked one of Alvaro's waiters to run after her and bring her back.

When she came into the restaurant I was not disappointed. She was an American named Suzanne Valier who lived in Switzerland but was en route to the Reading pop festival. She was in London looking up some friends but had had no luck and had nowhere to stay. Being the gentleman I was I offered to allow her to stay at the hotel. She was casually dressed in the hippie garb of the time but she seemed so sophisticated. I was captivated and hung on her every word. She had no idea who I was and I had to work that much harder than I was accustomed to. Time flew by and before I knew it I was due back at the hotel for the players' room check. I told her to stay on and chat to Alvaro and then come back to the hotel where I would have booked her a room and then when the players and manager were safely tucked up in bed I'd call her. Room to room.

Ten thirty came and went, as did eleven, twelve and one. There was no reply from the hotel room that I had arranged for her. I was now convinced that this wonderful girl had thought better of joining me and I started to try and get some sleep. At 1.30 the phone rang and it was Suzanne safely ensconced in her room. 'Alvaro, he is so charming. Time just simply flew by,' she explained.

'Hang on there,' I said. 'I'll be right up.'

Suzanne's room was two floors up and I decided to bound up the stairs rather than risk bumping into someone in the lift. Breaking curfews was a serious business at the time and with me the management were always extra vigilant. On Suzanne's floor I flung open some double doors only to see the back of Wilf McGuinness, my manager, as he appeared to be leaning out of a window. I doubled back. Now, I'm not sure whether Wilf was just getting some fresh air or if he was on the look out for me, but I was not going to risk trying again. I think he saw the back of me as I disappeared. Immensely frustrated I rang Suzanne and told her the problem and that I would have to see her at breakfast in the morning. She was not playing hard to get but she seriously was hard to get. At breakfast I introduced her to Wilf who looked her up and down knowingly. 'And how long have you known George?'

She pondered a while and then breathed, 'Long enough.'

We exchanged phone numbers and she continued on her English adventure to the Reading pop festival. I could not get her out of my mind. It was unlike me to become so smitten and although my friends told me it was only because I had not had my wicked way with her that I felt like I did, I was sure it was something deeper. I could have sworn she felt the same way and just could not understand it when she did not return my calls from her home in Switzerland.

Malcolm Mooney could see what a state I was getting myself in and volunteered to travel to Switzerland to see how the land lay and hopefully fetch her back to England. This was the running after the bus scenario in extremis. Armed only with her full name, the town she lived in and a phone number, he set off. The next day he called me from the hotel he was staying in and gave me the results of the surveillance he had already carried out. She lived with a guy in some style – apparently he was a count or something. Neighbours had told Malcolm that he was quite possessive about her. He then told me his strategy. The next day he knocked on her door and, seeing the boyfriend hovering in the background, went into a spiel about being a scout for a model agency in England and how he had seen her around town and wondered if she was interested in some modelling work. Malcolm said she looked at him strangely, knowing something was not as it seemed. Still wary of the boyfriend, Malcolm continued to bullshit as he pressed an air ticket to London into her hand. 'From George,' he whispered and then left.

I expected Suzanne to arrive imminently but a week went by and then a month and then a couple of months. I started to condition myself to rejection and fantasised that the count had her under lock and key and she was pining for me. Eventually I took another girlfriend and one day at my house I was sitting on the sofa with her when the phone rang.

'Hello, George,' she said.

My mind raced. I had recently had a brief fling with a Canadian girl and at first I assumed it was she. With my girlfriend sitting there I politely gave her the brush off. Only later did it dawn on me that the phone call was from Suzanne and she must have now thought I'd lost interest. When I tried to phone her when my girlfriend was not around I discovered the number had been changed. This was one relationship that was destined not to be but thanks for trying Malcolm, my old mate.

DEDICATED FOLLOWERS OF FASHION

Next door to Malcolm and my boutique Edwardia was a hair-dressing shop, the Village Barber, and one afternoon I popped in for a trim. Matt Busby had probably told me earlier to get my hair cut. He frequently did at the beginning. The guy that ran it and cut my hair on that first occasion was another Malcolm – Malcolm Wagner – so when we became friends he soon became known to all as Waggy to avoid any confusion. He had already lived a full and exciting life having, among other things, been a small part of the burgeoning beat group scene in the North-West. Although it was the Mersey sound and the Liverpool beat groups that led the charge, Manchester had its share of successful pop acts. Waggy had gone to school with a guy named Graham Gouldman and they and a couple of other guys had formed a band called the Whirlwinds. They enjoyed some local success but split up after their first record was released and failed to chart. Local groups that started up at the same time as them such as the Hollies and Herman's Hermits went on to massive international success. Graham then wrote hits for Herman, 'No Milk Today', and the Hollies, 'Bus Stop', besides penning the number one hit for the Yardbirds 'For Your Love'. The Yardbirds boasted a talented young guitarist called Eric Clapton. He would later become God. Graham, who remained Waggy's great pal, then went on to even bigger and better things when he formed Hotlegs, which evolved into 10cc, one of the biggest bands of the 1970s.

Another musician who was part of Waggy's set and drank with us all was Bob Lang, who had been in the Mindbenders. Their biggest hit had been 'Groovy Kind of Love' in 1966, which was covered a couple of decades later by Phil Collins. Bob and the Mindbenders had started out as Wayne Fontana's backing band but they went their separate ways and both enjoyed some success in their own right. Bob resurfaced in the 1970s with a band called Racing Cars and they had a top ten hit with 'They Shoot Horses Don't They?'. Another member of the Mindbenders was Eric Stewart who would later become part of Hotlegs and 10cc with Graham Gouldman. In those days in Manchester everyone was interconnected.

After we became friends I helped put Waggy's shop on the map when the press collared me in his shop one day. They knew I had been on holiday to Majorca and wondered what I was doing back in Manchester. 'I flew back to have my hair cut at Waggy's,' I quipped. 'I'm back to Spain this afternoon.'

They loved this. It was the height of footballing playboy extravagance for them and it made good copy – GEORGIE BEST FLIES HOME FROM HOLIDAY FOR A HAIRCUT! From that minute on Waggy's shop was certainly the most famous barber's in Manchester and he was suddenly in danger of becoming the North-West's answer to Vidal Sassoon. The trouble was that Waggy was expected to be at the forefront of hairstyling fashion but up until that time the most daring cut he had been asked for was a Tony Curtis and his staple order was for a short back and sides. He managed. Soon Waggy was partners with Malcolm Mooney and myself in business and partners with me, mainly, on the town.

Waggy looks back on those days and shakes his head now. Because we were living it we didn't think that anything special was taking place. He points to things like picking me up from Manchester Piccadilly railway station after an away game and me, Jimmy Murphy and Sir Matt Busby piling into his little car and discussing the game and other footballing matters. Or when Kenny Lynch, Michael Parkinson and others would come down to the training ground and work out with the team. It was all very irregular but we didn't realise it.

Wherever we went, everyone else seemed to follow. If we changed pubs or nightclubs then everyone else did. When pop groups, entertainers or other football teams were in town they'd seek us out. It was a heady time. When we alighted on a run-down, spit-and-sawdust pub called the Brown Bull, almost overnight it was transformed into the in-place in Manchester. The guvnor was serving brown and mild to railway workers one day and then found himself quaffing champagne with footballers, rock stars and the cast of *Coronation Street* the next. Besides the Manchester Rat Pack all sorts of people became regulars: Kenny Lynch, Jimmy Tarbuck, Germaine Greer, Michael Parkinson and countless visitors to the Granada television studios to name but a few. Actor Ian McShane, now most famous as TV's Lovejoy, was a good pal. His father Harry had been a professional footballer with United. We had a sort of initiation ceremony which involved soaking a new face with soda syphons when they came out the Gents toilet for the first time. Gerald Harper was a debonair, immaculately dressed actor at the peak of his powers. He had made it big as Adam Adamant on the TV and at this time was riding high in a series called *Hadleigh*. When he came out of the toilet after, no doubt, brushing his white cashmere suit down and combing his hair into an immaculate bouffant in the mirror, he was none too pleased when we drenched him good and proper. He must have got the joke in the end though because he came back again and again.

Ray Davies and his brother Dave of the Kinks were mates and always joined us when they were in town. I have read since that Ray wrote the Kinks big hit 'Dedicated Follower of Fashion' with me in mind. I have not seen him in recent years to ask him but looking at the lyrics it may well have been:

They seek him here, they seek him there,
His clothes are loud, but never square.
It will make or break him so he's got to buy the best,
'Cause he's a dedicated follower of fashion.

Oh yes he is (oh yes he is), oh yes he is (oh yes he is)
His world is built 'round discotheques and parties.
This pleasure-seeking individual always looks his best
'Cause he's a dedicated follower of fashion.

LYNCH MOB

Dennis Viollet, the former Manchester United and England forward, introduced me to Kenny Lynch. I believe he was working in the Granada studios on a TV show and he started to come into La Phonograph and other pubs and clubs I was using. We hit it off immediately and were soon sharing a flat together. Once we had the flat we shared a few girls too. Officially, though, I still lived at Mrs Fullaway's, although by this time I was only putting in token appearances. I think she understood. Matt knew of the flat but couldn't prove I was living there. He used to say to Kenny, 'About this flat?' and Kenny would change the subject like only he can.

Kenny is all energy and believes in working hard and playing hard. He loves life and laughing. You couldn't ask for better company. I used to pop into his dressing room in the Granada studios, waiting for him to finish work, and word would get round that I was there and this little room would fill up with actors, actresses and crew wanting to talk to me. There was barely more space than a couple of phone boxes joined together and we would be all crammed in and there would be Kenny pushing against the door, calling to be let in to his own dressing room. He always said this was the story of his life when with me. Even in London, which was his manor – and don't forget he had been a pop star and constantly on TV at the time – people almost shoved him out of the way to ask for my autograph or to share some words of wisdom with me.

Lynchie was born into a large family in working-class Stepney in London and he has never forgotten his working-class roots. He has always been an active supporter of the Labour Party. His sister Maxine Daniels is a popular standards singer. Kenny first started to make waves when he sang with the big bands in the dance halls in the late 1950s. In 1960 he made a record 'Mountain of Love' and enjoyed his first pop chart success. He became a teenage heart-throb along with Cliff Richard and a stable of other stars with names intended to stoke up teenage desires, like Eager (Vince), Faith (Adam), Wilde (Marty) and Kidd (Johnny) in the period between Elvis and the Beatles. Kenny was different from most of his contemporaries in three ways at least: his surname meant to hang someone (this may have gone above the heads of screaming teenagers); he wrote songs; and he was black. He penned 'Sha La La La Lee' for the Small Faces and in one heady week of March 1966 for us Manchester crowd 'Sha La La La Lee' with Kenny joining in on vocals, 'Groovy Kind of Love' with Bob Lang's Mindbenders and 'Dedicated Follower of Fashion' by the Kinks were all in the Top Ten in this country.

Kenny branched out further and his quick wit and friendly personality soon opened up doors for him in television. He became a feed man and regular guest to Bruce Forsyth and Jimmy Tarbuck, who became his closest friends. Bruce, Jimmy and Kenny found time between their golf and their work to make a record to rival Pavarotti's 'Three Tenors' release in Christmas 1996. They called themselves the Three Fivers and put out 'Winter Wonderland' only to find themselves on the end of legal threats from Pavarotti's record company. The record company alleged 'passing off', which amused Kenny no end. 'Even if all three of us got in the same suit we'd still look nothing like Pavarotti,' he mused.

When we first became friendly I asked Kenny to accompany me to Belfast where I was playing for Northern Ireland in an international match. When the game was over we were eager to get home for some party or another and decided to leave the international party and sneak off to the airport and nip back to Manchester as quickly as we could. This entailed leaving the ground and weaving our way through the back streets. In those days a game of kids' soccer would be going off in every street, just how it was when I had been playing on the Cregagh estate ten years earlier. As we hurried through the labyrinth of roads the boys began to recognise me and follow in our wake. They began to call out to each other, 'It's Georgie Best. Over here! It's Georgie Best.' At each turning we acquired more boys until I estimated there were a hundred kids pulling at our sleeves and jumping up and down beside us. Feeling like the Pied Piper of Belfast I stopped to talk to them and hopefully persuade them not to stray too far from their homes. Some were asking Kenny and me for our autographs but had no pens or paper to offer. A group of men came out into the road from a small bar to see what all the commotion was about. One of the bigger boys shouted over to them, 'Hey, come over here. It's Georgie Best and he's with Cassius Clay!'

Fifteen or so years later we had a kind of reprise of this story. My latest book about my career had just been published and it had been arranged for me to do a book-signing session at Foyle's, the large bookstore in London. By now I was living in Chelsea and so was Kenny. I rang him and asked him if he fancied coming with me and lured him by lies about there being drinks afterwards and a host of pretty young publishing executives on tap. Kenny didn't need too much persuading. At Foyle's I was sat up on a small podium with hundreds of books piled up on the table in front of me. A crowd had gathered and a long queue snaked out of the shop and into the street outside. 'This will take hours,' moaned Kenny.

'Shut up and sit down.'

The first person in the queue was an attractive middle-aged lady and I shook her hand. 'Who would you like it signed to?' I asked her.

'Just to me,' she smiled.

'But what's your name?'

'Sorry, how stupid, it's Valerie.'

I signed Valerie's book and jokingly pointed to Kenny sitting down next to me, twiddling his thumbs. 'Don't you want him to sign it as well?'

Valerie was being polite but it was clear she wasn't sure who Kenny was.

'That's Eusebio,' I explained, 'the great Benfica player.'

'Oh, of course,' she gushed looking at a bemused Mr Lynch, 'please sign it too. That's wonderful.'

Kenny duly signed as Eusebio looking at me sideways through gritted teeth as if to say, you bastard. Of course, the next person in the queue had witnessed this and duly asked for

'Eusebio's' signature as well as mine and before we knew it the joke was getting out of hand as one person after another requested the Portugal hero's autograph as well as mine. There was no going back. A few wise old birds in the queue quickly took their books from me and kept them well away from Kenny and others stared hard as Kenny signed. I'm sure they were thinking 'You're that bloke off the telly, I could have sworn it,' but could not bring themselves to challenge him. Some people tried to engage him in conversation but Kenny was clever enough not to let his strong cockney accent give himself away and just kept smiling and adopting the body language of one who has no grasp of the English tongue. So, dear users of Internet auction sites such as eBay, beware. Copies of rare George Best books signed by myself and Benfica rival Eusebio are not what they seem.

CALL FOR CARMAN

A somewhat unlikely member of our select bunch of drinkers on the Manchester night-time scene was the late George Carman, QC. He wasn't as famous then as he is now. At the time he was an up and coming youngish barrister and well-known only in the North-West. In later years he was to become the most famous advocate of recent times, defending Peter Adamson (Len Fairclough of *Coronation Street*) on child molestation charges; Jeremy Thorpe (the former Liberal Party leader) on a conspiracy to murder rap; and Ken Dodd over tax evasion allegations. He won all of these cases although Peter Adamson later admitted to a newspaper that he was guilty. He was also successful in winning substantial libel damages for Richard Branson, Elton John, Tom Cruise and Marco Pierre-White, among others. Indeed anyone who was anyone hired George if they found themselves in the law courts. It seemed he couldn't lose. But when he defended me he did.

Only I could manage to enter the legal record books as being the last person in England to be sued for breach of promise to marry. I had met a very pretty blonde Danish lady by the name of Eva Haraldsted on a United pre-season tour in Copenhagen but didn't manage to get anywhere with her, chiefly because she had a boyfriend in tow. I was quite taken with her beauty and when I returned to England I talked about her to the press. I lamented that I probably would never see her again. The papers liked this and thought it may be a good idea if they appealed to find her. It wasn't hard once my plea had appeared in the Danish press and before I knew it she was over in England. The 'romance' then took on a life of its own, principally driven by the tabloids. They dubbed her the 'Striking Viking' and Eva announced we were to be wed. I did not demur and must confess the idea appealed to me ... for a day or so. Eventually I plucked up courage to tell Eva that, much as I had enjoyed our little adventure, I had no intention of getting married, engaged or anything else hinting at permanence. She really did not take it very well and she stormed off into the arms of a waiting solicitor.

George Carman had carried out work privately for the Edwards family who owned United and for the club itself and once the papers were served on me for breach of promise we retained him to defend me. George obviously didn't believe in my innocence, nor did I, and he advised me to settle out of court by way of paying £500 and a ticket for Eva back to Copenhagen.

'It is one-way?' I asked.

Eva accepted and that I thought was that. When the press asked how I felt about it all my honest response was bandied all over.

'I fell in love with a pair of knockers. It could happen to anyone,' I told them.

In March 1970 I was drinking with Paddy Crerand in Blinkers, a popular Manchester nightspot, and Eva was in there with some friends. She obviously had not made use of her ticket yet. She asked the disc jockey to play 'I'm Leaving on a Jet Plane' by Peter, Paul and Mary and dedicate it to me. I responded by getting him to play 'Get Back' by the Beatles. This seemed like fun to me but some of the company she was with took exception and surrounded me in a threatening manner. A row broke out and Pat and I went outside with the male members of Eva's party. In the scuffle that ensued a twenty-three-year-old friend of Eva's got his jaw broken. The police arrived and Paddy was charged with grievous bodily harm. Call for Carman! After a two-day hearing in April, George managed to persuade the stipendiary magistrate that Paddy was acting in self-defence and he was acquitted.

We celebrated that night, George and I, but then again we celebrated every night. Besides people asking me who was the greatest player I ever played against they sometimes ask who was the greatest drinker I ever knew. I have to say it was George Carman. His legs were truly hollow. He could drink and drink and drink. Many a time he would phone for taxi at midnight to take him home from whatever club or pub we were in but then instruct the driver to wait outside while he had one for the road. At three or four in the morning when he had had a whole motorway of one for the roads he would finally emerge to take his taxi. The driver didn't care, George would have popped out at hourly intervals during those three or four hours to reassure him and permit him to keep the meter running. Now you know why George Carman had to set his fees so high.

Sadly our relationship soured after George took me back to his house. I think it may have been the night before the Eva Haraldsted case and he was concerned that if he didn't bring me home I might not turn up for court in the morning, but my recollection is unclear. His wife Celia was younger than him but not a great deal older than me and she was extremely pretty. I felt a strong physical attraction to her. So one night, a short time later, I rang her and arranged to go round and visit. I knew her husband wasn't in for the simple reason that he was sitting next to me in the bar. Celia told me that her and George's marriage was under strain and they slept in separate rooms. We embarked on a short affair.

Inevitably George Carman found out about the relationship and was extremely incensed, even though their marriage had reached the stage it had. He had complained about me to anyone who would listen including Manchester United and I did my best to keep out of his way. However, eventually, one lunchtime, he walked into the Grapes pub where I was drinking. He spotted me at the other end of the bar and walked towards me with a worrying sense of purpose. Fortunately, some friends and fellow-drinkers stood up to block his path. George stood there and boomed in his best law court voice, 'George Best, you black-guard, you fucked my wife.'

He and Celia divorced a few years after and George moved down to London to find real fame and fortune. I was delighted when we began to meet up again when he was living with his partner Karen in Wimbledon only a few years ago and I was with Alex. We could even laugh about all the old times. I was very sad when I heard of his death from prostate cancer in January 2001.

Blinkers, the club where the altercation with Paddy and the Danes took place, was owned by Selwyn Demmy. Selwyn was a local bookmaker who had sold his betting shop chain to one of the big players and was enjoying his new-found wealth and leisure with the same zest he did his business. His parties on a Sunday afternoon were something to behold. Selwyn rang every modelling agency in the vicinity and got them to send along their prettiest girls. Although they were paid to come, there was nothing seedy in it and many a happy couple met at one of Selwyn's bashes. He moved to Monte Carlo where all respectable tax exiles end up but missed the down-to-earth Mancunians and the simple pleasures of the north-west of England and soon returned. Last I heard he had rebuilt his chain of betting shops and no doubt will sell to William Hill or Joe Coral once again.

Jennifer Moss, who played Lucille Hewitt in *Coronation Street*, was a friend of both Waggy and me. Coincidentally, one long-running story line in the soap was when Lucille, who was the adopted daughter of Annie and Jack Walker the licensees of the Rovers Return, was having a romance with Gordon Clegg, who was the son of Betty Turpin. Betty, played by Betty Driver, is still serving hotpot in the pub to this day. A young Bill Kenwright, who was referred to earlier in this book and is currently deputy chairman of Everton Football Club, played Gordon Clegg. Jennifer's character Lucille had a following among young girls. She was probably the only rebellious female teenager portrayed on the television at the time. She and I were approached to front a new business venture, which was to be a teenagers' supermarket. I'm not sure how this would have differed from the boutiques we were already involved in because bread, milk and toilet paper were hardly high priority on the average teenager's shopping list then or now. Needless to say the idea came to nothing but it was indicative of the ridiculous ventures (or opportunities as the proposers preferred to call them) that were being put in front of us every day. Jennifer left the Street and fought some public battles with drink for some time afterwards. We haven't met up in ages but I am pleased to hear she has been clean for many years now.

It was an established supermarket that approached me with an offer that was staggeringly generous. I think it was Tesco and they had bought up a smaller rival and were rebranding the acquired company's stores as a Tesco. They wanted me to open each store as they were relaunched. This was going to be rolled out over an eighteen-month period, as there were a hundred stores countrywide. The great news was that they were offering me £500 a store. That came to a mouth-watering £50,000. In today's money that would have been half a million smackers on just this deal alone. Waggy spoke to the club on my behalf but they felt it was too big a commitment for me to take on especially as it would involve openings of the flagship stores on Saturday mornings. I expect that Sir Matt would have worried too about the effect such a high-profile deal might have on the other players. When Waggy broke the news to me I thought about it and said, 'Look, I'll do a bunk. Go back to Tesco and see if we can cram all hundred into a fortnight.'

HANGOVER

For me, and a few others, after the party came the hangover. It was a severe hangover and one that I am only now recovering from. I went from El Beatle to El Vino in five or six short years. When I was still at United people constantly told me I could not carry on burning the candle at both ends. Eventually I stubbed one end of the candle out. I stopped playing serious football. Then my drinking really took off. If my life was divided up into quarters you could say that I spent the first quarter on and around football pitches, the second in and around bars, and the third in and around hospitals and doctors. I am determined that the fourth quarter will be spent around my wife and my family and close friends. Hospitals are not places I like to be, most people in them tend to be ill for one thing. Nevertheless it is in these places you come across the good things about human beings (bravery, compassion and goodness to name but three) but when I'm in, I can't wait to be out. I must say though, being banged up in a hospital bed has not been without its lighter moments.

Not long before I left my house in Northern Ireland to return to England and settle in my lovely converted barn in Surrey, I was taken ill. I was rushed to the nearest hospital in Belfast and when stabilised ended up on a general ward for a night. A very pleasant and laid-back doctor came to the ward, perched on the side of my bed and we chatted. We touched on the subject of the importance and urgency of me getting my liver transplant. Waiting lists and the uncertainty of the whole process were under discussion. Suddenly a fellow Irishman in the bed next to me sat bolt upright and exclaimed in a loud Belfast brogue, 'Doctor! The man lying in bed there is my hero. We all love him. He's George Best, so he is. He can have one of my livers. I mean it, so I do. Take one now!'

Few people realise that Paolo Di Canio was ordered to stop drinking because of the damage it was doing to his liver. He was only twelve years of age at the time. His liver had deteriorated to the point that the rest of his body was having to work twice as hard just to keep it functioning. His parents banned his drink from the house but the young Paolo resorted to begging his friends to buy him his poison. Finally, he says, he accepted he had a problem and found the will to overcome it. He managed to cut right back and continue to develop his budding football career while indulging only in moderation. Paolo took his final drink of cola on Christmas Day 1998. 'I've been clean ever since. It was a very difficult thing to do and I am very proud of it,' he says.

HURRICANE

During that last short stay in hospital in Belfast, Alex Higgins, some say the George Best of the snooker world (or was I the Alex Higgins of the football world?), came to see me. By now he had been living back in Northern Ireland for some time. I knew he was in poor health and down on his luck. I also knew there would have been a reasonable chance he had taken a drink or two. It crossed my mind to tell the nurse to tell him I was not up to seeing him because sometimes Alex can be exuberant to say the least. But he had been thoughtful enough to come and see me and Alex had throat cancer and I had a failing liver. Who knows if the two Belfast boys would ever have the chance to see one another again? He was on top form, gibbering away in typical Alex Higgins style. Some of it I understood. Most I didn't. We exchanged failing health stories for a while and then wished each other the best. Perversely, as he shuffled out of the ward I felt so much better. I had just been having a one to one with a man who looked so much worse than I did.

When I was recovering in the Cromwell Hospital in London after my transplant one of the first things I remember after regaining consciousness was listening to the radio and being aware that the voice was talking about me and my operation. The presenter, whoever he was, claimed that day he had seen two housewives standing outside a butcher's shop in their local high street that afternoon looking at a sign in the window proclaiming – BEST LIVER. One lady turned to the other and said, 'I wondered what they would do with it.'

Being handed the newspapers the following morning, it was good to see that the printed media too had maintained their sense of humour over the whole thing. In reporting the difficulties the surgeons faced during my operation and the large amount of blood I required to get me through it, more than one headlined with GEORGE BEST NEEDED 40 PINTS. In the same paper, a columnist helpfully pointed out that my name is an anagram of GO GET BEERS.

GEORGE BEST

NUTS

I was warned about a number of possible side effects of my transplant but one thing the doctors neglected to talk to me about was the possibility of my scrotum swelling up. It just expanded and expanded and before I knew it it looked (and felt) like I was clasping two melons between my inner thighs. I laughed about it at first and so did Alex when I lifted the bedclothes to give her a peek, but I didn't see the funny side when the swelling continued. The doctors, nurses and physios were not too alarmed and pointed out that this was an occasional side effect of the treatment of my condition and that it should subside. Should? They could well be not too alarmed – it was not their bollocks that were taking over their body. Alex popped out to Marks & Spencer to purchase the largest boxer shorts in the store but even they could not contain my monstrous nuts. The nurses and Liz, the physiotherapist, who had to tend to me and generally get involved in my every movement, were very diplomatic. The nurses referred to my 'lower level' and Liz was very concerned I didn't knock my 'undercarriage'.

Liz had the task of getting me mobile and fit, big bollocks or not, and she was forever coaxing me: 'Come on George, that's the boy, good boy, just a few more steps …' She also coached me in breathing and balance; things I had always taken for granted but now seemed not so straightforward. Liz was lovely but because she was the person getting me to do the things my body did not want to do, sometimes I dreaded her coming and her soft coaxing tones occasionally jarred. Not since I was a boy in Belfast had anyone addressed me, as 'there's a good boy'. One day we were doing our 0.1 mph sprint up and down the corridor with Liz gently holding my arm when she pointed to a small puddle of liquid just in front of us (not me, Guv!) and said, 'Now George, be ever so careful, there's a little puddle just in front.'

'I'm in here for problems with my liver not my bloody eyes,' I blurted out. As soon as I said it I regretted it. This lady had been nothing but kind and patient but she bore the brunt of all my bottled up frustrations and fears. I think she knew this and before I had the chance to apologise for my ungrateful outburst she had dissolved into laughter herself and then so did I. She'd seen it all before.

A source of great support in the days after my operation and during the real touch-and-go period immediately afterwards was the hundreds of letters and cards that were pouring into the hospital each day. Now I know the difference between wishing someone well in your mind and sitting down, penning a letter, buying a stamp and sending it off – it's a big difference. Most of us don't do it, so I intend to work through all of these and reply because it meant so much to receive them all. Many were heartwarming, especially from those who had been through the same operation, and were obviously still around to tell the story. Others spoke of their alcohol addiction and identified with my condition. Many were football fans from all over the world and explained how they had watched me here or there and how the performance had impacted on them so much.

It was extraordinary how people remembered matches, scores and incidents that I had long forgotten. Some letters were so funny that they had Alex, Phil (my manager) and myself in fits of giggles. One lady sent me a photo of me, taken in my Manchester United heyday; she asked if I could sign it for her husband because it was his birthday this year. Surely it's his birthday every year? Phil pointed out. One lady wrote to let me know that she had only bought my book *Blessed* because she believed that it was the biography of the actor Brian Blessed. Seeing that there is a big picture of a fairly emaciated me on the front she must have thought he'd lost a good bit of weight. Nevertheless it wasn't a bad read, she said, and she wished me well. Another writer said they were praying for my recovery and hoped that my appearance would improve after the operation as these days to look at me it reminded them of Homer Simpson. Thanks for the boost.

Jimmy Tarbuck was among the wellwishers who phoned. Before I came into the hospital he had promised me some trees for our new garden. The nurse passed the telephone to me.

'Where's my fucking trees?' I said.

'I can tell you're feeling better,' replied Jimmy.

We small-talked for a minute or two and then he said, 'Guess who I bumped into in Specsavers today?'

'Who?'

'Everyone.'

I told him not to make me laugh because of the pain.

"Should I kick him up the arse or should you?". Me, Marshy and a linesman on our crowd-pleasing debut for Fulham in September 1976.

We've often revived our Fulham double-act as after-dinner speakers and still regularly cross swords as pundits on Sky Sports.

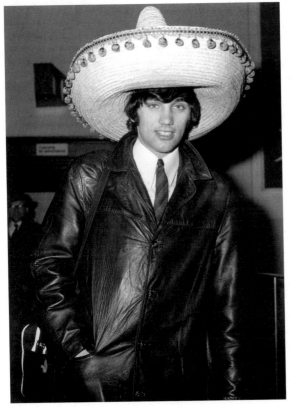

(above) Me and boxer Johnny Prescott enjoying a coke and a laugh, no doubt about some antics the night before, while on holiday with the usual gang in Majorca, July 1967.

(left) El Beatle returns victorious from Portugal after our 5-1 demolition of Benfica in the 1966 European Cup quarter finals complete with Sombrero.

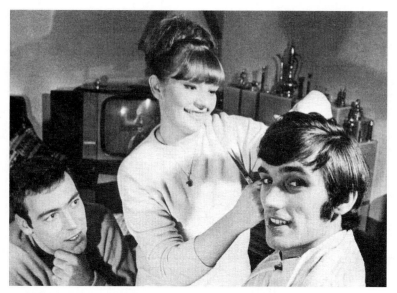

Getting my famous Beatle mop top trimmed at my beloved
Chorlton-cum-Hardy digs. Best mate David Sadler
is on hand to spot if Linda Gidman misses a bit.

© EMPICS/ALPHA

Some of my other great friends from the game –
Bobby Moore, Jimmy Greaves, Ray Wilson, Bobby and
Jack Charlton visiting a London gym during the 1966 World Cup.

An early incarnation of my swing sixties look, as posed outside Old Trafford,
now looks more like I was going for a bit part in the High Chaparral.

Ray Davies of the Kinks gives me some lessons in being a dedicated follower of fashion.

In many ways I was the first 'brand' footballer – sought by advertisers everywhere. Here I am modelling shirts with Rowena Hill in 1966.

Time out for a joke while training, during my
first spell at Fort Lauderdale Strikers in 1978.

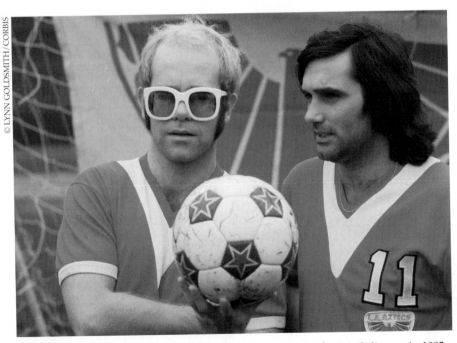

Watford enthusiast Elton John joins me for a warm-up at the LA Coliseum in 1982
for some of what had become run-of-the-mill star-spangled soccer circus marketing.

In action for the LA Aztecs.

Not the only woman's inside leg I took in my heyday. An innocent publicity shot
with actress Sue Whitman taken at the opening of my boutique Edwardia in 1966.

Eva Haraldsted, the Striking Viking, and me already looking
a little apprehensive. After I broke off our engagement she
ridiculously attempted to sue me for breach of promise.

Look at my delight at being involved in the Shape Up and Dance aerobics record in 1984 with (left to right) Patti Boulaye, Suzanne Dando, Mary Stavin, Lulu and Bucks Fizz singer Jay Aston.

A post-match shower and – note – not a girl in sight. This was actually taken after our winning second leg 3–3 draw in Madrid in 1968 and I was too exhausted to get my kit off never mind anybody else's.

Just another night out with yet another girl on my arm.
Me and latest flame Jan Locke outside Tramps nightclub in 1987.

My audience at 10 Downing Street in March 1970 when embarrassingly more people flocked to me than Huddersfield Town fan Harold Wilson.

(opposite top) Sold a dummy – the indignity of having my waxwork likeness at Madame Tussaud's replaced by that of the new European Footballer of the Year, Johan Cruyff in 1973.

(opposite bottom) Attempting to dribble my way through a Metropolitan Police first eleven with little success. Arrest in 1984 after failing to turn up in court for a drink driving offence.

The people who really matter. Mum and dad visiting
a youthful me in hospital after an early cartilage operation.

On Thames Television with Parkie in 1975. He has been a loyal friend
and his own show has allowed me to set the story straight at crucial times.

Me and Calum in 1988. I briefly helped him try his hand at
football but it wasn't to be. Now he uses the Best trademark
poise and balance to keep steady on the catwalk.

True happiness at last with my beautiful wife Alex.

Only a few years back Alan Hudson spent many months in hospital after being knocked over by a hit and run driver on the Mile End Road. This was very close to the London Hospital, which was handy because if they hadn't had got him there so fast he would surely have died. I first heard about the accident when I saw the headline in the paper – HUDSON SMASHED. This must rank as one of the cruellest headlines ever as the man lay on his deathbed. But maybe just to upset journalists like that, Huddy refused to die and over many weeks and months fought himself back to consciousness and then to mobility. He suffered terrible injuries and amazed his doctors with his stamina, strength and determination. They went on record as saying he was extraordinarily fit for a man of his age and that his body was in excellent shape – a statement that was one in the eye of the perceived wisdom that Alan Hudson was a drinker who did not take care of himself. He was a drinker but he also took care of himself. When in the hospital and on the road to recovery a TV team interviewed him sitting up on his bed. The camera zoomed in disapprovingly on a bottle of vodka standing among the medicine bottles on his bedside table. 'I only drink cranberry juice with my vodka these days, so I have adopted a healthy lifestyle,' Alan explained in his defence.

I do not believe for one minute that Alan was drinking vodka or any other alcohol while in hospital, although, knowing him, he probably does believe that the cranberry juice offsets any ill-effects of the vodka, but he would have placed the bottle there to wind the interviewers and the audience up. He really does not care one iota what the press or public think and if they want to perpetuate and believe a certain image of him he will play up to it. It was that obstinate quality of his that led to him not fulfilling his full potential in the game, not his drinking or lifestyle. He was possibly the best English footballer I played against. Certainly one of the top five. But he didn't suffer fools gladly and had no time for imposters and bullshitters. He wouldn't call a manager 'boss' if he had no respect for them and if a coach was talking bollocks he'd tell them.

Alan has had his differences with Ken Bates although there have been small spells over the years when they have got on better. On one occasion Ken was showing Alan around the Stamford Bridge complex when the ground and surrounding area were being redeveloped. Ken was pointing to various structures and constructions and trying to help Alan visualise how the new stadium would look.

'We're determined to recognise the history of the club,' stated Ken, pointing in one direction, 'over there we're having a bar called Bentley's after Roy Bentley, the 1955 League Championship hero, and over here is going to be another bar called Tambling's after Bobby.'

Alan was beginning to think perhaps the old boy wasn't so bad after all.

'And here, Alan, we're building a bar called Huddy's,' Ken slapped Alan on the back and looked closely at him to gauge his reaction.

Pride welled up inside and for once Hudson was lost for words, until Ken added, 'I've always been a great fan of Roy Hudd.'

FORD SIESTA

The place other than hospital where my drinking led me was prison. Following my non-appearance in court on a drink-driving charge the police sent the cavalry to arrest me and one thing led to another and I was charged with assaulting one of the arresting officers. I got a three-month sentence, the equivalent of a whole close season, and was terrified at the prospect. Hugh McIlvaney, the brilliant sports writer and a good friend, tells the story of how we were having a cup of tea in the canteen at Southwark Court before sentencing and we feared the worst. 'I suppose that's the knighthood fucked,' I said. My attempt at humour at that time was pure bravado. Fortunately for me I was sent to serve my sentence at Ford Open Prison, which lay in a quiet backwater on the south coast.

Ford prison was a holiday camp. In fact it was better than some of the holiday camps I have visited. The facilities were good, the food reasonable and the entertainment tolerable for a start. If you really wanted to leave, you could, it wouldn't do much good in the long run, but you could. With the exception of women you could get pretty much anything you wanted. Most of the inmates were decent enough, friendly people. I knew nothing about the prison game when I found myself in there and was completely gobsmacked when I saw other prisoners ordering takeaway foods and wandering out in the grounds to pick up the bags as they were tossed over the wall. It all reminded me of an old black and white British film *Two Way*

Stretch they used to show on the TV when I lived at Mrs Fullaway's. The joke was that Bernard Cribbins and a host of other British comedy actors playing the lags ran the prison. The scene I remember is when Bernard and others are sitting in their cell in their arrows prison uniforms playing cards when the screw, played by Lionel Jeffries, knocks on their cell door. 'Come in, it's not locked,' shouts Cribbins.

One of the screws in Ford was known as Drunken Duncan. He had his coffee topped up with brandy but other than that I don't know if he was a drinker. I never saw any evidence that he was, but when a nickname is as good as that, who cares? He had a reputation for being a hard man and barked and charged around a bit but he was always okay with me. One of my little tasks was to make tea and coffee for the screws and one day when I was sugaring his coffee he asked me to follow him to the holding cells. The office adjacent to the holding cells was empty and he pointed towards a large desk with a telephone. 'If you tell anyone about this, you're in the shit. Understand? You've got fifteen minutes. Ring whoever you want.'

He left me alone in the office and I got busy dialling. I rang my girlfriend but she was obviously out. I tried my dad but it was engaged. I tried my sister – no reply. I tried a couple of friends again with no luck and then I sat there trying to think of someone to ring. I nearly resorted to ringing the speaking clock. There I was, George Best, in prison with free use of a telephone with no one to call. Drunken Duncan came back into the room.

'All right?'

'Thanks very much.' I was too embarrassed to tell him that I hadn't actually got through to anyone.

'One day you'll get money for writing about this,' Duncan laughed.

'I doubt it.'

Like me, Tony Adams, the Arsenal and England defender, hit his all-time low when he served fifty-six days in Chelmsford prison. Tony's drinking was out of control and his sentence came when he crashed his car while drunk and demolished a brick wall. The joke doing the rounds at the time was that Tony wasn't pissed, he was just trying to get the wall back another ten yards. Things didn't get any better when he was arrested and handcuffed to another prisoner who objected by saying, 'This is a nightmare. I'm a Tottenham fan and I get cuffed to you.' When asked to comment on whether he thought his team-mate and pal would beat his addiction, Ian Wright helpfully said, 'Tony has a lot of bottle.' With the help of the AA (Alcoholics Anonymous not the Automobile Association) Tony finally faced his demons and has been clean for a few years now.

Duncan Ferguson, the big Scottish striker, did forty-five days in a Scottish prison. This was during his time with Everton and was the culmination of a number of court appearances for fighting. His propensity for a row and general argy-bargy earned him the nickname Duncan Disorderly. These days I'm pleased to note his physical exuberance is being channelled more legitimately, as not once, but twice, he has physically

restrained (to put it politely) burglars caught in the act of robbing his house. This raises questions about the general intelli-
gence levels of the criminal fraternity around Duncan's neck of
the woods.

5

THE FAME

KICK-OFF

After being in the public eye for so many years I occasionally fall into the trap of assuming that people automatically know who I am. Only recently I hailed a taxi from central London to take me to Heathrow Airport. The cabbie was one of the few taxi drivers who chose not to talk and I sat quietly in the back reading a newspaper. As we got close to the airport I noticed him looking at me intently in his driver's mirror. Eventually he said, 'Okay, I give up. Give us a clue.'

I looked up from my paper. 'Football,' I said.

The taxi driver's brow furrowed. 'Come again?'

'Manchester United.' I smiled, folding my paper into my lap so he could get a long look at me. No reply.

'Irish.'

I could see he was now looking at me as if I was mad. He

gripped the wheel firmly and turned around and faced me. 'Look mate, I only want to know what bloody terminal you want.'

COOL BRIT?

One day as I was lying in hospital immediately after my liver transplant, Phil, my manager and best friend, passed me a copy of the *Daily Mail*. They had carried out a survey among the public as to who are the 'Coolest Brits'. I was genuinely surprised when Phil pointed out that I had been voted the fifteenth coolest Brit. David Beckham was top, followed by Sean Connery and Robbie Williams. The poll had been taken some time before my hospitalisation so it wasn't a sympathy vote. I reflected on this for a time after. Why were people considering me as cool, now in the twenty-first century? It has been thirty years or so since I kicked a football meaningfully and since then mainly my tempestuous love affair with drink has kept me in the public eye. Okay, for some drinking may be cool but no other celebs with a big drinking reputation figure in the top thirty so I don't think it is that. I reach the conclusion that I must have got the nostalgia vote. I'm a survivor of the 1960s and the 1960s remain the decade that provokes the most affection and nostalgia among the population. Deservedly or not I have become a personification of that era. So I think that, combined with the British custom of feting and honouring the recently dead, is why I got the vote. I know I'm not recently dead but I guess many of those people polled thought I might be by the time the votes were in.

People are generally very discreet and laid-back when they see me these days. Alex and I took a holiday in Malta shortly before I was called into the Cromwell Hospital for my liver transplant. Holidaymakers came up and spoke to us but none invaded our privacy unduly and most just wanted to say 'Good luck', which was kind. I find that many people just nod and say 'Hello George' when they see me and then don't give a second glance. Like I'm the ticket collector at their local railway station. It is easy to forget that just because I don't know someone's face they still know me and often it is an instinctive reaction to speak. They see me coming and just as the brain is sending the signal as to where they know me from they are level and auto-matically smile or speak.

From my position at the pool in the Malta hotel I could see into the bar. Sitting on a stool most days was a young man hold-ing a pint of lager. One afternoon he spotted me looking at him. He wasn't within speaking distance but he held up his glass and pointed at it and then me. He was saying, 'Do you want one?' I shook my head and smiled. He was not being clever or nasty, he was having a joke and it made me laugh, especially as he did it at about the same time every day.

One way or another, due to my celebrity, I got to meet most of the leaders, movers and shakers and icons of the twentieth century but I always preferred the company of my small but close-knit bunch of mates. I think fame really does go to your head when you only surround yourself with other famous people. And famous people are no different from anyone else when it comes down to it. Some are fantastic to be around but many are boring, tiresome, self-centred, drunk or drugged. Like everyone else.

Mind you, I was thrilled to meet some people. I remember in a hotel in New Zealand, during a talking tour, being sent mad by the person in the next room playing the piano at all hours. When a note of apology was passed under the door from Dudley Moore I invited him over and we had a magical evening together drinking and laughing. Sadly Dud died recently and his death attracted a fraction of the attention that his former comedy partner Peter Cook's did a few years before. Dudley had proved himself as a good musician and top Hollywood box-office draw as well as comedian but for some reason his talents were always perceived to be inferior to those of Peter Cook.

Another time Michael Jackson invited me backstage to meet him following a concert. Even then, while I loved his music, I felt distinctly uneasy about him as a person and declined.

ALL IN THE FAMILY

One time I was visiting home and took Dad along with me when we went travelling the Irish countryside. We were staying in a sleepy village and one Sunday morning decided to take a stroll. As we passed one cottage a man was leaning on his gate and he bid us good morning and engaged us in conversation. Finally he asked for my autograph and said, 'I know your Uncle Bill in Canada and he'll be thrilled that I've met you after all he has told us about you.'

'Uncle Bill in Canada? That's a new one on me.' I looked at Dad.

'We don't have an Uncle Bill in Canada,' confirmed Dad.

'No, you have. Bill Best, lives in Toronto,' insisted the man.

'Well, I've never heard of him or met him,' laughed Dad. The man didn't seem able to accept this and went inside and fetched his address book as if that proved anything.

'Yes, yes,' said Dad, 'you clearly have a friend in Toronto called Bill Best but we don't know him, we have never heard of him and we have never met him.'

The penny dropped with this man. 'The dirty bastard. He's been living off stories about you and your family for years.'

We all laughed and then my dad asked with a twinkle in his eye, 'Have you got a camera in the house?'

'Yes.'

'Well, get it, take some snaps and when you see your friend Bill next show him the photos and tell him you had a long chat with us about him and old times and see how he reacts to that.' We all had a long chuckle at the thought of old Bill Best, whoever he was, wriggling under the pressure.

Once I became famous it was not uncommon for people to claim to know my family or me and sometimes they would do it to my face. Rather than risk a scene I would quietly go along with it. It seems to happen with so-called 'cult heroes'. If all the people who were in John Lennon's class at school in Liverpool jumped off a wall at the same time there would be an earthquake. When was the last time you met someone from the East End of London over the age of fifty who didn't know the Kray Twins? My road on our little council estate must be a hundred bloody miles long if it really housed all the people who claimed to have lived there.

Dad still lives in the same house on the Cregagh estate in Belfast where I was raised. The only thing that has changed is the blue plaque on the wall saying that I lived there once. As if he needs reminding. Wags have said to my dad that the plaque was put there to help me find the house during my drinking days. He has recently recovered from a heart operation. He's eighty-four now and still going strong and full of life. The nurses in the hospital told me that once he was feeling better after the operation he perked up so much they considered putting him back on morphine because he just wouldn't shut up. I've had plenty of time to think about him and our early life while I've been recovering from my operation and I have had to smile and laugh at some of the memories that have returned. It warms my heart when I think how he used to stick up for me as a kid. Just as he still does now.

When I was little I was always in bare feet. Now this had nothing to do with poverty – we children had shoes, it was just the sharing of them that was the problem. My sisters didn't like my sandals and I didn't like their high heels. Seriously, I just preferred pottering around in bare feet until one day I stepped on some broken glass just after Mum had dropped a milk bottle. I felt a sliver of glass enter my foot but when we cleared the blood away we couldn't see anything. Dad took me up the hospital where a nurse poked around my foot for some time and eventually declared there was no glass in my foot.

'If my boy says he can feel glass in his foot, there is glass in his foot,' argued Dad, but we were sent on our way. A couple of weeks later I was running home from school when I felt a pain in my foot so I stopped and took my shoe and sock off to examine it. I was surprised to see, because I had forgotten about it, that a quarter-inch slice of glass had worked its way through the skin and was sticking out the sole of my foot. I showed Dad as soon as I got in and he promptly took the glass off me and marched back up to the hospital looking for the unbelieving casualty nurse.

Another time I was playing outside on some wasteland around a bonfire we had built and the street bully came along and started to kick away our efforts. Maybe because I was the smallest among us and I figured the older boy might not hit me I remonstrated with him. He was a good five inches taller but that didn't stop him knocking me to the floor and falling on top of me. As we rolled around the ground his arm caught on some broken glass and he yelled with pain. When he saw the blood running out of his sleeve he ran off home. Later that evening there was a knock at the door and it was the boy's father. Fortunately I had told Dad earlier what had happened.

'Your son has maimed my boy,' shouted the man. Dad wasn't a loud man, or a violent one, but his face reddened and he thrust it towards the man on the doorstep.

'Your son is a bully and everyone knows it. Get away from my door. Now!' He guided me into the man's line of vision so he could see just how much smaller I was than his son. The man was not going to argue with Dad.

There was a downside to my celebrity that thankfully seems to have passed although it probably has more to do with how I live my life these days than a sea change in attitudes towards me from some quarters. This downside was the problem of people wanting to fight me. It happened often, more so in London than Manchester. Most of the time I was able to get away unscathed and talk my way out of situations, but sometimes I was belligerent with drink and went for it, other times I just didn't see it coming. Like the time a man smashed me over the head with a glass beer jug in a London pub. He never even introduced himself. Once, when I was with Alex, a man became aggressive when I beat him at pool. I think it was about the eleventh time I'd beaten him when he started to turn. When he threatened me I was past caring and let him come to me.

'Do you know who I am?' he spat. That was a new one on me. The landlord and a couple of other guys bundled him out and told me on their return that he was well known locally and was ex-SAS. If someone tells everyone that, it normally means they are a complete prick and I felt a good deal less tense about him returning.

It makes me cringe now to think of some of the silly scraps that were down to me. Thankfully Johnny Gold and his late partner Oscar Lerman (Oscar was married to Jackie Collins), former owners of Tramps, have forgiven my childish misdemeanours. Like the time I took offence over something Michael Caine said when I was at his table with my girlfriend, Mary Stavin. He was drunk and so was I and our argument was a classic one between drunken men. Over nothing. I lunged at him and we ended up rolling around the floor. Another evening I went for Tim Jeffries, who was heir to the Green Shield stamp fortune (remember Green Shield stamps? I don't). He had committed the terrible crime of being in there with my ex-girlfriend. Tim became very famous when he went out with the erotic film actress Koo Stark. Koo Stark became very famous when she went out with the Queen's middle son, Andrew. Andrew became very famous when he married Fergy.

FAMOUS FANS

Celebrity supporters are a much-scorned breed it seems. Apparently if you are a celebrity it is not on to go and watch your club play. If you do you risk being accused of promoting yourself and using the club as a vehicle to do so. In my experience this is rarely the case. Danny Baker, the cockney radio pundit, summed it up well when he told the story of how he was at his beloved Millwall one afternoon when a belligerent supporter approached him, 'How come you only started coming down 'ere once you were famous,' he spat accusingly.

'But, before I was famous and my face wasn't known, you wouldn't have known whether I was coming down here or not,' Danny pointed out.

And, of course, that was true. Danny Baker had been going to Millwall, man and boy, rarely missing a home game.

The fact is that in the midst of a football crowd no one really cares who you are. Everyone is there to watch the match and immerse himself or herself in willing on their team to victory. The sorts of people who go to football are not, as a rule, celebrity watchers.

One of my favourite, I assume apocryphal, jokes conveys the footballing communites sentiments on the subject perfectly. It 'runs' as follows: Sebastian Coe, the former Olympic 1500m runner and now a Conservative MP, presented himself at Old Trafford. A steward looked at his ticket and told him that he could not gain entry at this point in the ground and needed to walk to another gate all the way around on the other side of the stadium. Coe was frustrated because he was a guest this day, at the box of some well-heeled friends, was running late and he knew it was only a short walk from the entry point where he stood. The steward would have none of it.

'Do you know who I am?' he asked.

'I don't care who you are, sir.'

'I'm Sebastian Coe.'

'Well, if you're Sebastian Coe,' the steward coolly replied, 'it won't take you long to sprint round the corner to get to your correct gate, will it?'

Some years back I met the acclaimed Shakespearean actor Kenneth Branagh, a Belfast boy like myself. It was in Australia and we were in a hotel foyer. He wasn't the big star he is now but had been in some plays in Northern Ireland and I recognised him as he recognised me. When he spoke I noticed he had a very English accent, in fact it was more English than English people themselves have.

'What happened to your accent then?' I asked and Ken seemed more than embarrassed. Every time I have seen him since he always talks to me in the broadest Belfast imaginable.

The celebrity supporters that *do* deserve the stick they get are the politicians. When all of a sudden they pretend to be a passionate supporter of a club in a cynical and patronising attempt to ingratiate themselves with parts of the electorate it makes me sick. Our own Prime Minister, surprise, surprise, is the ultimate example of this. Although no one around Tyneside knew it, Tony Blair declared himself to be in love with Newcastle United and suddenly started popping up at matches with his best interested and intense face on. Naturally the cameras were there to catch these precious leisure moments. It wasn't long before he gave himself away, as people who genuinely love football knew he would, when he waxed lyrically about being hooked since he first saw the Geordie hero Jackie Milburn play. Jackie Milburn retired four years after Tony Blair was born. Maybe an early case of the PM getting out of his pram?

In the interests of political balance I have to point out that the current leader of the Conservative Party is guilty of similar crassness. Iain Duncan Smith was only recently speaking to an invited audience on Wearside when he praised their local team Newcastle's renaissance under Sir Bobby Robson and congratulated them on a European victory the previous evening. If he had known anything about football at all, or known anything about the regional cultures of the people he seeks to lead, he would have known that Wearside is Sunderland territory and that Sunderland and Newcastle football fans hate each other with a vengeance. It was lucky for his own personal safety that IDS was addressing an invited audience and most of them were asleep.

George W. Bush suddenly took an interest in the game when one of his aides told him that the USA were doing rather well in the 2002 World Cup. He sent a message to the players: 'A lot of people, like me, that don't know anything about soccer are all excited and pulling for you.' No need to go quite that far, Mr Bush.

Harold Wilson, Prime Minister twice in the 1960s and then

again in the 1970s, did know a thing or two about football, despite supporting Huddersfield Town. He wrote to me after seeing me play against his club and congratulated me on a good performance. I didn't write back, I'm afraid, I wasn't great with fan mail in those days, so I was a bit surprised when he invited me to a cocktail party at 10 Downing Street not long after. I went along with Kenny Lynch, who knew more about these things than I, and also knew Harold a bit, I learnt. I think it was at this function that I realised just how famous I had become. I knew I was big in the world of football but the moment I walked into that reception room at Number Ten I was backed up against a wall and could barely move for the duration. Willy Brandt, the German Chancellor, was the guest of honour, and his bodyguard was told off for abandoning his boss and coming across the room to chat with me. Almost everyone else present seemed to want to shake my hand and tell me how good I was. This was enormously flattering but also very embarrassing especially as I could see Harold Wilson, second only to the President of America among world leaders, shuffling awkwardly as he stood alone filling his pipe on the other side of the room.

Kenny reminded me recently of something else about that evening. He had seen Henry Moore among the throng and approached him respectfully. 'Mr Moore, what an honour to meet you. I'm a great fan of your work.'

'Why, thank you, Kenny,' Henry Moore responded. 'Would you be able to do me a great favour?'

'Of course.'

'Could you introduce me to Georgie Best?'

Taken aback a bit, Kenny came over to me, where the Number Ten waitresses were keeping me occupied signing napkins.

'George, come with me. Someone wants to meet you.'

'Who?' I asked.

'Only Henry Moore, George.'

'Who's he?' I really had no idea. For a minute it crossed my mind it was Bobby Moore's father.

'Only one of the most famous people in the world,' explained Kenny but giving me that look. The one that said you really are in a world of your own. 'He is a sculptor, you berk.'

And I went over and met Henry Moore, who was very charming and told me he was an ardent Tottenham Hotspur fan. I'm afraid I still can't tell you who or what he has sculpted.

I really was that naive about many things in those days. I had left school sharpish and gone straight into football and therefore did not develop my formal education. Once at Manchester United I was straight on the merry-go-round and there was almost no time to read newspapers or watch television as most people did. After football I pursued my liquid career so my general knowledge outside of football was poor. I can remember when I first knew Kenny Lynch and he said me to, 'I'm a socialist, you know.'

'I know you are, mate. So am I. That's why we are here in this bar together.'

It was probably the first time Kenny gave me that look: I thought a socialist was someone who enjoyed going out.

However, in my thirties I started to read books and my hunger for autobiography and non-fiction has never diminished. These days my favourite pastimes are crosswords and TV quizzes and my thirst is for knowledge rather than drink. I was amused just the other day when watching *Fifteen to One* on afternoon television and the questionmaster asked, 'With which industry is the English town of Sheffield traditionally associated?'

A contestant buzzed and answered, 'Snooker.'

I suppose in this day and age he is right.

Fame is fickle. Because of the soap opera my life became I was never really out of the public eye but for some the shock of being well known, even adulated, and then in the space of a few years becoming an 'ordinary' person again must be difficult. Geoff Hurst, now Sir Geoff Hurst, recently illustrated an extreme example of this. He was visiting Upton Park with his former manager Ron Greenwood. Ron, you will remember, managed West Ham during their golden period in the 1960s and 1970s and also managed England for a spell. Geoff scored three fairly vital goals for England in the World Cup Final of 1966. The two men enjoyed the game on offer and decided to make their way to a private reception room afterwards. The room was called the Ron Greenwood Suite. As they approached the door, a steward barred their progress.

'Sorry, gents, members only.'

'This is Ron Greenwood,' explained Geoff. The steward's face remained blank and his arm still stretched across the doorway.

'No, seriously this is Ron Greenwood. Ron Greenwood of West Ham. The man this suite is named after,' Geoff persisted.

The steward snorted and replied, 'And don't tell me, you're Geoff Hurst.'

People like Carl Hoddle, brother of Glenn and a player with Barnet, had it bad from the beginning. After signing an autograph hunter's proffered book the guy looked a bit disappointed. 'Can you sign it as your brother please, sorry.'

AFTER-DINNER

One of the many plus points of my fame has been that I have been able to join the after-dinner circuit and develop a career in that direction. I've been at this now probably as long as I played professional football and many a 1960s and 1970s football star has found a living on the speaking circuit. Rodney Marsh and I formed a very successful partnership for a number of years and for a while our crowds were almost as big as the ones when we partnered together before – playing for Fulham. Of course, for a man fighting (or, as was often the case, not fighting) alcoholism, it was a dangerous way of making a living. A drink or two before would loosen me up and give confidence to a basically shy man and then a drink or two after would help me wind down. That was my excuse anyway. The reality was, during my darkest days, if I turned up to a gig at all, I was often pissed. Very often, the more pissed I was, the more the audience liked it. Somehow I convinced myself that if I wasn't arseholed I would be letting my audience down. Maybe, for some of them, I would have been.

Rodney remembers the drunken episodes better than me and tells of one occasion when he was pleading with the hosts of one after-dinner to allow me to speak before dinner because he could see I was getting paralytic fast. Unfortunately they didn't want to interrupt the running order and Rodney was proved correct when my head fell into my soup. It went downhill from there. Poor Marshy had to get me out (with help) and into a cab and away because the audience who had all paid good money were none too pleased that they had been short-changed. In the cab I was slumped with my head on Marshy's knee when apparently I looked up and said in all seriousness, 'Did you get the money?'

We were up near Manchester one evening when Denis Tueart, who was Rodney's colleague at Manchester City, came up to him. I knew Rodney disliked Denis from their playing days although I was never sure why. This will be interesting, I thought. They hadn't crossed each other's paths for about twenty years and Denis held out his hand but Rodney refused it. Denis pulled a face as if to say, 'Oh come on, don't be childish. We're a lot older now.'

Marshy read his mind. 'Piss off, Denis. I still think you're a bastard but I can't remember why.'

Rodney and I enjoyed parallel careers really. Both flair players. Both drank. Both went to America. Both joined the after-dinner circuit. Indeed there was a time when my star was falling and Rodney's was rising to such a point the unthinkable happened. Madame Tussaud's announced that my waxwork dummy was being melted down and I was being replaced by a likeness of Rodney Marsh. I was even asked for my reaction to this at a general press conference in America.

'Who is Rodney Marsh?' I wisecracked, but the really funny thing was I could tell by the way it went quiet afterwards that no other person in the room really knew who he was either.

In the end Madame Tussaud's snubbed us both and decided to shelves their plans for Marshy and replace me instead with the new European Footballer of the Year, Johan Cruyff.

One time I was doing a question and answer session when a man from the audience really threw me. I just got through three or four typical queries – 'Who was the dirtiest player you ever came up against?' and so on – when this man addressed me in real David Dimbleby *Question Time* fashion.

'Is Ian Ure still alive, and if so, why?'

What was that all about? Ian Ure was a solid but now largely forgotten Scottish defender who plied his trade in the 1960s with Arsenal, Manchester United and Scotland. It was a strange question, almost Monty Pythonesque, and no one laughed including the questioner. I moved on to the next question.

When I first got up there in front of an audience and spoke I was terrified. I am a very shy person who was thrust at a very young age into the spotlight and for many years even being interviewed for TV was an ordeal. I believe now that my initial drinking was partly a subconscious effort to overcome my shyness. Drink changed my personality and helped a private young man deal with a very public life. Yet drink or no drink, if someone had told me when I was a young man that one day I would be on stage delivering speeches I would have just laughed. It just sort of developed. I was being offered money to present awards, attend functions and dinners and I was being required to 'say a few words'. My act evolved from there. I found that humorous stories went down a treat and that also I could react competently in a question and answer environment. Soon I had become the reason for the dinner and the central attraction rather than the 'name' hired to shake a few hands.

I think I was one of the first footballers to become an after-dinner act although, and not a lot of people know this, players in previous decades used to appear in theatre and music hall during the close season to add to their incomes. Eddie Hapgood, the Arsenal and England full back from the 1930s and 1940s, and Stanley Matthews were just two of the big names who would share a bill on a seaside pier or a provincial theatre with the likes of Tessie O'Shea, Flanagan and Allen or Tommy Handley, during the summer months. I don't think they did a lot of speaking though. Basically the curtains would open and they'd be standing there in their kit and then proceed to demonstrate their ball control or balance the ball on their heads. Audiences these days demand a little more.

On the subject of football personalities doing a bit of extracurricular to bring the money in, Alex James, who was a forward in Herbert Chapman's super Arsenal side of the 1930s, made up his meagre earnings by becoming a demonstrator at the Selfridges store in London. Imagine that. Alex was one of the most famous players of his day, people from my dad's generation talked about him in reverential tones yet there he was standing in the store in full kit, feeling a bit of a prat no doubt, persuading mums to buy their boys the latest footballs.

I had a fund of stories from my own experience and I soon realised when playing to an audience having this bank of anecdotes was not enough and that things like timing, delivering punchlines and sounding and acting naturally were just as important. It made me realise how talented the guys were who got up and did an act. Bob Monkhouse, for example, is a joke man and nobody can touch him for his memory, range and quick-fire delivery but you could not say he was natural. Billy Connolly, on the other hand, is a storyteller and he appears to ramble quite naturally but his act is no less structured, organised and timed than Bob Monkhouse's. It just looks that way. Those attributes did not come easily to me at all and friends in the world of show business were very helpful in offering advice and tips. Jimmy Tarbuck's was 'stick to playing football'. Nowadays it is the question and answer sessions I enjoy the most. I can get the scripted stuff out the way and then just hoof it. Many of the questions are the ones that come up every time and I use the same patter to respond to them but always someone will come up with something original and I like the challenge of finding new and, hopefully, entertaining answers. Often these sessions are like settling down in a pub and having a good old chinwag about the game.

Before long, dozens of us were on the circuit and it was the so-called mavericks – football's bad boys – who seemed to be in particular demand. Audiences were more interested, it appeared, in drunken escapades and womanising, than accounts of historic goals, games and seasons. I caught Frank Worthington's act one time and he had pinched some of my material. Right from his opening line when he talks about my drunken appearance on the *Wogan* show and Oliver Reed calling me up the next day when it was all over the papers – 'I don't know what all the fuss is about George. You looked okay to me' – through to 'Bill Wyman couldn't be here tonight, he's at the hospital attending the birth of his next wife.' I couldn't complain. Frank has always had the cheek of the devil and I would have lifted some of his material if I'd fancied it.

Duncan McKenzie, who was a highly skilful forward when he played the game, was sometimes criticised for being lightweight and inconsistent on the field. They are qualities that could not be levelled at him in his career as an after-dinner speaker. I would say he is the best on the circuit among the ex-footballers. He is a storyteller as opposed to a joke man but he is interesting and funny and very, very natural. Another guy who is a master of this craft is a chap called Bob 'The Cat' Bevan. He never was a professional footballer, so why he has assumed Peter Bonetti's nickname I can't say, but he works with many of us and if you ever get the opportunity to see him, you should. One of the funniest men around.

The best nights are when something happens impromptu. When Rodney and I were touring, sometimes guests would turn up unannounced. We were playing Slough one time and Kenny Lynch appeared from nowhere (we knew nothing about it, he lived nearby in Henley-on-Thames and he just turned up off his own bat) and walked up to the stage carrying champagne and glasses on a silver salver. He rocked them in the aisles that night with his tales and ad-libbing. Another time, a couple of years later, we were taking questions from the audience at the Shaw Theatre, Kings Cross. A lad stood up and said, 'Dennis Lawrence, Finsbury Park. What are your views on the current Nigeria team and do you think they can become a serious force in world football?'

Both Rodney and I became quite disparaging about Nigeria

as a football team and in order to get a cheap laugh I took it a bit further. 'Last time I was there people were still eating each other.' At that a familiar face stood up at the back of the theatre. 'Kenny Lynch, Nigeria,' he boomed and it brought the house down.

6

THE MEDIA

KICK-OFF

On the whole the press have not been too bad to me. If they had really tried they could have got photos of me lying in the gutter, literally, but they didn't – nevertheless we have endured strained periods. One morning after one drinking binge, when I did God knows what, my telephone rang at 7.30 in the morning. As I hadn't got to bed yet I answered it. My voice was obviously instantly recognisable.

'Good morning, George, I'm from the *Sun* ...'

'And I'm from Earth, now fuck off.'

PRESSING QUESTIONS

Some quarters of the media think ethics is a place, east of London, where they sell a lot of papers. But I'm not complaining because the rules are pretty clear. I'm part of it these days anyway. I write for a newspaper and I broadcast on television. I am old enough and wise enough to appreciate how it all works. There is some truth in the adage 'Never let the truth get in the way of a good story', but the celebrity industry uses the media unashamedly to promote their product (themselves) and they can't complain when the media take them apart when they get caught with their pants down or with white powder up their noses. The rules, hypocritical as they are, are well known. If you have a dark moustache you don't sniff cocaine in public places.

A couple of years back I was taken ill while on holiday in Cyprus. The English press got to hear about it and they managed to get through to me on the telephone in my room. 'Can we ask what is wrong you with, George?'

'Yes,' I told them truthfully. 'I have picked up a virus and I am not very well. The hospital and doctors are great and are looking after me excellently. I hope to be out in a couple of days.'

You could almost hear the sigh of disappointment in a London newsroom. They had hoped I had fallen off the wagon or better still was on my way out. They obviously didn't take my word for it and phoned again to the administrator of the hospital who was just not used to this type of thing. He came into my room clearly distressed.

'Meester Best, they are asking if there is any truth in the rumour that you have HIV,' he told us.

'Don't worry,' I laughed, 'it's wishful thinking. Tell them yes I am HIV – Heavily Into Vodka – that'll shut them up.'

When footballers come across the press for the first time they are more often than not young boys and wet behind the ears. It takes a while to appreciate the media game. Stories get made up to fill space. Stories get placed by the players themselves (or these days their agents). Some journalists champion particular players or managers and others are out to destroy and undermine particular individuals. There is a web of special relationships and there is an income stream for many writing and supplying stories to newspapers and journalists. When Rodney Marsh was first on the verge of making the England team, the press were building up a head of steam in calling for his inclusion in the international side. One Sunday tabloid offered him a substantial fee to give an exclusive along the lines of RODNEY MARSH SAYS I AM READY TO PLAY FOR MY COUNTRY. Marshy had the sense to seek advice before accepting the Fleet Street pound and went to see his manager at the time – Alec Stock. Now Alec was a wise old stick and advised the young player firmly against selling his story.

'One thing Alf Ramsey doesn't like is players or the papers telling him just who he should pick. Don't risk your international future for a grand,' he counselled.

Rodney saw the sense in this but was gobsmacked when he opened his Sunday paper the next week. RODNEY MARSH IS READY

TO PLAY FOR ENGLAND SAYS ALEC STOCK screamed the headline. Wise old stick indeed.

Rodney didn't get on too well with Bedford Jezzard, who was his first manager at Fulham, not a village just outside Milton Keynes. He played his natural game and this included attempts to try and do one or two clever things with the ball. Sometimes they worked and sometimes they didn't. This day one of Marshy's clever bicycle kicks led to an own goal. The manager was furious. 'What the hell were you trying to do out there?'

'Entertain,' replied Marsh.

'If I wanted entertainers, son, I'd contact Billy Smart and sign two clowns.'

'You've got a first team full of them, what do you want two more for?' returned Rodney.

As I said earlier the press boys, and sub-editors especially, are not without their sense of humour. A favourite headline about me was in a North-West paper following an incident when I broke down in my car in the Mersey Tunnel after an Everton/Manchester United fixture. As luck would have it, Alan Ball and his lovely wife Lesley were passing through and they very kindly towed me out to the nearest garage. Someone must have tipped off the press about this momentous incident and a small article the following day was captioned BEST DRAGGED OUT OF TUNNEL BY THE BALLS.

During the 1960s and 1970s there was a sports reporter on the *Manchester Evening News* who David Meek once told me about. He was an unashamed United nut and try as he might he just could not disguise his bias towards us in his reporting. United games always got more space than City and our football was described as wonderful, flowing, brilliant. City on the other hand got better write-ups than the opposition outside Manchester but not that much better. When the unthinkable happened in one match and an unfancied Newcastle team absolutely destroyed Manchester United by five goals to one we all wondered how he would deal with it. The headline set the tone – UNITED IN SIX-GOAL THRILLER.

MICK AND TEL

Television chat shows have been good and bad for me. My early appearances on the *Parkinson* show I think were a huge success. They came at a time when most of the publicity surrounding me was negative – unreliable, drinking, womanising, arrogant, wastrel, etc. Michael, like he did with most of his guests, brought the best out of me and let the audience and viewers see that I was not that person and the situations I found myself in were not so black and white. I believe that the *Parkinson* shows helped cement the relationship I have enjoyed with the British public ever since. *Parkinson* was a chat show. I'm not sure chat shows nowadays can really be described as such. There is not a lot of chatting being done, is there? If you watch *Graham Norton*, for example, you'll notice that if you take out commercial breaks and lead-ins, guests are lucky to get more than seven minutes. Nine times out of ten the guest is unashamedly pushing a product (a book, a film, a play, a new TV series) and the conversation has to get around to that very quickly. There is a very thin dividing line nowadays between chat shows and the shopping channels where fading celebrities push lines of jewellery or plates with garish pictures of themselves on them. Alternatively they are merely a vehicle for this year's fad chat show presenter and the guests are no more than mere decorations.

The *Wogan* show in 1990 was a different kettle of fish from my *Parkinson* appearances altogether. I was very drunk after hitting the bar with Omar Sharif in the BBC hospitality room beforehand. I was that drunk I started thinking Omar was Sacha Distel. Then I walked out and took my chair, puffy-eyed and giggling, opposite Terry Wogan on live TV and with an audience of many millions. We talked about my spell in Ford prison, Paul Gascoigne and Italia 90, although little that I said was very coherent. At home the viewers started paying serious attention realising someone was in the process of making a real fool of himself. The latter part of the interview went like this:

TW: At the risk of being sycophantic, not everybody has your talent.

GB: That's correct, yeah. Correct! No, it's just a shame because I still love the game, I love it, I'll watch it and they've got no idea what they're doing ... and they keep bringing these managers in who've got no idea what they're talking about ... a load of ....

TW: Please ...

GB: Is this live?

TW: Almost.

GB: Can I say shit?

TW: I don't think so, I don't think so but tell me about ...

GB: He panicked!

TW: I do, yeah. You can see it in my eyes. Now you were saying it's very tough on Gazza and people like that. In your day, as a footballer, was it easier to express yourself? Was it easier to give rein to your talent?

GB: Yes, it was.

TW: Why was that?

GB: Cos we could play.

TW: You don't think players now are any good? That makes you sound cynical and old, George.

GB: It's not just cynical, it's just ... I actually believe when I played it was nice. It was fun, it was lovely ... and I watched that show you did with Gazza ... can I say this?

TW: Well, I don't know – what are you going to say? Want to whisper it to me first? So it's not as good? Yeah, moving right along here, George. Yes, I'm spooling on. Tell me, in the book that you have written, why did you leave Old Trafford?

GB: Tommy Docherty.

TW: What happened?

GB: I don't like people who tell lies, and he told lies to me.

TW: What did he tell you?

GB: I'm Irish.

TW: Get away. But I mean tell me about ...

GB: Don't people bullshit ...?

TW: Yeah.

GB: Is that live?

TW: No, no, we can edit that out in a minute.

GB: People bullshit. I don't like people who bullshit.

TW: Do you still bear a grudge?

GB: Yeah, yeah.

TW: Do you still feel that your playing career was cut short?

GB: No.

TW: You feel you gave your money's worth?

GB: I don't like bullshitters.

TW: Yeah ... So tell me, in your book you were saying that you'd a reputation for knocking about with lots of girls.

GB: Screwing.

TW: Yeah.

GB: Yeah.

TW: And to put it delicately. Yes, now, in that case, you were saying that when ...

GB: He's not sure, is he?

TW: Can you blame me? You were saying that every time any one of them want to make any money they write about their years with George Best?

GB: Terry, I like screwing, all right?

TW: All right. So what do you do with your time these days?

GB: Screw.

And that was that. The show caused a tremendous uproar at the time especially because of its early evening broadcast slot. Thirteen years later it all seems pretty tame with the most offensive word used being 'screw' and the above text underlines what it was – the incoherent and embarrassing ramblings of a pissed man. Now, early evening BBC viewers are subjected to murder, drug addiction, prostitution, incest and paedophilia and that's just in *EastEnders*. One good thing came out of it, however; Omar Sharif and myself became engaged that evening.

Poor Terry, or at least his researchers, were had on his show by another football-related thing just after my performance. A seventeen-year-old boy had announced he was buying Aldershot Football Club and therefore saving them from the liquidation that was looming. Something didn't ring true about the whole story but when he appeared on the show in his suit and waistcoat he was terribly self-assured and claimed he had made his millions 'in computers'. You have to go some to make your millions in computers by the age of seventeen but this bit of logic seemed to have passed the *Wogan* people by. The boy was treated seriously and courteously. Such was the hype about yuppies and self-made men and women under the Thatcher revolution anything was possible. However, the most basic digging by a newspaper discovered afterwards that the boy was a fantasist who hadn't even started work. He was a top bullshitter, you had to give it to him, and for a few days he took everyone in. I wonder where he is now? Spin doctor for the Government perhaps?

The chat show I was most nervous about was when I was invited to appear on *Johnny Carson* in the US. This was the biggest chat show in the world and I was due on to publicise the British football game in America. It was not like Parky or Terry Wogan – it was a fast-moving format where you had a limited time to get over whatever it was you were getting over and you were followed and joined on the couch by real live Hollywood legends. (On *Wogan* you'd be following the Singing Nun or a man who didn't answer any questions correctly on *Mastermind*.) Out here and in this company I was a nobody. No one in America really knew who George Best was. I had a couple of drinks in the Green Room with actor and film director Mel Brooks, who I had met before in Tramps in London, and wished him luck as he went on. But now as I was one guest away my stomach tightened up and I felt really scared. I really didn't want to go on. Watching Mel on the TV screen he was hilarious, storytelling and ad-libbing. There was no stopping the man and thank God for that because the producer came into the Green Room and said, 'We're terribly sorry, George, but Mel's doing great out there, we'd like to run with him. Would you mind if we had you back another time?'

I could have kissed the man.

THESE ARE MY LIVES

Perhaps the most rewarding television I have ever done has been the two *This Is Your Life*s where I have been the subject. The first was in 1971 when I was only twenty-five and the second was thirty-two years later, in 2003. I had no idea either time that anything was afoot. In fact only a few weeks before the second one I was sitting at home watching Michael Aspel pounce on someone with his red book when I remarked to some of Alex's family, 'They'll never catch me with that one again.'

Of course, at that time everyone in the room except me knew I was about to be captured. They caught me very easily by simply asking me to film an appeal for the Liver Foundation with Professor Williams, something they knew I would not turn down, and therefore I went to them and a waiting audience and guests at Teddington Studios. It was a lovely day and I thoroughly enjoyed it although I did reflect poignantly afterwards on those who featured in 1971 who were not around this time. My mum most obviously and painfully, but also my nans, my old landlady Mrs Fullaway, Sir Matt Busby and not forgetting the presenter Eamonn Andrews himself. I was astounded though that the producer Jack Crawshaw who was on the first one was still there thirty-two years later. And they say there is no job security in this day and age. I am particularly pleased about the second one because, rather than making a programme celebrating my life, I'm sure plenty of television companies had my obituaries ready to use at very short notice – a sort of *This Was Your Life*.

The first programme though caused everyone except me a great deal of stress. At the time I was knocking around Manchester with a clothes designer named Harold Tillman. Like me he enjoyed the night-life and we drank, played and did bits of business together. It amuses me that people think Manchester only became fashionable with the advent of the Gallagher brothers, Madchester and the 1990s nightclubbing scene. Rubbish. Manchester in the 1960s and 1970s was *the* in-place, more so than London even. Harold had working for him a certain Paul Smith, now Sir Paul Smith, whose name has become one of the biggest shirt brands of all time. The fashion house they worked for was called Kilgore, French and Stanberry and in the knowledge that I was going to be targeted for *This Is Your Life* they made me a beautiful suit which was going to be the centrepiece of their latest range. They co-operated in setting me up but at the same time they were ensuring that their product would be showcased on prime-time television. I was told that the new range was being launched to the press following a party at a penthouse flat in London. The idea was that the press launch they took me to the morning after the party would really be the Teddington Studios. I was assured of plenty of gorgeous women and even more booze at the party. They knew that was the only sure way of making me turn up.

They got me down to the flat near Park Lane in London and I tried the suit on before the party got swinging. There is nothing like a well-cut, made-to-measure, quality suit to make you feel good and once I put it on I did not want to take it off. 'Come on, George, hang it up and leave it fresh for the morning,' urged Harold, mindful though not to arouse my suspicions.

I would have none of it and by now guests had began arriving and the champagne was starting to flow. My boredom threshold has always been low and I also had a fear of enclosed spaces, so before long I was itching to leave the party. I fancied going to Tramps. Whenever I was in London I liked to go there. Johnny Gold, the owner, was good to me and tolerated my more drunken moments and you were always sure to bump into someone interesting. It might be a Beatle, a Stone or a Kink or a Sean Connery or a visiting Hollywood star. Never a dull moment. A girl at the party had a car. It was probably a Mini and she agreed to drive us both to the club. I didn't know it then but as I eased out of the door a look of horror spread across Harold Tillman's face. A great deal of effort and expense had gone into preparing the programme and Harold and others had given ATV all sorts of assurances about being able to ensure they'd deliver me. Once I was out in that night air they knew that like a Smith's crisp packet I could blow anywhere. With this unpalatable eventuality in mind they had two private detectives waiting in a car who were watching the door and they followed the young lady and myself to the club. I spotted them but remember thinking to myself that the press should have better things to do.

I cannot recall who was in that night but I do know that shortly before dawn broke, and now incapable of anything, the girl agreed to drop me back at the penthouse. Outside, the private detectives who I thought were press were waiting and followed us. Out of devilment I got the girl to lose them and this she did with ease. I hope the TV people didn't pay too much for them because those 'detectives' couldn't follow a bus. At the flat the party had long finished and even Harold had given up waiting for me. So as not to disturb anyone I flopped on to a sofa and went to sleep.

We all overslept, although in those days none of us kept to conventional sleeping patterns. Harold was up and rushing around, pleading for me to come to the car for the 'launch'. I remember him fussing around my jacket and trousers and worrying about creases. He seemed unusually worried. The upshot was that they got me to Teddington, where Eamonn pounced, and then promptly kept me locked in a room until the evening when the programme was going to be shot. It crossed my mind to escape if I could, not so much because I didn't want to do the programme, but because I needed a hair of the dog. I did it and enjoyed it but the suit looks terrible. Unfortunately no videos were available then but I do have the commemorative album that the production team present to you and my suit looks like it had been slept in, which, of course, it had.

I suppose I'm like anyone else when I watch *This Is Your Life*. It is a great programme and a durable idea but I am often left wondering why it is so short. Covering someone's life in less than half an hour is difficult. These days I often wonder too just who the person *is* whose life is being celebrated. I think it's a shame how guests are graded by the size of their celebrity and not by their relevance to the subject, meaning that the final guest is often a big star now who may have appeared briefly in panto with the subject twenty years earlier. (And is Lionel Blair really the great friend of every single person in show business?) In the old days it would be a long lost brother, or dear school friend not seen in quarter of a century. I love it though when a voice comes over the speakers and it is obvious that the subject does not have the foggiest idea who the person is. I was terrified this would happen to me. On the first one it did.

When Nurse Ruth Anderson spoke I went cold and thought I was going to have pretend to know her but as she recounted her story it all came back to me. As a young child I had to go to hospital to have my tonsils removed and Nurse Ruth took a shine to me. My favourite TV programme at the time was *Quatermass and the Pit* and she allowed me to stay up and watch it. One night as she tucked me in she gave me a little kiss on the forehead and to my horror this was witnessed by the other boys on the ward who did not leave me alone thereafter. At that age you wouldn't admit to still being kissed good night by your parents let alone a nurse on a general hospital ward and I thanked God the boys who had witnessed this terrible incident were not from my school or my estate. Ironically I need never have been in the hospital in the first place. At the time I was unhappy at school and I tried to kid my mum that I was sick. I used to buy red gobstoppers from the penny sweetshop and suck them until my throat area was visibly red and then complain of a sore throat. Because it happened so regularly my mum became genuinely concerned and took me to the doctor. The doctor, who couldn't identify a malingerer when he saw one, referred me to the hospital and the tonsil specialist. When she decided I needed an operation to have them removed I was tempted to come clean. But events had overtaken me and I judged going into hospital for two weeks and having an unnecessary operation a lesser evil than confessing to my mum (and then my dad) that I had been deceiving them all this time.

FORE FRONT

I've been used in some advertising campaigns in my time and endorsed many a product. Who can forget George Best football boots whose laces did up at the sides and 'E for B and Georgie Best', the campaign to encourage people to buy eggs? There was also the *George Best Annual* which was the same as any other football annual except it had my picture on the cover and a letter from me to the readers at the front. At its peak it was selling an incredible 120,000 copies in the run-up to Christmas. Up there with the *Dandy* and the *Beano*. I cringe a bit now when I look back on the sausage advertisement I did back in the 1960s. My whole family got roped into that one and we all sat around a breakfast table feigning a Best family breakfast and I then look at the camera and beam: 'Cookstown are the Best family sausages.' The thing was, by that time, I hadn't lived at home for years and the kitchen that the ad was filmed in was bigger than our entire downstairs at home. I don't really understand the advertising game but although I can see how me endorsing football boots or clothes could have a direct impact on sales, I cannot believe that my mugshot really persuaded housewives to switch sausage brands.

I was even in Playtex bra adverts for a period, but the strangest campaign I got involved in was an aftershave called Fore. Long before Henry Cooper and a heavily permed Kevin Keegan were splashing Brut all over, I was the marketing face of Fore. Their logo was a golf ball and to this day I do not know the significance of that. I didn't care at the time – I just took the money. (I've never taken up golf, by the way. Unlike many of my peers, I cannot bear being separated from the ball for those long periods. I have no time for cricket either. It must be the only contact sport where you can put on weight while playing.) They wanted to shoot a film of me driving down the Kings Road in a sports car with a couple of dolly birds in the back and an Afghan hound sitting up regally on the passenger seat next to me. I never understood the significance of the Afghan hound. Were they suggesting I went out with old dogs? However, I didn't make that shoot, having spent a very heavy night in Tramps nightclub.

Waggy told me later that the agency responsible for the advertisement were furious because they had flown me by helicopter from Newcastle, where I had been playing, to the Carlton Tower Hotel in London. They were threatening all sorts of legal action. Waggy didn't tell me at the time because he knew that if I knew that they were all incandescent with rage at me I would have just walked away. I hate bad feelings. The next shoot Waggy made sure I was there by fetching me from my bed and taking me to Hyde Park. The new idea was I would walk through the park and among various sunbathing ladies who would get a whiff of me and my Fore and start to follow me. A sort of play on the Pied Piper. The Afghan had taken the rap for the first debacle. Just as the cameras were about to roll a youth ambled into camera view and leant up against a tree, chewing gum and watching the proceedings.

'Do you mind moving please?' called out one of the crew.

'Na,' replied the yobbo.

'Why not?'

'Free country.'

I had had enough of this, especially as I had a raging hang-over and wanted to get the whole afternoon over so I could get to the pub and resume drinking again. I walked over to him and whispered in his ear, 'If you don't piss off out the way I swear I'll put you in hospital.' And I meant it. I think the teenager sensed this and he swaggered off.

'What did you say to that yob?' asked the director when he had finally wrapped up.

'Oh, I gave him a tenner to make himself scarce.'

One of the girls in the advertisement was Vivian Neves. Vivian was famous for being the first nude to appear in *The Times* when she advertised a product for Fisons, the chemical company, in 1971. She was a very pretty, sexy girl and helped establish Page Three of the *Sun* as a national institution. Tragically Vivian died from multiple sclerosis a couple of years back.

Another ad I did, or at least I nearly did, was for a new car being launched by Renault called the Dolphin. Why they chose this name I'm not sure. Perhaps it had a hole in the roof. This time I was ensconced in Regent's Park with a similar bevy of beautiful ladies. As with all of these things there were hours of waiting around for half an hour's worth of filming which in turn would be distilled into fifty seconds of commercial. These production crews seem to spend more time setting up their mobile canteen and eating and drinking from it rather than making films. The boredom was getting to me and halfway through the shoot, I shot off. I told someone I was just going to buy a paper but instead walked the few streets to where my car was parked on a meter, got in it and drove off. I went for a couple of swift drinks in Chelsea and then later that afternoon turned up at Kenny Lynch's place. I told Kenny what I had done and he tried to persuade me to go back. 'I'll come with you,' he coaxed, 'we'll knock the thing out and then take a couple of the girls out.' The problem was that once I had let someone down I couldn't face them and I was determined not to return. As I sat next to Kenny on the sofa his phone rang. It became obvious from his side of the conversation that the people on the other end were the advertising agency for the Renault Dolphin.

'No, I haven't seen or heard from him … no idea … yes, of course, I'll let you know … why did you call here?'

'Because, we've been told that when he does a disappearing act he often comes to you.'

'Well, he's not here, I can assure you,' ended Kenny, looking straight at me. To cap it all he switched the television on and there was an item on the London regional news about me disappearing. To put a spin on what had now become a tedious occurrence they even suggested I might have been kidnapped.

When Great Universal Stores approached me to become the male face of their clothing catalogue, I wasn't sure. These were the days before credit cards and three-quarters of the population purchased their wardrobe from mail-order catalogues. The problem was that the quarter of the population I belonged to didn't. Nevertheless I turned up at the photographic studios on a regular basis to model comfortable cardigans, polo-neck jumpers and sensible slip-on shoes. For me, it was excruciatingly boring standing around all day with a pack of women crawling around my feet with pins in their mouths attending my turn-ups. I put up with this because the money was fantastic and it got better. Sales in that first season went through the roof and GUS wanted me to continue and upped the money to ensure that I did. They kept telling me how well the catalogue was doing and how many units of this and that they had moved. I was delighted for them and myself but to this day I can put hand on heart and say that I never ever wore any of the clothes I modelled socially and more significantly I never ever saw one person wearing any item from the range. I can only conclude that there was a large chunk of the male population who bought their clothes from the catalogue and either kept them neatly folded in their chest of drawers or they lived at home with Mum and never left the house.

BEST FILM?

Films about football never seem to work. I suspect it is because it is so hard to transfer the spontaneity and atmosphere of a football match, stadium and supporters to a contrived situation and the big screen. Who can forget *Escape to Victory* where Bobby Moore, Pele and Mike Summerbee were unlikely pitch partners of a muscle-bound Sylvester Stallone and a middle-aged Michael Caine. Curiously though, to this day, Summerbee regards his part in this film as the highlight of his entire career, possibly his life.

When I was told they were making a film about me, *Best*, I was flattered but nervous of the outcome. If someone decides to make a film about you there is a not a lot you can do. It wasn't me making a film about me, yet I still worried. However, there was a good cast, including John Lynch who was playing me. Linus Roache (son of William Roache, *Coronation Street*'s Ken Barlow and a highly regarded actor in his own right) was playing Denis Law, Jerome Flynn was Bobby Charlton and the veteran film and TV star Ian Bannen was playing Sir Matt Busby.

I was invited to a private screening before the release date and all my fears were realised. I thought the film was shit. It just didn't work on any level for me and I found myself searching for a side exit to escape from. From a personal point of view the bit that really got to me was a scene where I am being ejected from a nightclub or bar and I shout at the bouncers, 'Don't you know who I am?' Yuk. I felt sorry for the director, the producer and especially John Lynch and the rest of the cast because they had tried so hard and after the screening I could not bring myself to tell them what I really thought. Deep down though I think everyone knew. Sadly Ian Bannen died shortly after the film was completed although I'm sure the two events were not connected.

This Boy's Story was a far better film. It told the tale of two young boys and their adventure in getting to a Manchester United v Liverpool fixture and to see me play. It was a short film made by the National Film School in 1991 on a shoestring budget but it went on to win a BAFTA. It starred Steven Arnold, now familiar on our television screens thrice weekly as the beleaguered Ashley Peacock in *Coronation Street*. It was a modest, charming film and I made a cameo appearance at the end when one of the boys, now grown up, sees me just as his wife is telling him she is pregnant. 'I can't wait to go out and tell everyone,' he beams. The wife is unsure whether he wants to go out and tell everyone about the pregnancy or the fact that he has just met George Best.

Besides that cameo appearance I only got to speak in one other film. This was a spin-off from the hugely popular *Till Death Us Do Part* TV series starring Warren Mitchell and Dandy Nichols. If you ever wonder or have forgotten what things were like before political correctness, try and catch this movie on a gold satellite channel. It is quite shocking. As in the TV programme, Alf Garnett's daughter Rita was played by Una Stubbs but instead of the Prime Minister's father-in-law Tony Booth playing her boyfriend it was, wait for it, Kenny Lynch. This gave

Alf plenty of mileage on the racial abuse front. In one scene he is watching his club West Ham United and Clyde Best, their Bermudan winger (no relation) comes in for a stomach-churning stream of invective. In my scene I am in the toilets with Bobby Moore having a quick wee after the game and Alf is spouting off again. I approach him and whisper something in his ear. Piss off, I think it was or meant to be. That same year, 1968, I was offered a more substantial part in *The Virgin Soldiers*, the film adaptation of Leslie Thomas's best-selling book. The film, starring Hywel Bennett, was a huge box-office hit and I sort of wished I'd got involved but I think even the mere suggestion of it would have sent Matt Busby into despair.

NO COMMENTATE

We've had some wonderful commentators and presenters in this game of ours. Dear old Kenneth Wolstenholme, lovely Brian Moore and John 'Motty' Motson to name but a few. They are not with us now. Well, Kenneth and Brian are dead, Motty is just not with us. Can't forget David Coleman, either, whose faux pas over the years, thanks to *Private Eye*, became famously known as Colemanballs. Their distinctive voices and off-the-cuff, on-the-hoof commentaries provided the soundtrack to our footballing careers. Some of their exclamations have become indelibly linked with certain footballing moments. Kenneth Wolstenholme's 'They think it's all over – it is now' at the end of the 1966 World Cup Final between England and West Germany is arguably as famous a saying as any from English history – Shakespeare's 'My horse, my horse, my kingdom for a horse' from Richard III and Churchill's 'We'll fight them on the beaches' included.

Gabby Yorath, daughter of Terry Yorath, an old adversary at Leeds United, was the first lady to break through into this closed, sheepskin, male-orientated world and thank God she did, because lovely as all those guys were and are, she is far more pleasing on the eye. But even the glamorous Gabby follows in the great tradition of Colemanballs. Only recently, when England went out of the World Cup to Brazil and David Seaman made a couple of serious errors, she sat in the studio eliciting opinions from her panel of experts. When they had finished defending the Arsenal keeper she looked straight into the camera to wrap up.

'Well, one thing is for sure,' she said, 'it'll be Seaman all over tomorrow's papers.'

More recently Alan Brazil was speaking on TalkSport radio. 'I was sad to hear yesterday about the death of Inspector Morse, TV's John Shaw.'

His co-host Mike Parry was quick to correct him. 'No, John Thaw, Alan.'

'I've been doing that all morning. John, if you're listening, sorry mate.'

So as to be fair to all concerned, what follows are my favourites from our commentators and presenters past and present and across the board:

'With the very last kick of the game, Bobby McDonald scored with a header' – Mike Parry.

'… and Southampton have beaten Brighton by 3 goals to 1; that's a repeat of last year's result when Southampton won 5–1' – Desmond Lynam.

'Thank you for evoking memories – particularly of days gone by' – Mike Ingham.

'Kilmarnock versus Partick Thistle, match postponed … that, of course, is a latest score' – Frank Bough.

'And there will be more football in a moment, but first we've got the highlights of the Scottish League Cup Final' – Gary Newbon.

Ian St. John: 'Is he speaking to you yet?'

Jimmy Greaves: 'Not yet, but I hope to be incommunicado with him in a very short space of time.'

'Julian Dicks is everywhere. It's like they've got eleven Dicks on the field' – Metro Radio.

'If you can't stand the heat in the dressing room – get out of the kitchen' – Terry Venables.

'And I honestly believe we can go all the way to Wembley, if we don't get knocked out on the way' – Dave Bassett.

Richard Keys: 'Well, Roy, do you think you'll have to finish above Manchester United to win the League?'

Roy Evans: 'You have to finish above everyone to win the League, Richard.'

Live radio and now television phone-ins are a relatively new phenomenon for pundits to deal with. At least in a studio, you sort of know what is coming but to let loose mad members of the public is asking for trouble. Rodney Marsh has done phone-ins on radio for some time now and he is sharp and can dispatch the idiots, the abusive and the downright boring rapidly and with ease.

It is footballers though, rather than commentators, presenters or pundits, who when interviewed have provided some of the best Colemanballs. What follows are a few of my favourites:

Neville Southall, the former Everton goalkeeper, showed just how those footballers favourite clichés can get in the way when he replied to an interviewer's question with, 'If you don't believe you can win, there is no point in getting out of bed at the end of the day.'

Paul Gascoigne couldn't understand why Gerald Sinstadt looked puzzled when he stated, 'I've had fourteen bookings this season, eight of which I hold my hands up to but I think the other seven are debatable.'

Alan Shearer was deadly serious when he said, 'I am committed to Newcastle. I never want to leave. As far as I'm concerned I'm here for the rest of my life and hopefully after that as well.'

'My father was a miner and he worked down a mine' – Kevin Keegan.

Jonathan Woodgate demonstrated his commitment to Leeds when he declared, 'Leeds is a great club and it's been my home for years even though I live in Middlesbrough.'

Stan Collymore was obviously in a confused state of mind when he told an interviewer, 'I faxed a transfer request to the club at the beginning of the week, but let me state I don't want to leave Leicester City.'

Ade Akinbiyi: 'I was watching the Blackburn game on Sky on Sunday when I saw that George [Ndah] had scored in the first minute at Birmingham. I went to call him on his mobile to congratulate him but then I remembered he was out there playing.'

Paul Gascoigne: 'It was a big relief off my shoulder.'

Stuart Pearce: 'I can see the carrot at the end of the tunnel.'

Les Ferdinand: 'I was surprised, but I always say nothing surprises me in football.'

Gary Lineker: 'There's no in between – you're either good or bad. Today we were in between.'

It is so easy though to say inane and stupid things on camera. You don't have time to think and there is no bigger crime in the world of television sound bites than silences. Therefore you cannot help but say the first thing that comes into your head. I'm sure I spouted similar rubbish in my time but in those days there was far less football coverage, fewer pundits and generally fewer opportunities to make a fool of yourself. And there wasn't videotape so your every word and slip of the tongue could be scrutinised. In my early days at Sky, though, I came out with a classic – 'When they first installed all-seater stadiums everyone predicted that the fans wouldn't stand for it.' Another time I made the astute observation that 'in football you're flavour of the month for a day'.

My Sky colleague Chris Kamara is about as enthusiastic a commentator as you will find these days. He can almost convince us that a 0–0 tie between Rochdale and Swindon on a muddy, rainy day really is exciting, as he probably believes it is. That's the thing about Chris, unlike Stuart Hall, for example, who must spend the entire match thinking up clever, flowery, topical prose rather than watching the game, Chris just allows the enthusiasm to tumble from his lips. I much prefer that approach even if it is not so polished. Only recently I heard him raving about 'Big' Wayne Allison playing for Sheffield United – 'the manager has done a great deal, he got him for nothing but Wayne must have paid him back at least five times over ...'

Bob Wilson was one of the first to make the successful transition from player to TV commentator and presenter. He once told of how, when he was making one of his very first

TV appearances as a match reviewer, he had been dispatched to Arsenal to watch a game and was hurrying across London after the match to deliver a match report before the end of *Grandstand*. After which he was to hurry home to catch *Baywatch* on the other side. In the car over and over again he practised his patter:

'... I've just arrived hotfoot from Highbury where Liam Brady has just won the game for the Gunners almost single-handedly ...'

At the studio he sat patiently for Frank Bough to intro him in and he continued to repeat his few lines over and over in his head. Finally Frank looked at the camera and said:

'And now over to Bob Wilson who has just returned from Highbury where it seems Liam Brady has almost single-handedly won the game for Arsenal.'

Older readers will remember Sam Leitch. He was a journalist with the BBC during the 1960s and 1970s. He was a matter-of-fact, down-to-earth man who never embraced sensationalism. Sam was also a decent man who never said a bad word about anyone. I remember after Manchester United had played Leeds United in 1967, he came into the players' lounge where Jack Charlton was sitting quietly alone with a pint of beer.

'Hello, Jack.'

'Hello, Sam.'

'How's your Bobby?'

No one could say that Jack resented his brother Bobby's success but it was 1967 and Jack had been in the World Cup winning England side too and his Leeds United team were reaching their peak yet people still insisted on asking him about his brother.

'Sam, how is it that whenever you see me you ask how our Bobby is. Bobby this, Bobby that. I'm Jack Charlton, not Bobby Charlton's brother.'

Sam was embarrassed that he had clearly hit a raw nerve.

'Jack, I am sorry. Of course, you're absolutely right. Please accept my apology for being so tactless.'

Jack shrugged his shoulders; a little embarrassed himself at his own outburst.

'How are you, Jack,' Sam continued.

'I'm fine, Sam,' replied Jack and the two men sat in silence for several seconds before Sam added, 'And how's your Bobby?'

One of the most bizzare things that happened to me in my role as a TV pundit was when I was invited to be one of a panel commenting on a game featuring Brazil. I am being deliberately vague about the TV company and the year because I do not want to identify them. You see, they are still around and these days I never like closing avenues of potential work. They sent a driver for me and we arrived at our London base a couple of hours before kick-off. I was surprised to be asked to change my jacket and shirt for a Hawaiian beach shirt. I obediently did so. When I was shown into the studio I was immediately hit by the heat and the perspiration running down the presenter's forehead.

'What's going on?' I whispered.

'We're meant to be in Brazil,' he told me. 'We're not actually saying it but that's the impression we're trying to give.'

I sweated through the next two hours and went along with the whole ridiculous charade.

These days Sky also very kindly send a driver for me when I'm doing my commentating. One afternoon the car turned up and it was a driver I had never seen before. He opened the door for me to get in the back but I barely got a hello out of him so I decided against engaging him in conversation. I was happy enough to read my paper but when he seemed to get lost in the countryside near my house I tried to attract his attention. When he didn't respond to my voice I put my hand on his shoulder. He almost crashed the bloody car and snapped, 'Don't fucking do that!'

I apologised although I wasn't sure why I should and eventually he said, 'I'm sorry about that, it's my first day on the job.'

'Don't worry about it.'

'Yeah, up until yesterday I drove a hearse for seventeen years.'

7

THE
FAIRER SEX

KICK-OFF

When the veteran American comic George Burns was asked how it felt to still be enjoying sex at seventy-four he replied, 'Fantastic. Especially, bearing in mind, as I still live at number seventy-five.'

Nothing to do with me or football but I like it.

SCORING AT HALF-TIME

It is no surprise that footballers and women are the source of many a story. Footballers reach their peak around the time they are most interested in the opposite sex and as young, athletic men in their prime with money, fast cars and fame, they often prove a strong target for women. For the single men the opportunities were enormous, for the married ones, the temptations worrying. It is a surprise really, that over the years so few scandals have reached the public domain.

I try to be discreet about my past liaisons and tend to have only spoken about any relationship or fling only when the other party has decided to do so first. In my heyday there were many, many women – many who I targeted but just as many who targeted me. I have nothing but respect for the vast majority who have never felt the need or desire to make public our private liaisons. Maybe they were instantly forgettable for some, who knows?

OLD QUEENS

Marjorie Wallace was the American lady who won the Miss World contest and who I had a brief affair with shortly after. When we were spent she had no problems in going to the press with stories about me and our stormy relationship. One newspaper called me and said that she had only awarded me 6 out of 10 in the bedroom performance stakes. That was 4 more than I gave her, I told them. Our falling out has been well documented elsewhere. Marjorie went on to have a fairly long affair with Tom Jones thereafter, although I think they had known each other before her fling with me. I heard that when we had our spat Tom offered to come over from the States and sort me out. That would have been a Northern Ireland v Wales clash with a difference.

It was another Miss World, Mary Stavin, who I was lying on a posh hotel bed with, sipping champagne and counting casino winnings, when the room-service man uttered the now legendary words, 'Where did it all go wrong, George?' It wasn't that I went out hunting beauty queens; other people seemed to delight in putting us together. Not an evening went by for many years where I was not invited to a celebrity function of some sort and it was inevitable that my path (and sometimes my legs) would cross with the great beauties and icons of the time. Mary Stavin and I made a record together, it was an LP called *Shape Up and Dance* and we are featured on the cover wearing headbands and grinning inanely. If you come across this in a second hand shop anywhere, please buy it and destroy it straight away. Thanks. Mary went on to become a Bond girl in the film *Octopussy* and has developed a career in Hollywood.

CARRY ONS

I remember being asked to open a shopping centre in Manchester back in the late 1960s and was astounded to be met by thousands of screaming fans. It was amazing: even though this was the age of Beatlemania, this was the first time a foot-baller had received such predominantly female adulation. Being a red-blooded male, the realisation at that time that I could have sex with almost whoever I wanted, whenever I wanted it, was a head-turning experience. It takes a long while for that to work through the system.

That day in Manchester was a surreal one, as I recall, and not unusual for the period. Barbara Windsor, then the busty cockney sparrow star of the Carry On films, now more famous as Peggy Mitchell in *EastEnders*, was doing the gig alongside me. As my eyes travelled along the line of hysterical, screaming girls in front of me, my eyes alighted on a slight man in late middle age with neat hair and small round John Lennon glasses. Like the girls he was throwing his arms around and screaming. Unlike the girls, he scared the life out of me. It was Barbara's Carry On co-star Charles Hawtrey – he had tagged along with her and it seems joined in the spirit of the occasion. In the days before Graham Norton, Dale Winton and a host of other in-your-face gay stars, Charles was one of the few 'celebrity gays', although then he would only be described publicly as 'a the-atrical type' or maybe 'effeminate'. When we spoke after he was quite crude and made no secret of his desire to get to know me better. I was relieved to get away and disappear with the far more desirable Barbara, whose bits were definitely all in the right places. We enjoyed a good night together, as she says in her recent autobiography *All of Me*.

TAKING THE MICHAEL

During one of my intensive periods on the drink Michael Parkinson kindly invited me to come and stay with him and his family in their home in Bray. Parky was probably worried about me and hoped that by having me live in a stable family environment away from the temptations of London I would get my head together. Michael and Mary are truly a lovely, caring couple who are the best friends anyone could wish for. Helping me was all they wanted to do, Michael never really spoke about me publicly and he knew more than most. It worked too. I felt relaxed in their comfortable, loving home in Bray and I liked having Michael's boys around me. Sometimes I walked down to the pub nearest the house but did not get rat-arsed. One night though my mind turned to female flesh and it dawned on me I had gone some days without any physical contact. I decided to get a takeaway. I phoned a girl who I had been having an on/off relationship with and asked her to get straight into a cab to Bray and I would settle the bill at this end. By the time she arrived, Michael and Mary were in bed and I sneaked her into my room without anyone being any the wiser. In the morning I had planned to rise first and get her out before my hosts realised and avoid any embarrassment. But my friend got up first and pattered into the kitchen for a drink in just her knickers and bra. As luck would have it Mary had decided to rise at the same time and the two strangers met in the kitchen. Mary worked the situation out very quickly and as

I heard the embarrassed introductions I pulled the quilt over my head.

I often used to go to Parky's magnificent house on the River Thames in Bray for quiet weekends. It was like an oasis of calm in my mad existence. Not that Parky was in any way boring, he and Mary could party with the best of us, but he was firmly anchored with his family and young children and I liked nothing better than kicking a ball around his garden with his young boys on a sunny Sunday afternoon. Often there was a host of other celebrities around and if anyone had peered over the garden wall they could have been forgiven for thinking they were watching a loose rehearsal for the Royal Variety Performance. I can remember Michael Caine, Frank Bough, Susannah York, Sarah Miles, Jimmy Tarbuck and Marion Montgomery among many others all sitting out on the lawn at various times.

GROUPIES

Like the pop groups of the period some of the high-profile football teams attracted groupies. In the world of pop these were the girls that attached themselves to a band, particularly during times of touring, and made themselves available for every sexual whim of the stars and often their entourage as well. It wasn't quite the same with footballers but what tended to happen was that a girl would target a player and then slowly but surely she would work her way through the entire squad. Or, at least, those that were interested. It wasn't quite a one-night stand each time but it didn't seem to take too many weeks for these girls to have been passed around.

There was one particular girl who was more striking than most. She had been a beauty queen in Manchester and had the most startlingly large breasts. I suppose she was the Jordan of her time although the only Jordan around at the time had no teeth and played centre forward for Leeds. She had started by going out with one of the Manchester City players and then had come over to us. One of the younger players at United had just broken into the first team and he was still finding his feet and was in awe of us older players. One morning after an away match he came down to breakfast with this girl on his arm. This young lad swaggered in with the look of the cat that got the cream. Their canoodling over the cornflakes was a clear message to us all that they had spent a night of passion together. When we boarded the coach back to Manchester she had to make her own way home. On the journey the young player was dying for us to press him about his conquest but we said nothing. Finally he piped up. 'I pulled a cracker last night,' he boasted. 'Did you see her? The bird at breakfast with me?'

'Yeah, we saw her,' I said.

'Lovely birthmark at the top of her thigh,' said one of the other lads.

'Doesn't stop telling you about when she was beauty queen.'

'Snores like a pig.'

The more anecdotal evidence we threw at him the more he realised that half the people on the coach had enjoyed nights of passion with this girl and the more his face dropped.

YOU'RE DEAD

One year when United played down at Southampton I was surprised when the hotel receptionist told me there was a message for me and handed me an envelope. When I opened it, I was shocked to see it was a death threat. Not so much a threat but a promise. I took it seriously because the letter referred to a girl who I had met in Southampton the previous season. We had enjoyed a pleasant evening together and had consummated our relationship. I was surprised when she managed to get in contact with me after I had returned to Manchester and asked when we'd be meeting up. She was all for coming straight up the motorway. I tried to let her down gently but she became angry and then hysterical. Afterwards I did not return her calls or answer her letters and after a couple of months she got the message. I thought. This letter appeared to be from a male member of her family. He was accusing me of using this girl and 'ruining' her life and because of this he was going to shoot me during the game tomorrow. I knew it was unlikely anyone would do this but I couldn't help worrying. Should I go to the police? Should I just ignore it? Maybe the writer was a Saints fan who had knowledge of this fling and just wanted to put me off my game? Maybe not. I decided to go and see Matt Busby. The boss read the letter and then sat back in his chair puffing on his pipe. After a few minutes of contemplation he eventually said, 'Tomorrow afternoon, George, go out there and play. Keep running and running,' he said as I regarded him with a slightly puzzled expression. 'Because, George, a moving target is much harder to hit.'

This reminds me of another death threat I received before a Manchester derby. The police took this one very seriously because it purported to be from an Irish political group. For some reason the threat and the subsequent protection and security was leaked to a newspaper. I know for a fact it wasn't from me, I would rather have kept it under wraps other than informing the police. The papers and television were full of it but as I ran out on to the pitch at Old Trafford I did my best to put it out of my mind. Before the kick-off the teams were both kicking the ball around in their own halves and I crossed the halfway line to have a brief chat with my drinking mate Mike Summerbee. As I approached him he started walking backwards. And backwards.

'Hello, Mike,' I said.

'Fuck off, Bestie, keep away from me, he might have a machine gun.'

THE DOG'S BOLLOCKS

I hope I haven't given the impression that my young life was just a series of one-night stands: there were a few regular girl-friends as well, some of whom I was head over heels in love with. One such girl was Jackie Glass. Not only was she wonderful looking but she was witty, intelligent and resourceful. One night we went to San Lorenzo, then the in-restaurant in Knightsbridge, London. Sat at the next table was a couple of very camp French men complete with moustaches, neckties knotted at the side and white poodle. For a minute I thought I might have walked on to the set of an Inspector Clouseau film. The two old queens looked us up and down and obviously didn't like what they saw. Their sneers would have done Kenneth Williams proud. They began to pick us apart in French not realising that Jackie was fluent in their language or believing that an English couple would be too arrogant or thick to know a second language. Jackie translated everything they said to me. Things like 'mutton dressed as lamb ... he could have shaved' that type of thing. I wanted to lean over and thump one of them there and then but Jackie restrained me, assuring me she would deal with them. When we finally left the restaurant Jackie accidentally on purpose gently stepped on the dog who let out a small yelp. She appeared to be apologising in French but the two men's faces expressed only horror.

'What exactly did you say to them' I asked as we got outside.

'I said I was sorry and I hope I didn't step on the dog's cock.'

Jackie, I think captured my personality better than most when she was asked by a journalist to reflect on our relationship.

In response to the question, 'What was special about your time with George?', she commented, 'We had some beautiful silences.'

TELEVISION TENNIS

I sometimes used to drop in to a small hotel in Manchester run by Philomena Lynott, the charming mother of Thin Lizzy front man and fellow Irishman, Phil Lynott. She had a small bar in the front room of her old Georgian house and it was somewhere I could go for a drink but also some peace and quiet. One night Phil himself was there along with some musicians when I dropped in with another regular girlfriend, Kate, who I was seeing at the time. Now you might think, early hours of the morning, notorious footballing drinker, drug-crazed musicians, pretty women, equals some sort of orgy of drink, drugs and sex but nothing could have been further from the truth. Not this night anyway. The forerunner of the computer game had just arrived then – television tennis – and we played against each other fervently until the sun came up with only Coca-Cola and orange juice for refreshment.

Us boys were having a whale of a time but my girlfriend got very fed up with being ignored and she finally grabbed the keys to my beloved Jaguar and said she was going to throw them in the canal. I assumed she did this and carried on playing. When I went out to the car the traffic was building up as the early morning rush hour was now approaching. When a police car approached I had a hell of a job getting them to believe the reason why I couldn't move my car off the yellow line it was parked on. It was an even harder job to get them to believe I had only been drinking orange juice all night while playing television tennis.

A few years later Phil Lynott, who was a good man, died from a drugs overdose. He had married Liz Crowther, the daughter of Leslie Crowther. I remembered Leslie as the squeaky-clean presenter of *Crackerjack* on the TV when I was a teenager. He himself died not so long later and I was surprised to learn that he too had wrestled with a serious drinking problem for some years.

GEORGIE GIRL

About the time of my boutiques, 'Dedicated Follower of Fashion' and all of that, the *Daily Express* gave me a column where I talked about young people and the various issues surrounding them. It was their attempt to woo a teenage audience I guess. After a while they thought it would be more interesting if there was a female perspective too and they plucked a suitably beautiful young model by the name of Georgie Lawton from the streets of Manchester. Predictably the column was called 'George and Georgie' and we had great fun writing it. We had great fun not writing it too and became good mates as well as occasional lovers. One day she came to me with a worried look on her face and said she needed to tell me something. That normally does not bode well. But it was nothing like that.

'I'm telling you first because the press are on to me and it'll be all over the papers soon,' she confided.

'What?' I couldn't imagine what this nice young girl could have done that may have been of interest to the tabloids.

'I'm Ruth Ellis's daughter,' she gulped.

'Ruth, who?'

I genuinely didn't know who Ruth Ellis was but Georgie soon told me the whole sad story. Georgie's mother had been the last woman to be hanged in England in 1955. She was a nightclub manageress in London who had fallen in love with a dashing young motor racing driver, David Blakely. Their relationship was volatile to say the least and when David tried to end it Ruth became insanely jealous. Her state of mind was probably badly affected by the miscarriage she had just suffered. Whatever, she obtained a handgun and waited for David to emerge from a north London pub where he was drinking with a male friend. Ruth emptied a number of bullets into him and her lover was dead. When police asked her if she meant to kill him, she looked at them incredulously. 'Of course, I meant to kill him.' That didn't help her case. Despite nationwide protests she was found guilty of murder and sentenced to hang. It was one of the last executions carried out by Albert Pierrepoint, who I had heard of.

Georgie was very upset and worried that it was all going to come out and feared her career would be damaged by it. It probably was. Although I didn't see why it should make a jot of difference. These days it would have been a positive plus on her curriculum vitae. We drifted apart as Georgie had to cope with a whole lot of unwanted media attention and I didn't see or hear of her for years. About ten years ago she walked into the Phene in Chelsea and we had a chat. I was shocked at how her appearance had changed and no doubt the feeling was mutual.

Lynsey dePaul was a talented songwriter and a smashing girlfriend. Although she was very tiny (maybe because) she was fiercely independent and knew what she wanted from life. She had a Top Ten hit with 'Sugar Me' in 1975 and wrote and sang the theme song to the John Alderton/Pauline Collins TV sitcom *No Honestly*. She lived in a curious place that seemed to be slap in the middle of Highgate Cemetery and we had a nice relationship for a while. Lynsey had also enjoyed quality time with

James Coburn, the Hollywood star, and ex-Beatle Ringo. My abiding memory of Lynsey was her unwarranted dissatisfaction with her body. Well, it was her knees actually. She would sit there and look at them and moan, 'I've got Jewish knees.' Answers on a postcard please.

Coincidentally James Coburn appeared on the cover of Paul McCartney and Wings' acclaimed 1970s album *Band on the Run*. He was among a group of random and seemingly unconnected celebrities featured. John Conteh, the boxer was one along with Christopher Lee and Clement Freud, but the other two were two of my best friends: Michael Parkinson and Kenny Lynch.

LADY JANE

With the ladies it didn't go all my way by any means. I had my share of rejections. Dusty Springfield said no. When I learnt later she preferred women that repaired my damaged ego a little but there were no excuses with Jane Asher, actress and former girlfriend of Beatle Paul McCartney. When I pursued her Jane had not hitched up with Paul but was very much part of the Chelsea set. I had tried to impress my charms on her a couple of times but she politely declined. With an arrogance that comes of having women throw themselves at you many times a day (as was the case at that time) I assumed she was playing hard to get.

When I was invited to a well-known TV producer's party at his house in Chelsea, I accepted, because I figured Jane would be there. She was and so was just about anyone who was anyone at the time. You couldn't move for political satirists. To loosen my tongue and to try and compete with the sharp wits that surrounded me I gulped back the champagne like there was no tomorrow. This led to an embarrassing and clumsy pass by me on Jane as she tried to leave the bathroom and I tried to enter it. Still, I would not be thwarted and I was determined not to leave before Jane, so I just sat on a sofa with a stupid grin on my face and demolished whatever drinks were brought to me. Finally Jane and a friend fetched their coats to leave and I drilled my eyes into her back as she kissed our host goodbye but there was no response. Not even a glance sideways. I went to the toilet again, despondent and feeling sick. I sat in there for a while as I tried to regain my composure because by now I was as pissed as a fart.

When I came back into the main room I plumped myself back down on the sofa and looked at the producer who was sitting on a sofa opposite. Then I looked around the room. It was spinning a bit but what was clear was that no other guests remained. It was just him and me and I was paralytic. He was a lovely guy, and was openly gay. When I say openly gay, I mean among his friends. The closet was still jam-packed with gay people frightened to come out lest their lives and careers became damaged. There were no public gay figures. Some people suspected Liberace of not being a red-blooded heterosexual, but that was about as far as it went. The other misconception was that all gay people were sex maniacs and would jump on you given the slightest opportunity and I am afraid as a young Irish footballer I knew no better. I truly believed he was about to engage me in a theatrical discussion. I had never sobered up so fast as I did at the end of that party when I managed to pull myself up from that sofa and thank my host for a lovely party and sprinted out into the crisp, night air.

SHE MADE ME
WANNA SHOUT

It was a similar story with Lulu. Her brother Billy had an interest in a club in Manchester and I started to meet up with her here and there. Unlike Jane Asher, Lulu seemed interested in me and I felt I was getting the right signals. Only later did I realise that Lulu is lovely to everyone and has this bubbly, infectious personality that can lead people in her company to believe they are the most important thing in the world to her. Lulu could thank the postman for a recorded delivery letter and he might go home and leave his wife on the strength of it. She came to Old Trafford a few times to watch the match and we went to places together afterwards but Lulu always made sure she was safely tucked up in bed without me before midnight.

One day after a game she said I could drop her back at her hotel in Didsbury. I was hoping that I might be on the verge of a breakthrough but having played a very energetic First Division match and having had no refreshment I was deeply dehydrated and absolutely knackered. When we got to the hotel I dropped her at the door and motored home fast to my bed. We went out a few more times, and the papers got hold of it. I started to become besotted by her and I think I was growing on her. But Lulu was really what it said on the packet – a nice girl. She knew that there was no getting any commitment or loyalty out of me at the time and despite my protestations moved on gracefully. Lulu went on to marry the late Maurice Gibb and in doing so passed over a GB for a BG.

Kenny Lynch introduced me to Pat Booth, a top model. Pat and I had a special relationship. When I came down to London I would simply turn up at her flat and we would resume where we had left off. We were totally comfortable with one another and if she wasn't there I was fine and if I didn't turn up she was fine. When we were together we sparked so well that I have to confess I was cut up when I turned up at the flat one Saturday night and her girlfriend opened the door and said, 'Pat's gone, George. For good.'

Pat went off abroad and I never saw her again until she had found fame and fortune as a romantic novelist. Her books like *Palm Beach* are up there with Jackie Collins in that genre and she now lives in America but has a home in England. She is also a great friend of Cilla Black and occasionally I bump into each of them.

Carolyn Moore was a serious girlfriend. She was from Nantwich, Cheshire, and had won the Miss Great Britain crown. I think she was extraordinarily beautiful and when I saw her dressed in a man's suit I was smitten. There is something about women in men's pinstriped suits that does it for me. We dated for a long while before we went our separate ways. Stephanie was another model who I went out with for a while. Steph always told me she would end up with someone rich and famous and once she got shot of me, she did. She married top motorcyclist Barry Sheene and eventually emigrated to Australia where they raised their family. Tragically Barry died in 2003 from cancer. Stephanie's sister married Lulu's brother. It was all very incestuous.

RUNAROUND SUE

I met Susan George while she was filming *Spring and Port Wine* with James Mason in the north of England. This was a strong British movie about a dictatorial father and his wayward daughter who falls pregnant. Although Susan was a very young girl (maybe because) we hit it off straight away. Susan invited me to meet her parents at their hotel in Maidenhead, which is sometimes a good sign. Depends what you are looking for from a relationship. When everyone had retired for the night I sneaked into Susan's room. It seemed I had again misread the situation. Susan sat up in her bed and said firmly, 'Would you mind going away,' or words to that effect. Still, I was not one to give up easily and when she rang me to ask if I would pick her up from the airport in Majorca as she had arrived on 'my' island for a holiday I thought I should be in with a chance. Her plane landed in the early hours of the morning and she was waiting by the taxi rank with a friend. She gave me a piece of paper with the address of the villa where she was staying.

'No, don't worry, Sue,' I said casually. 'You can stay at our villa tonight and then I'll drive you to your place in the morning when it's light.'

'No thanks, George, we'd like to get settled in tonight.' She wasn't falling for that one either.

It took two hours to find the bloody place. First of all we had to find someone who spoke English, and then someone who knew where this place was. At three in the morning this was no easy task. When we did finally locate their villa down some unlit dirt track, Susan asked if I wanted to come inside. I could barely keep awake. I told her where we met during the day and that I would see her there tomorrow.

When Susan turned up the following afternoon there were a few press around and they snapped away and then sent the pictures back to Fleet Street. The story was that Susan had flown out to join me in the sun. We were having a romance, they said. If only. The romance story persisted off and on for a few years and Susan and I would both laugh about it. We never did get it together and it was because of this, I think, that we have become really close friends.

Back in Manchester there was a pretty girl who ran one of the shops in the village where our boutique was, in Bridge Street. I used to wander over to her shop to chat her up and we soon got on like a house on fire. At the same time a man who was running one of the other shops was pursuing her and to top all this she had an attendant husband-in-waiting. Let's call the shop manageress Sue and the shop man chasing her James. Sue and I reached an agreement that we would enjoy the occasional liaison but we swore each other to secrecy. This worked fine until the boyfriend got into the habit of coming into our shop and began confiding in me.

'Something's not right,' he moaned. 'I think Sue is seeing that James character, you know. He's always sniffing around.' I did my best not to be drawn.

'What would you do, George?'

I couldn't believe my ears as I heard myself respond, 'You'll have to confront him.'

James did and the shop man protested his innocence vehemently, as did Sue. The shop man withdrew, our liaisons continued although they became less frequent, and Sue and James got married. In the years that followed I would bump into James around Manchester. 'How's Sue?'

'She's fine. Often talks about you actually. You've been a good friend. Thanks, George.'

'Don't mention it.'

I'm afraid to say, in those days, when it came to women who were willing, I had no morals and very little conscience. I'm not sure many young men do. I lived life on the edge, which made it all the more exciting, but I was at constant risk from rightfully jealous enraged husbands, fathers and boyfriends.

FOOTSTEPS IN THE SNOW

Kenny Lynch tells a story, which I am sure is true, but I don't really remember it. In fact that goes for most of Kenny's stories. With 30 years of drinking between then and now, neither of us has any right to remember anything. But the true reason I don't really remember this specific incident is because it happened so many times. Maybe it happened only the once with Kenny.

This one is best coming from Kenny Lynch himself: 'George and I had been to the Time and the Place nightclub and we had pulled two nice young birds and persuaded them to come back to our flat. I remember the night well because it was just before Christmas, freezing cold, and the snow was inches thick on the ground. Driving back to the flat in George's Jaguar was even more hair-raising than normal. Once in the flat I poured a couple of drinks but George was impatient and had already pulled his girl by the arm over in the general direction of his bedroom. Left alone, my girl and me got straight down to some serious nookie. We were interrupted only about fifteen minutes later when George's girl switched the light on and said, "I'm sorry to disturb you but have you seen George?"

'"What do you mean, have you seen George?" I said, rolling off my new girlfriend.

'"Well, he said he was going to the toilet, but that was ages ago."

'"Maybe he's ill or something." I got up and checked the toilet but there was no sign of him having been there. I looked back in his bedroom and still no George. I then went to the spare bedroom where we used to dump our rubbish and felt a cold chill and noticed the window open. I walked over and looked out into the night. The snow was like a smooth white blanket except for a trail of footprints leading from the house over to George's Jag. The bastard. He was probably pulling up outside the Time and the Place that very second.

'He was always getting me into situations like this. When he was on the run from Manchester United one time he was holed up in a flat we used and the press got wind of it. He didn't want to be seen leaving with any girls in the mornings so he'd call me and I'd come round the back and leave out the front door with the girl on my arm. The press fell for it a couple of times but soon they were winking at me andsaying, "You're a right Rudolph Valentino, you are Ken." Another time my phone rang at 4.30 in the morning. I knew it would be George. No one else calls you at those sort of hours and thinks nothing of it.

'"Lynchie," he says, "you've got to help me out. I've hit a lamp post. The car's a write-off. Can you get here? The police will be here soon and the papers. When Matt reads about this I've had it."

'When I got there, George and his girl were standing there looking forlornly at the wreckage of his car. They looked okay.

'"Can you get in it, Kenny. Say you were driving, please. You haven't had a drink have you?"

'I hadn't. So I got into the car and sat and waited for the police as George and his girlfriend scuttled off into the night. As

I sat there in George's car, adopting George's accident at five in the morning and preparing the pack of lies I was going to have to tell the police, I thought, What the fuck am I doing? Half an hour later there was still no sign of the police so I too buggered off into the night and back to bed.

'But this was George. He was unreliable, always in trouble, lurching from one crisis to the next, but you couldn't stop loving him. He has this vulnerability about him. I remember when he got nicked and locked up the newspapers rang me and asked me if I had any comment. I didn't but got straight on to the phone to Parky.

'"George is in trouble," I said.

'"I know," said Parky. "I've had the papers on."

'We discussed a few things we could do to help but ended our conversation getting all reflective.

'"Where does all this end, Mike? The man's nearly fifty and we're still trying to sort him out."

'I remember when he told me about these fantastic parties with wall-to-wall crumpet Selwyn Demmy was having on a Sunday afternoon up in Manchester. By this time I was working and living in London.

'"Don't worry about that. Just get a plane to Manchester and I'll be waiting to pick you up at the airport at two o'clock and drive us straight to Selwyn's."

'I'll have some of that I thought and duly arrived at Manchester Airport for two. No George. Two thirty, no George. Three p.m., no George. Eventually I got in a cab and made my own way to Selwyn's. When I walked in George was on a settee with a glass of champagne in one hand and a pretty blonde's buttock in the other.

'"Where were you, George?"

'"Ah shit. The airport. Sorry, Lynchie, I clean forgot."

'You couldn't stay angry with George long. Although the next week, following all sorts of reassurances and promises, he did it again and I felt like wringing his neck. After the third week of this charade I didn't bother waiting outside the airport, I just walked straight out and into a cab. How he manages now, in the age of mobile phones when people can call him and find out where he is, I'll never know. Bet he doesn't have one.'

And finally, there is the story about the beautiful girl who I had wonderful sex with in the changing rooms at Old Trafford during the interval of a First Division match. This is a famous story, that I have now heard many, many times. Almost as much as 'Where did it all go wrong, George?' The title of this very book comes from that apocryphal tale. It never happened. Where were Nobby, Alex, Paddy, Bobby, Denis, Shay and the others when this happened? Looking at the floor discreetly while washing the mud from their shins? Was I standing behind Sir Matt holding my breath as he delivered his half-time pep talk? It is an urban myth, I'm afraid, not started by myself, I hasten to add.

However, there was the time on a coach on the way home from Ipswich when ...

CAREER STATISTICS

Team	Season	League A	G	FA Cup A	G	Lge Cup A	G	Europe A	G
Manchester United										
(5/63 – 1/74)	63/64	17	4	7	2	-	-	2	0
	64/65	41	10	7	2	-	-	11	2
	65/66	31	9	5	3	-	-	6	4
	66/67	42	10	2	0	1	0	-	-
	67/68	41	28	2	1	-	-	9	3
	68/69	41	19	6	1	-	-	8	2
	69/70	37	15	7	6	8	2	-	-
	70/71	40	18	2	1	6	2	-	-
	71/72	40	18	7	7	6	3	-	-
	72/73	19	4	-	-	4	2	-	-
	73/74	12	2	-	-	-	-	-	-
Jewish Guild										
(5/74 – 6/74)	1974	5	n/k	-	-	-	-	-	-
Stockport County										
(11/75 – 12/75)	75/76	3	2	-	-	-	-	-	-

Cork Celtic

(12/75 – 1/76)   75/76 3 0 - - - - - -

Fulham

(9/76 – 5/77)   76/77 32 6 2 0 3 2 - -

(9/77 – 11/77)   77/78 10 2 - - - - - -

Hibernian

(11/79 – 4/80)   79/80 13 3 3 0 - - - -

(9/80 – 10/80)   80/81 4 0 - - 2 0 - -

AFC Bournemouth

(3/83 – 5/83)   82/83 5 0 - - - - - -

Brisbane Lions

(7/83)   1983 4 0 - - - - - -

Tobermore United

(1/84)   1984 - - 1 - - - - -

CAREER RECORD IN NASL

Team	Season	Regular Season				Play Offs			
		A	G	As	P	A	G	As	P
Los Angeles Aztecs									
(4/76 – 8/76)	1976	23	15	7	37	1	0	0	0
(5/77 – 8/77)	1977	20	11	18	40	5	2	4	8
(4/78 – 6/78)	1978	12	1	0	2	-	-	-	-
Fort Lauderdale Strikers									
(6/78 – 8/78)	1978	9	4	1	9	5	1	2	4
(3/79 – 7/79)	1979	19	2	7	11	-	-	-	-
San Jose Earthquakes									
(4/80 – 8/80)	1980	26	8	11	27	-	-	-	-
(3/81 – 8/81)	1981	30	13	10	36	-	-	-	-

Key

A = Appearances

G = Goals (2 points)

As = Assists (1 point)

P = Points (Total points for goals and assists combined)

CAREER RECORD EXCLUDING NASL

Team	League		FA Cup		Lge Cup		Europe	
	A	G	A	G	A	G	A	G
Manchester United	361	137	45	23	25	9	36	11
Jewish Guild	5	n/k	-	-	-	-	-	-
Stockport County	3	2	-	-	-	-	-	-
Cork Celtic	3	0	-	-	-	-	-	-
Fulham	42	8	2	0	3	2	-	-
Hibernian	17	3	3	0	2	0	-	-
AFC Bournemouth	5	0	-	-	-	-	-	-
Brisbane Lions	4	0	-	-	-	-	-	-
Tobermore United	-	-	1	-	-	-	-	-
TOTALS	440	150	51	23	30	11	36	11

CAREER RECORD IN NASL

Team	Regular Season				Play Offs			
	A	G	As	P	A	G	As	P
Los Angeles Aztecs	55	27	25	79	6	2	4	8
Fort Lauderdale Strikers	28	6	8	20	5	1	2	4
San Jose Earthquakes	56	21	21	63	-	-	-	-
TOTALS	139	54	54	162	11	3	6	12

INTERNATIONAL APPEARANCES

Date	Opponents	Venue	Result	Goals
1964				
15th April	Wales	Swansea	3–2	
29th April	Uruguay	Belfast	3–0	
3rd October	England	Belfast	3–4	
14th October	Switzerland WC	Belfast	1–0	
14th November	Switzerland WC	Lausanne	1–2	1
25th November	Scotland	Glasgow	2–3	1
1965				
17th March	Netherlands WC	Belfast	2–1	
7th April	Netherlands WC	Rotterdam	0–0	
7th May	Albania WC	Belfast	4–1	1
2nd October	Scotland	Belfast	3–2	
10th November	England	London	1–2	
24th November	Albania WC	Tirana	1–1	
1966				
22nd October	England EC	Belfast	0–2	
1967				
21st October	Scotland	Belfast	1–0	
1968				
23rd October	Turkey WC	Belfast	4–1	1

1969

3rd May	England	Belfast	1–3	
6th May	Scotland	Glasgow	1–1	
10th May	Wales	Belfast	0–0	
10th September	USSR WC	Belfast	0–0	

1970

18th April	Scotland	Belfast	0–1	
21st April	England	London	1–3	1
25th April	Wales	Swansea	0–1	
11th November	Spain EC	Seville	0–3	

1971

3rd February	Cyprus EC	Nicosia	3–0	1
21st April	Cyprus EC	Belfast	5–0	3
15th May	England	Belfast	0–1	
18th May	Scotland	Glasgow	1–0	
22nd May	Wales	Belfast	1–0	
22nd September	USSR EC	Moscow	0–1	

1972

16th February	Spain EC	Hull	1–1
18th October	Bulgaria WC	Sofia	0–3

1973

14th November	Portugal WC	Lisbon	1–1

1976

| 13th October | Netherlands WC | Rotterdam | 2–2 |
| 10th November | Belgium WC | Liege | 0–2 |

1977

27th April	West Germany	Cologne	0–5
21st September	Iceland WC	Belfast	2–0
12th October	Netherlands WC	Belfast	0–1

NORTHERN IRELAND PLAYING RECORD

Appearances	Won	Drawn	Lost	Goals Scored
37	13	8	16	9

EUROPEAN APPEARANCES

Season	Opponents	Round	Venue	Result	Goals
63/64					
Feb 26	Sporting Club Lisbon	ECWC QF	Hone	4–1	
Mar 18	Sporting Club Lisbon	ECWC QF	Away	0–5	

64/65

Sept 23	Djurgaarden	ICFC 1st rd	Away	1–1	
Oct 27	Djurgaarden	ICFC 2nd rd	Home	1–1	1
Nov 11	Borussia Dortmund	ICFC 2nd rd	Away	6–1	1
Dec 2	Borussia Dortmund	ICFC 2nd rd	Home	4–0	
Jan 20	Everton	ICFC 3rd rd	Home	1–1	
Feb 9	Everton	ICFC 3rd rd	Away	2–1	
May 12	Racing Strasbourg	ICRC QF	Away	5–0	
May 19	Racing Strasbourg	ICRC QF	Home	0–0	
May 31	Ferencvaros	ICFC SF	Home	3–2	
June 6	Ferencvaros	ICFC SF	Away	0–1	
June 16	Ferencvaros	ICFC SF P-off	Away	1–2	

65/66

Oct 6	HJK Helsinki	EC Prel rd	Home	6–0	2
Nov 17	ASK Vorwaerts	EC 1st rd	Away	2–0	
Dec 1	ASK Vorwaerts	EC 1st rd	Home	3–1	
Feb 2	Benfica	EC QF	Home	3–2	
Mar 9	Benfica	EC QF	Away	5–1	2
Apr 13	Partizan Belgrade	EC SF	Away	0–2	

67/68

Sept 20	Hibernians (Malta)	EC 1st rd	Home	4–0	
Sept 27	Hibernians (Malta)	EC 1st rd	Away	0–0	
Nov 15	FK Sarajevo	EC 2nd rd	Away	0–0	
Nov 29	FK Sarajevo	EC 2nd rd	Home	2–1	1
Feb 28	Gornik Zabrze	EC QF	Home	2–0	
Mar 13	Gornik Zabrze	EC QF	Away	0–1	

Apr 24	Real Madrid	EC SF	Home	1–0	1
May 15	Real Madrid	EC SF	Away	3–3	
May 29	Benfica	EC FINAL	Neutral	4–1 a.e.t	1

68/69

Sept 18	Waterford	EC 1st rd	Away	3–1	
Sept 25	Estudiantes	WCC	Away	0–1	
Oct 2	Waterford	EC 1st rd	Home	7–1	
Oct 16	Estudiantes	WCC	Home	1–1	
Feb 26	Rapid Vienna	EC QF	Home	3–0	2
Mar 5	Rapid Vienna	EC QF	Away	0–0	
Apr 23	AC Milan	EC SF	Away	0–2	
May 15	AC Milan	EC SF	Home	1–0	

Key

ECWC = European Cup Winners Cup

ICFC = Inter City Fairs Cup

EC = European Cup

WCC = World Cup Championship

EUROPEAN PLAYING RECORD

Appearances	Won	Drawn	Lost	Goals Scored
36	21	8	7	11

CHRONOLOGY

1946
22nd May. George Best born in Belfast.

1961
16th August. Joins Manchester United as an amateur.

1963
22nd May. Sign professional forms with Manchester United.
14th September. Makes league debut in home fixture against West Bromwich Albion, aged 17. United win 1–0.
28th December. Scores first league goal versus Burnley at Old Trafford.

1964
15th April. Makes Northern Ireland debut in 3–2 win against Wales in Swansea.
14th November. Scores first goal for Northern Ireland in a 1–2 away defeat against Switzerland.

1966
9th March. Scores twice in a 5–1 away win against Benfica in the 2nd leg of the European Cup quarter-final tie. Many observers believe Best's performance in the match to be his finest ever.

1967
4th May. Scores a hat trick in a 6–0 home win against Newcastle United.
21st October. Plays in what many observers believe to be his finest game for his country as Northern Ireland defeat Scotland 1–0 in Belfast.

1968

4th May. Voted British Footballer Of The Year.

29th May. Scores in Manchester United's 4–1 victory against Benfica in the final of the European Cup at Wembley Stadium.

16th October. Sent off for the first time in his playing career against Estudiantes at Old Trafford.

December. Named European Footballer Of The Year.

1969

19th April. Presented with the European Footballer Of The Year trophy by Paris magazine *France Football*.

28th July. Plays for the Rest of the UK against Wales in Cardiff.

3rd December. Knocks the ball from the referee's hands at the end of the League Cup semi-final 1st leg match against Manchester City at Maine Road.

1970

2nd January. Suspended for four weeks and fined £100 after knocking the ball out of the referee's hands after the League Cup tie against Manchester City.

7th February. Scores six goals in Manchester United's 8–2 win against Northampton Town (away) in the 5th round of the FA Cup. It is Best's first game after suspension.

18th April. Sent off playing for Northern Ireland against Scotland after spitting and throwing mud at the referee.

1971

4th January. Appears before an FA disciplinary commission after acquiring three cautions for misconduct in a period of 12 months. Best arrives three hours late. He is fined £250 and given a six week suspended sentence.

8th January. Misses the train taking the Manchester United team to play Chelsea in London. Best takes a later train though but spends the weekend with actress Sinead Cusack. The episode makes the front and back pages of the National newspapers for three days.

11th January. Manchester United suspend Best for two weeks following the incident in London.

27th January. Plays and scores for a Rangers/Celtic select side in a benefit game for the 66 victims of the Ibrox disaster.

21st April. Scores his only hat trick for Northern Ireland in a 5–0 win against Cyprus in Belfast.

18th September. Scores a hat trick in a 4–2 home win against West Ham United.

13th October. Refused permission by Manchester United to play for Northern Ireland against USSR in Belfast after Best receives death threats.

23rd October. Best receives further death threats that he will be shot whilst playing for Manchester United in an away game at Newcastle United. Best plays and scores the only goal of the game. Security is tight and Best receives police protection after the match.

17th November. Best is subject of 'This Is Your Life'.

27th November. Scores his second hat trick of the 1971/72 season in a 5–2 away victory against Southampton.

1972

4th January. Misses training all week.

8th January. Dropped for the home game against Wolverhampton Wanderers after missing training. Best flies to London and spends a much publicised weekend with current Miss Great Britain, Carolyn Moore.

10th January. Best returns to Old Trafford and is fined two weeks wages (about £400). He is instructed to do extra training and ordered to move from his home to his previous digs with Mrs Mary Fullaway.

16th February. Tells Daily Express journalist John Roberts that he is fed up playing in a poor Manchester United side and as a consequence he would like to play elsewhere.

1st May. Plays for a Rest of Europe side against Hamburg SV in a testimonial match for Uwe Seeler in Hamburg.

20th May. Best is in Marbella when he announces that he has decided to retire from football. He declares that he has been drinking a bottle of spirits a day.

1st June. Rumours circulate that Best will return to football as he flies out to Majorca.

7th July. Flies back to Britain and announces he will again play for Manchester United. The Club suspend him for two weeks for a breach of contract and the Marbella affair and order Best into lodgings with Pat Crerand. This arrangement is short-lived when Best's house is put up for sale and he moves back into digs with Mrs Mary Fullaway.

10th July. Reports for pre-season training.

12th August. Plays in Manchester United's first game of the season against Ipswich Town at Old Trafford.

18th October. Sent off playing for Northern Ireland in an away match against Bulgaria for kicking an opponent.

30th October. Following Manchester United's 1–4 home defeat against Tottenham Hotspur, Best announces he will seek a transfer if his team is relegated.

18th November. Plays in the Manchester derby at Maine Road. United are beaten 0–3.

22nd November. Fined by Manchester United for missing training.

25th November. Makes his last appearance of the 1972/73 season in the home game against Southampton.

29th November. Best sees United manager Frank O'Farrell after missing training earlier in the week. He is subsequently dropped from the team as rumours prevail that Best will be transfer listed.

4th December. Leaves Manchester without permission from the Club and is later seen in a London nightclub.

5th December. Suspended for two weeks by Manchester United and transfer listed at a fee of £300,000. Derby County declare interest.

6th December. Bournemouth show an interest in Best but he announces that he would like to join Chelsea.

7th December. New York Cosmos show interest in Best.

11th December. Manchester City manager Malcolm Allison shows interest in signing Best.

14th December. Best is presumed to have been taken off the transfer list when Manchester United chairman Louis Edwards announces that the Irishman will commence training.

16th December. Manchester United are beaten 0–5 at Crystal Palace and speculation mounts that manager Frank O'Farrell will resign.

19th December. O'Farrell is sacked by Manchester United. Best sends a letter to the Club directors to say that he is finished with football. This is the second time that he announces his retirement.

1973

4th January. New York Cosmos again express an interest in signing Best.

11th January. Found guilty of assaulting waitress Stefanja Sloniecka and causing actual bodily harm during an incident the previous November in Ruebens nightclub.

16th January. Flies to Toronto to discuss the possibility of playing in the World Indoor Soccer League but it comes to nothing. New York Cosmos approach Manchester United for permission to negotiate terms to sign Best but the proposed deal fails to materialise.

26th March. Best declares an interest in playing for Northern ireland but his Club say that they would block his intention.

11th April. Crystal Palace make a bid for Best.

13th April. Queens Park Rangers hold transfer discussions with Manchester United about a possible transfer of Best to Loftus Road.

27th April. Best resumes training four months after announcing his retirement.

7th May. Admitted to hospital in Manchester after suffering from thrombosis in Marbella whilst on holiday.

19th June. Best declares that he will not play football again and says it is his intention to write a book with Michael Parkinson.

27th August. Manchester United Chairman Louis Edwards states that the Club would like Best to start training again.

28th August. Best announces that after talks with Manchester United manager Tommy Docherty that he would like to give football another try.

10th September. Reports to Manchester United for training.

25th September. Plays for 45 minutes in Eusebio's testimonial match in Lisbon as Benfica play the Rest of the World.

3rd October. Plays in Denis Law's testimonial game for Manchester United against Ajax.

6th October. Plays for Manchester United Reserves against Aston Villa Reserves at Old Trafford. 7,126 spectators attend to watch Best's latest comeback game.

15th October. Plays in a friendly match away against Shamrock Rovers.

20th October. Plays in his first team comeback game against Birmingham City at Old Trafford.

24th October. Plays in Tony Dunne's testimonial match for Manchester United against Manchester City.

November. Opens club 'Slack Alice' in Manchester.

1974

1st January. Best plays in his last ever game for Manchester United in the fixture away at Queens Park Rangers. United lose 0–3.

4th January. Best fails to turn up for training.

5th January. Omitted from the Manchester United team to play Plymouth Argyle in the FA Cup 3rd Round tie at Old Trafford. Best walks out of the ground vowing never to play for the Club again.

12th January. Suspended for two weeks and transfer listed by Manchester United.

16th January. Tonbridge are keen to sign Best and offer Manchester United £100,000. United manager Tommy Docherty dismisses the move as a publicity stunt. Crewe Alexandra also make enquiries about Best.

21st February. Best is arrested in Manchester and later charged in London with stealing a fur coat, passport, cheque book and other items from the flat of Miss World, Marjorie Wallace. He is later released on bail of £6,000.

24th April. Cleared of all charges relating to the Marjorie Wallace incident.

May/June. Best plays in five games for Jewish Guild in South Africa including:

5th June. Hellenic Versus Jewish Guild.

5th August. Plays for Dunstable Town in a friendly fixture against Manchester United Reserves.

12th August. Plays for Dunstable Town in a friendly fixture against Cork Celtic.

29th October. Plays in Jeff Astle's testimonial match.

27th November. Plays in Tony Book's testimonial match.

1975

29th October. Plays for Dunstable Town in a friendly match against Luton Town.

7th November. Banned by FIFA from playing anywhere in the world.

8th November. Released from his Manchester United contract and FIFA lift Best's worldwide ban.

10th November. Signs for one month to play home games only for Stockport County. Best plays and scores in a friendly game for the Edgeley Park Club against Stoke City. The match attracts 8,000 spectators.

24th November. Scores twice in Peter Osgood's testimonial. Chelsea are reported to be interested in acquiring Best although refuse to meet his wage demands. Queens Park Rangers and Southampton also declare an interest in the player.

26th November. Plays in Pat Crerand's testimonial game.

28th November. Best makes his league debut for Stockport County against Swansea City and scores in front of 9,220 spectators.

4th December. Chelsea are again rumoured to be interested in signing Best on a match fee basis linked to attendances.

12th December. Plays and scores for Stockport County against Watford. The game attracts a crowd of 5,055 spectators.

26th December. Plays the last of the league games for Stockport County against Southport. 6,321 fans watch the game.

Late December. Best signs for Los Angeles Aztecs for the 1976 NASL season.

28th December. Plays in the first of three League of Ireland games for Cork Celtic in the home fixture against Drogheda.

1976

11th January. Plays for Cork Celtic in the home fixture against Bohemians.

18th January. Plays for Cork Celtic in the away fixture at Shelbourne.

19th January. Best is sacked by Cork Celtic due to his 'lack of enthusiasm'.

20th February. Arrives to play for Los Angeles Aztecs.

17th April. Makes his debut for Los Angeles Aztecs in a 1–2 away defeat against San Jose Earthquakes.

18th July. Scores a hat trick in a 8–0 home win against Boston Minutemen.

12th August. Best signs a contract to play for Fulham.

18th August. Plays his last game of the 1976 NASL season in a 0–2 play off defeat away to Dallas Tornado.

2nd September. Best is registered to play for Fulham.

4th September. Makes his league debut for Fulham in the home fixture against Bristol Rovers. Best scores after 71 seconds in front of a 21,127 crowd.

2nd October. Sent off in the away match at Southampton for using 'foul and abusive language'.

13th October. Makes 'comeback' appearance for Northern Ireland in an away fixture against Holland almost three years after his last international game.

1977

14th May. Plays his final league game of the 1976/77 season as Fulham lose 0–1 at Blackburn Rovers.

20th May. Returns to Los Angeles to play his first game of the 1977 NASL season for the Aztecs. His team lose 0–1 at Portland Timbers.

25th August. Plays his last game of the 1977 NASL season in a 0–1 play-off defeat at Seattle Sounders.

30th August. Best returns to England but is unable to appear for Fulham due to the London Club owing Los Angeles Aztecs compensation.

3rd September. Plays for Fulham in the home game against Blackburn Rovers.

8th September. Returns to Los Angeles until a problem of who owns Best's registration is resolved.

18th September. Returns to London.

24th September. Plays again for Fulham in the 1–3 defeat at Cardiff City.

12th October. Wins his 37th and final cap for Northern Ireland in the home game against Holland.

12th November. Plays his final game for Fulham in the 0–2 away defeat at Stoke City.

29th November. Best is suspended by Fulham for not attending training sessions. Best had already returned to Los Angeles.

1978

24th January. Marries Angela MacDonald Janes, aged 25, in Las Vegas.

2nd April. Best plays in his first game of the 1978 NASL season for Los Angeles Aztecs in a 2–3 home defeat against Houston Hurricane.

May. Suspended by Los Angeles Aztecs for missing training.

20th June. Plays his last game for Los Angeles Aztecs in a 0–4 defeat at Washington Diplomats.

June. Transferred to Fort Lauderdale Strikers.

24th June. Best scores two goals on his debut for Fort Lauderdale Strikers as his new side beat New York Cosmos 5–3 at home.

23rd August. Plays his last game of the 1978 NASL season for Fort Lauderdale Strikers in a 1–3 play-off defeat away to Tampa Bay Rowdies.

September. Best guests for Detroit Express on a European tour playing two games for them in Austria. Disagreement over his registration surface when Fulham announce that Best is only able to play for them outside America.

11th October. At the request of the FA, Best is banned by FIFA from playing anywhere in the world until the registration dispute with Fulham is resolved.

12th October. Best's mother, Ann, dies.

1979

28th March. FIFA lift Best's ban and he is cleared to play for Fort Lauderdale Strikers.

31st March. Best plays his first game of the 1979 NASL season for Fort

Lauderdale Strikers in a 2–0 home win against New England Teamen.

25th July. Plays his last game of the 1979 NASL season for Fort Lauderdale Strikers in a 6–3 away win at California Surf.

July. Suspended by Fort Lauderdale Strikers for missing both training and matches.

October. Manchester United refuse Best a testimonial match.

13th November. Best guests for Ipswich Town in a testimonial match for manager Bobby Robson.

16th November. Best signs for Hibernian from Fulham.

24th November. Makes his Hibernian debut in the away match at St Mirren. Best scores though his new team lose 1–2. 13,670 spectators attend the game.

15th December. Best fails to appear for the away game against Morton.

1980

9th February. Best fails to appear for the home game against Morton.

11th February. Suspended by Hibernian.

17th February. Best deemed unfit to play in the home game against Ayr United in the 4th Round of the Scottish Cup. He is dismissed by Hibernian.

24th February. Best re-engaged by Hibernian.

13th April. Best signs to play for San Jose Earthquakes for the 1980 NASL season.

19th April. Plays his final game of the 1979/80 season for Hibernian at home to Dundee United before flying out to join San Jose Earthquakes.

27th April. Plays his first game for San Jose Earthquakes in the away game at Edmonton Drillers. His new side lose 2–4.

1st June. Best fails to appear for the game against California Surf.

23rd August. Scores in his last game of the 1980 NASL season for San Jose Earthquakes in a 1–2 home defeat against Los Angeles Aztecs.

September. Signs a new two year contract with San Jose Earthquakes.

9th September. Best plays his first game of the 1980/81 season for Hibernian in the away fixture against Dundee.

11th October. Plays in his final game for Hibernian in the home match against Falkirk.

1981

6th February. Son, Calum Milan Best, is born in San Jose.

29th March. Best plays his first game of the 1981 NASL season for San Jose Earthquakes in a 0–3 home defeat to New York Cosmos.

22nd July. Best scores one of his finest ever goals playing for San Jose Earthquakes against Fort Lauderdale Strikers in a 3–2 home win.

19th August. Plays his last ever game in the NASL for San Jose Earthquakes in a 1–3 away defeat to Vancouver Whitecaps.

8th September. Best guests for Middlesborough in a testimonial match for Jim Platt.

26th September. Manchester United consider re-signing Best.

October. Middlesborough show interest in signing Best during San Jose Earthquakes British tour.

11th December. Middlesborough prematurely announce that a deal has been done to sign Best.

14th December. Best announces that he will not be joining Middlesborough.

1982

November. Best is declared bankrupt.

1983

24th March. Signs for AFC Bournemouth after receiving clearance from San Jose Earthquakes.

26th March. Best makes his debut for AFC Bournemouth in the home game against Newport County watched by a crowd of 9,121 spectators.

16th April. Best makes his final away league appearance in England when AFC Bournemouth visit Southend United. 4,275 spectators watch the game.

7th May. Best makes his final league appearance in England for AFC Bournemouth in the home game against Wigan Athletic 15 days short of his 37th Birthday. 4,523 spectators are present.

3rd July. Best plays in the first of four league games for struggling Brisbane Lions in Australia. His new team win 2–1 in the home game against Sydney Olympic.

8th July. Plays in the 0–3 home defeat against St. George.

10th July. Plays in the 1–1 draw away to Marconi.

17th July. Best plays in his final game for Brisbane Lions in the home fixture against Adelaide City. His side is beaten 0–4 in front of 1,600 spectators.

24th July. Best plays for Australian side Osbome Park Galeb and helps them to a 2–1 home victory against Melville Alemannia. A crowd of approximately 2,000 watch the game.

10th October. Best guests for Linfield against Everton in a testimonial game for Peter Dornan.

1984

28th January. Plays for Tobermore United in an Irish Cup match at home to Ballymena United.

5th August. Plays for Hibernian in a testimonial match for Jackie McNamara against Newcastle United.

3rd November. Best is charged and then bailed for a drink driving offence. He later fails to turn up at court, is subsequently arrested and assaults a policeman.

3rd December. Receives a three month prison sentence for drink driving and the assault on a policeman. He is bailed pending an appeal.

17th December. Best's appeal is dismissed and he is sent to Pentonville prison though eight days later he is transferred to Ford open prison in Sussex.

1985

8th February. Released from prison after serving eight weeks of a twelve week sentence.

17th May. Guests for Aston Villa in a match against West Bromwich Albion in a benefit game to help victims of the Bradford City fire disaster.

1986

17th February. Plays in the George Dunlop testimonial match.

7th May. Plays in the Gerry Peyton testimonial game.

3rd December. Best plays in a testimonial game for Pat Jennings at Windsor Park, Belfast.

1987

December. The Irish FA refuse to grant Best a testimonial game.

1988

11th January. Ulster Television screen a tribute programme entitled 'Best Intentions'.

June. Plays in a charity match in Tokyo to raise money for Aids research.

8th August. Best has his own testimonial match played at Windsor Park, Belfast. Approximately 25,000 spectators watch the game.

1989

June/July. Promotional work in Australia.

June. Working relationship ends with former agent Bill McMurdo.

1990

19th September. Appears on the Wogan show.

1992

5th May. Receives bankruptcy discharge.

1995

24th July. Marries for a second time; to Alexandra Jane Macadam Pursey, aged 23, at Chelsea Town Hall, London.

1996

22nd May. BBC2 devote an entire evening's viewing to celebrate Best's 50th birthday.

1999

May. Best's former home in Bramhall, Cheshire is put up for sale by the owners at an asking price of £450,000. He originally had the house built in 1970 at a cost of £30,000.

26th May. Best leaves the European Champions' League final four minutes early and misses Manchester United's two late dramatic goals which seal a 2–1 victory for his old team against Bayern Munich.

2000

23rd January. Best honoured by the Football Writers' Association with a unique services to football award.

9th March. Rushed to Cromwell Hospital in west London with suspected liver failure.

13th April. Leaves hospital after almost five weeks.

2001

11th April. Returns to Cromwell hospital to have anti-alcohol pellets inserted into his stomach.

20th May. Named the top Manchester footballer of the past fifty years by a Manchester Evening News Sunday Pink Panel.

28th May. Best appears at a celebrity six-a-side tournament at Chelsea's Stamford Bridge. He does not play but presents the trophies.

17th September. Best's autobiography 'Blessed' is published by Ebury Press.

22nd November. Falls ill in Cyprus from a viral infection and is admitted to a Limassol clinic.

25th November. Commences contributing a weekly column to the *Mail on Sunday's* 'Night and Day' magazine.

29th November. Leaves the clinic in Cyprus after recovering from illness.

13th December. Best presented with an honourary degree from Queen's University in Belfast.

2002

11th March. George is one of the baton carriers for the Queen's Jubilee relay race in London.

3rd April. Awarded the freedom of Castlereagh, the area of east Belfast where Best grew up.

30th July. George undergoes a 10-hour liver transplant operation at the

Cromwell hospital in London. He suffers massive internal haemorhaging and requires 40 pints of blood.

16th August. George is discharged from hospital only 17 days after receiving his life saving transplant.

17th August. Rushed back to Cromwell hospitall 18 hours after being discharged. George is suffering from severe stomach pain caused by his bile duct leaking toxins into his body.

8th December. Receives a lifetime achievement award at the BBC Sports Personality of the Year evening.

2003

10th January. George appears on the 'Patrick Kielty Almost Live' show in his native Belfast and receives a wonderful reception from his home audience.

8th March. The subject of 'This Is Your Life' for a second time.

7th April. Theatre tour with Jimmy Greaves commences.

INDEX

10cc 181, 182
Abbott, Bud 12
Aberdeen 85
AC Milan 38, 303
Adams, Tony 207
Adamson, Peter 190
Adelaide City 315
AIDS 316
Ajax 57, 106, 308
Akinbiyi, Ade 260
Albania WC 130–1, 299
Alcoholics Anonymous (AA) 207
Aldershot Football Club 240–1
Alderton, John 282
Alexander, Albert 110
Ali, Muhammad 146–7
    see also Clay, Cassius
All of Me (Windsor) 270
All Star charity games 64
Allison, 'Big' Wayne 261
Allison, Malcolm 26, 42, 44–5, 106,
    110–11, 112–13, 307
Alvaro's restaurant 177–8
Anderson, Ruth 247
Andrew, Prince 217
Andrews, Eamonn 243, 246
Anfield 103, 105, 127
Are You Being Served? (TV programme)
    125
Armfield, Jimmy 124
Arnold, Steven 255
Arsenal 9, 12, 13–14, 46, 57, 58, 91, 98, 99,
    165, 169, 177, 207, 227, 228, 258, 262
Arsenal Stadium Mystery, The (film) 99
Asher, Jane 284, 286
ASK Vorwaerts 302
Askey, Arthur 103
Aspel, Michael 243
Asprilla, Tino 65–6
Astle, Jeff 310
Aston Villa 117, 309, 315
Atkinson, Ron 74, 105, 126–8

Atletico Madrid 127
ATV 245–6
Ayr United 313

Bader, Douglas 101
Bahrain 106–7
Bailey, Gary 126
Bailey, Roy 126
Baker, Danny 218
Baldwin, Tommy 40
Ball, Alan 57, 76, 96, 121, 122–3, 150, 165,
    166, 235
Ball, Alan (father of Alan Ball) 121
Ball, Lesley 121, 235
Ballymena United 315
Band on the Run (album) 283
Banks, Gordon 9, 19, 79
Banks, Leslie 99
Bannen, Ian 254, 255
Barnet Football Club 123, 224
Barnsley Football Club 61, 120
Bassett, Dave 259
Bates, Ken 78, 169, 204
Baxter, Jim 143, 153–4
Bayern Munich 317
Baywatch (TV programme) 262
BBC2 316
Beagrie, Peter 166
Beano (comic) 7, 249
Beardsley, Peter 67
Beatlemania 269
Beatles, The 105, 135, 141, 175, 186, 191,
    245, 284
Beckenbauer, Franz 124
Beckham, David 6, 7, 13, 82, 99, 210
Belfast 6, 19, 31, 130, 187, 214, 304, 317
Belgium WC 301
Bell, Colin 9
Ben Sherman fashion 26, 27
Benfica 188, 189, 302, 303, 304, 305, 308
Bennett, Hywel 256
Bentley, Roy 204

Bentley's bar 204
Best, Alex (*née* Macadam Pursey)
  (George's second wife) 31–2, 33–4, 193,
  200, 202, 211, 216, 243, 316
Best, Angela (*née* MacDonald Janes)
  (George's first wife) 111, 139–40, 149,
  312
Best, Ann (George's mother) 215, 243
Best, Bill 213–14
Best, Calum Milan (George's son) 58, 94,
  314
Best, Clyde 172, 173, 256
Best (film) 254–5
Best, Dickie (George's father) 213–16
'Best Intentions' (TV programme) 316
Bevan, Bob 230
Beverly Sisters 6
Bingham, Billy 56, 95
Birmingham City 9, 136, 260, 309
Black, Cilla 287
Blackburn Rovers 79, 260, 311
Blackpool 12, 121, 122, 124, 172
Blackpool incidents 171–3
Blair, Lionel 246–7
Blair, Tony 219–20
Blakely, David 281–2
Blessed, Brian 202
Blessed (George's autobiography) 1, 202,
  317
Blinkers nightclub 191, 193–4
Bloye, Ray 113
Bobby Charlton School of Excellence
  58–9
Bohemians 310
Bolton Wanderers 12, 53, 93
Bonetti, Peter 19, 38, 41, 230
Book, Tony 109, 125, 310
Booth, Pat 287
Booth, Tony 255
Borussia Dortmund 302
Boston Minutemen 311
Bough, Frank 258, 262, 272
Bournemouth, AFC 43, 44, 88, 296, 298,
  307, 314
Bournemouth Evening Echo (newspaper)
  70
Bovington, Eddie 86–7
Bowles, Stanley 63–5
Bowyer, Lee 51–2
Bradford City 315
Bradford Park Avenue 120
Brady, Liam 262

Bramhall residence, Cheshire 316
Branagh, Kenneth 219
Brandt, Willy 221
Branson, Richard 190
Brazil 55, 257, 263
Brazil, Alan 258
Bremner, Billy 47, 49
Brennan, Liz 24
Brennan, Shay 24–5, 102, 294
Brent Walker leisure 139
Bresslaw, Bernard 140
Bridges, Barry 171
Brighton & Hove Albion 79, 258
Brisbane Lions 296, 298, 314, 315
Bristol Rovers 311
British Academy of Film and Television
  Arts (BAFTA) 255
British Broadcasting Corporation (BBC)
  237–40, 262, 316
  Sports Personality of the Year Award
  318
British Footballer of the Year 305
British Transport Police 167
Brooks, Mel 241–2
Brown Bull pub, Manchester 183
Brut aftershave 249
Buckingham, Vic 56–7
Bugner, Joe 138
Bulgaria WC 300, 307
Bull, Steve 42
Burn, Colin 135
Burnley 31, 73, 82, 83, 84, 171, 172, 304
Burns, George 265
Burtenshaw, Norman 61
Burton 175
Bury 167, 168
'Bus Stop' (song) 181
Busby, Sir Matt 23–4, 29, 42, 48–9, 54, 95,
  96, 125, 181, 183, 185, 195, 243, 254, 256,
  275–6, 292, 294
Bush, George W. 220

C&A 175
Caine, Michael 104, 217, 254, 272
California Surf 313
Cambridge 40
Campbell, Bobby 95
'Candle in the Wind' 51
Cantwell, Noel 29
Cardiff City 167, 312
Carlton Tower Hotel, London 250
Carman, Celia 192–3

Carman, George 190, 191, 192, 193
Carry On films 140, 269–70
Castlereagh 317
Celtic 17, 27, 63, 85, 103, 132, 306
Chamberlain, Tosh 119–20
Channon, Mick 160, 161
Chapman, Herbert 98, 99, 228
Charles, John 158
Charlton Athletic 91, 111
Charlton, Bobby 7, 16, 27, 29, 34–5, 47, 99,
  102, 254, 262–3, 294
Charlton, Jackie 23, 49, 126, 262–3
Chelmsford prison 207
Chelsea Football Club 9, 38, 40–1, 51, 63,
  78, 87, 100, 132, 143, 163, 168, 169, 171,
  172, 305, 307, 310, 317
Chelsea Registry Office, London 33
Chelsea Town Hall, London 316
Cher 140
Chicken Shack, Algarve 32
China 142
Churchill, Winston 257
Clapton, Eric 181
Clarke, Allan 72–3
Clay, Cassius 172, 187
  see also Ali, Muhammad
Clemence, Ray 46
Cliff training ground 62
Clough, Brian 60–1, 61–2, 91–2, 97, 98,
  114–16
Cobbold, John 77
Coburn, James 283
Cocker, Les 54
Coe, Sebastian 218–19
Cold Blow Lane ground 61
Coleman, David 257
Coleman, Tony 107–8
Collins, Jackie 217, 287
Collins, Pauline 282
Collins, Phil 182
Collymore, Stan 260
Connery, Sean 210, 245
Connolly, Billy 229
Conteh, John 283
Cook, Elisha 7–8
Cook, Peter 212
Cooke, Charlie 40, 41, 143–5
Cookstown sausages 249
Cooper, Henry 138, 172, 249
Cooper, Terry 47, 49
Cork Celtic 296, 298, 309, 310–11
Coronation Street (TV programme) 21,

183, 190, 194, 195, 254, 255
Costello, Lou 12
Crackerjack (TV programme) 280
Craven Cottage 72, 118
Crawshaw, Jack 243
Cregagh estate, Belfast 187, 214
Crerand, Noreen 27
Crerand, Paddy 25–6, 27, 28–9, 97, 132,
  191–2, 193, 294, 307, 310
Crewe Alexandra 309
Cribbins, Bernard 206
Crimewatch (TV programme) 26
Cripps, Harry 72
Crocker, Lt Bobby 148
Crompton, Jack 134
Cromwell Hospital, London 1, 198–202,
  211, 317–18
Crowther, Leslie 280
Crowther, Liz 280
Cruise, Tom 190
Cruyff, Johan 226
Crystal Palace Football Club 112–13, 308
Currie, David 61–2
Currie, Tony 9
Curtis, Tony 182
Cusack, Sinead 305
Cyprus 123, 124, 164–5, 300, 306

Daily Express (newspaper) 281, 306
Daily Mail (newspaper) 69
  coolest Brits poll 210–11
Daily Mirror (newspaper) 79
Daley, Steve 42
Dalglish, Kenny 79
Dallas Tornado 311
Dandy (comic) 7, 249
Daniels, Maxine 186
Darlington 65
Davies, Dave 184
Davies, Ray 184
Davies, Ron 143
Dean, Dixie 7–8
Dear, Brian 172
'Dedicated Follower of Fashion' (song)
  184, 186
Demmy, Selwyn 193–4, 293
Den, The 61
dePaul, Lynsey 282–3
Derby County 40, 106, 114, 115, 120, 307
Detroit Express 312
Di Canio, Paolo 128, 197
Diamond, Anne 24, 25

Diana, Princess of Wales 51
Dicks, Julian 259
Dimbleby, David 227
Distel, Sacha 238
Djurgaarden 302
Dobson, Kevin 148
Docherty, Tommy 20, 95, 96–8, 100, 101, 114, 127, 160, 171–2, 239, 308, 309
Dodd, Ken 190
Dolphin cars 251–2
Doncaster Rovers 158
Dooley, Derek 10–11
Dornan, Peter 315
Dougan, Derek 26, 50, 164–5
Doyle, Mike 9–10, 108–9
Doyle, Pat 163
Drewery, Eileen 67
Driver, Betty 194
Drogheda 310
Drunken Duncan (screw) 206–7
Drury, George 14
Dundee United 313
Dunne, Tony 27, 102, 309
Dunphy, Eamonn 62, 70, 71, 72
Dunstable Town 309, 310

Eager, Vince 186
Eagle (comic) 7
EastEnders (TV programme) 127, 240, 269
Eastham, George 93
Ebury Press 317
Edgeley Park Club 310
Edinburgh 85, 86
Edmonton Drillers 313
Edwardia (boutique), Manchester 176, 181
Edwards family 191
Edwards, Louis 307, 308
egg advertising campaign 249
Elizabeth II, Queen of England 118
Elland Road 48
Ellis, Ruth 281–2
Elm Park 167
England 7, 9, 10, 14–15, 16, 17, 38, 53, 64–5, 72, 73, 87, 90, 106, 111, 117, 119, 122, 123, 124, 125, 126, 185, 207, 223, 228, 234–5, 257, 262, 299, 300
England, Mike 96
Escape to Victory (film) 254
Estudiantes 303, 305
European appearances 301–3
European Champions' League 317

European Cup
  1966 304
  1967/68 21, 302–3, 305
European Cup Winners Cup
  1964 301
  1970 37, 78
European Footballer of the Year Award 305
Eusebio 188–9, 308
Evans, Roy 259
Evening News (newspaper) 118
Everton Football Club 7–8, 9, 56, 73, 81, 103, 104, 123, 142, 160, 166, 194, 207, 235, 259, 302, 315
Exeter City 68

FA Cup
  1953 12
  1956 9
  1963 30
  1964 73
  1966 104
  1969 43
  1970 78, 305
  1974 309
  1978 58
  1992 169
FA (Football Association) 83, 113, 125, 305, 312
Faith, Adam 186
Falkirk 313
Farr, Chick 120–1
Fenerbache (of Turkey) 111
Ferdinand, Les 260
Ferencvaros 302
Ferguson, Sir Alex 35, 98–9, 127
Ferguson, Duncan 207–8
Ferguson, Sarah 217
FIFA (Fédération Internationale de Football Association) 310, 312
Fifteen to One (TV programme) 223
Finney, Tom 14
First Division 9, 43–4, 116, 124, 158, 286, 294
Fisons 251
Fitzpatrick, John 62
FK Sarajevo 302
Flanagan and Allen 228
Flynn, Jerome 254
Fontana, Wayne 182
Football Writers' Association 317
'For Your Love' (song) 181

Ford Open Prison 205–7, 238, 315
Fore aftershave 249–51
Forsyth, Bruce 186–7
Fort Lauderdale Strikers 86, 142, 297, 298, 312–13, 314
Foulkes, Bill 49, 102
Foyle's book store, London 188
France Football (magazine) 305
Francis, Trevor 9, 115
Franklin, Neil 6–7
Fratton Park 86
Frazier, Joe 147
French, Graham 167–8
Freud, Clement 283
Friday, Robin 167
Fugler, Bryan 94
Fulham 57, 72, 86, 119–20, 225, 235, 296, 298, 311, 312, 313
Fullaway, Mrs Mary 157, 185, 206, 243, 306, 307

Gabriel, Jimmy 160
Gallacher, Hughie 15
Gallagher brothers 244
Gary (boutique assistant) 176
Gascoigne, Paul 53, 238, 239, 260
Gatorade 144
Geller, Uri 68
Gemmell, Tommy 132
George Best Annual (football annual) 249
George Best football boots 249
George, Charlie 9
George Dunlop testimonial match 315
George, Susan 288–9
Gerry Peyton testimonial match 315
'Get Back' (song) 191
Gibb, Maurice 287
Gibson, Mr 134
Gigg Lane 167
Giggs, Ryan 82, 99
Gigi's restaurant 32–3
Giles, Johnny 47, 48, 49
Glasgow Rangers 85
Glass, Jackie 277–8
Glover, Brian 16
Gold, Johnny 95, 217, 245
Good, the Bad and the Bubbly, The (Best) 187–8
Goodison Park 103
Gordon, Flash 12
Gornik Zabrze 302
Gouldman, Graham 181, 182

Grace, Mr 125
Graham, George 91, 171–2
Graham Norton (TV programme) 237
Granada Television 183, 185
Grandstand (TV programme) 262
Grapes pub 193
Gray, Eddie 20
Great Universal Stores 252–3
Greaves, Jimmy 9, 38–9, 172, 259, 318
Green Shield stamps 217
Greenwood, Ron 172, 173, 223–4
Greer, Germaine 183
Gregg, Harry 19, 91
Gregory, Jim 98
Griffith, Walter 110
'Groovy Kind of Love' (song) 182, 186

Hadleigh (TV programme) 184
Haffey, Frank 17–18
Hall, Stuart 261
Hamburg SV 306
Handley, Tommy 228
Hapgood, Eddie 228
Haraldsted, Eva 190–2
Harding, Matthew 76
Harley, Alex 136–7
Harper, Gerald 183–4
Harris, Ronnie 'Chopper' 51, 52, 53, 63, 78
Hart, Tom 85–6
Hartson, John 63
Harvey, Joe 56
Hateley, Tony 100–1
Hawthorns 149
Hawtrey, Charles 269–70
Hayes 167
Haynes, Johnny 7, 93, 119, 120, 121
Heathrow Airport 209
Hector, Kevin 120
Hellenic 309
Hemery, David 64
Herd, David 30
Herman's Hermits 141, 181
Hermosa Beach 148
Heslop, George 146
Hibernian 296, 298, 302, 313, 315
Higgins, Alex 198
Highbury 13, 99, 262
Hill, Gordon 72
Hill, Jimmy 93, 120
HIV 234
HJK Helsinki 302

Hobson, Valerie 112
Hoddle, Carl 224
Hoddle, Glenn 67, 224
Hold Tight (film) 141
Holiday Inn, Birmingham 155
Holland 311, 312
    see also Netherlands WC
Hollies, The 181
Hollins, John 41
Holton, Jim 96
Holton, Mrs 96
Honved 16
Hope, Bobby 'Paleface' 149
Hotlegs 181, 182
Houston Hurricane 312
Hudd, Roy 204
Huddersfield Town 99, 221
Huddy's bar 204
Hudson, Alan 40, 58, 123–4, 165, 203–4
Hughes, Charlie 54–5
Hughes, Emlyn 65, 102
Hughes, Phil 202, 210
Hungary 16
Hunt, James 64
Hunter, Norman 46–7, 49
Hurley, Charlie 167
Hurst, Sir Geoff 223–4
Hutchinson, Ian 40–1

Ibrox disaster 306
Iceland WC 301
ICI factory, Teeside 14–15
Iglesias, Julio 25
'I'm Leaving on a Jet Plane' (song) 191
Imperial Hotel, Blackpool 172
Ingham, Mike 258
Inland Revenue 94
Inter City Fairs Cup 302
Ipswich Town 58, 77, 126, 307, 313
Irish Football Association 316
Italia 90 238

Jackson, Michael 212
Jacobs, Laurie 140
Jagger, Mick 156
Jago, Gordon 35–6
James, Alex 228
James, Sid 140
Jeffries, Lionel 206
Jeffries, Tim 217
Jemson, Nigel 60
Jennings, Pat 316

Jesus Christ 102, 105
Jewish Guild 295, 298, 309
Jezzard, Bedford 235
Joe Coral 194
Johanneson, Albert 158–9
John Collier 175
John, Elton 51, 62, 190
Johnny Carson (TV programme) 241–2
Johnson, Peter 81
Jones, Tom 267
Jones, Vinny 53
Jordan 273
Joy, Bernard 14

Kamara, Chris 261
Karen (partner of George Carman) 193
Kate (girlfriend of George Best) 279
Keane, Roy 53, 61, 62
Keegan, Kevin 9, 63, 65–6, 67, 68–9, 90,
    249, 260
Keeler, Christine 111–12
Keith, John 104
Kelly, Johnny 120
Kelly, Pat 120
Kendall, Howard 73
Kenwright, Bill 81, 194
Kes (film) 16
Keys, Richard 259
Kidd, Johnny 102, 186
Kilgore, French and Stanberry 244
Kilmarnock 258
King, Bryan 70–1, 72
Kinks, The 184, 186, 245
Knowles, Cyril 68
Kojak (TV programme) 148
Kray twins 214

La Phonograph pub 185
Labone, Brian 73, 104
Labour Party 186
Lane, David 'Bronco' 91
Lang, Bob 182, 186
Law, Denis 7, 16, 17–18, 23–4, 27, 31–4,
    35, 99, 102, 105, 108, 254, 294, 308
Lawrence, Dennis 230
Lawrence, Tommy 75
Lawton, Georgie 281
Lawton, Tommy 14, 15, 175–6
Layne, Bronco 92
League of Ireland 7, 310
Lee, Christopher 283
Lee, Francis 93–4, 106–8

Lee, Gordon 56
Leeds United 9, 20, 46, 47, 48–9, 54, 72,
    104, 114, 122–3, 124, 158, 260, 262–3
Leicester City 43, 260
Leitch, Sam 262–3
Lennon, John 214
Lerman, Oscar 217
Lewinisky, Monica 110
Liberace 285
Lincoln City 117
Lincroft 176
Lineker, Gary 260
Linfield 315
Liver Foundation 243
Liverpool 7–8, 9, 27, 46, 54, 68, 81, 101,
    103, 105, 114, 160, 255
Liz (physiotherapist) 200–1
Lloyd, Barry 87
Lockhead, Andy 73
Lofthouse, Nat 53
Loftus Road 308
London, Brian 138, 172
London Underground 99
Longleat safari park 131
Lord, Bob 83–4
Lorimer, Peter 20
Los Angeles Aztecs 142, 143, 146, 148,
    297, 298, 310, 311, 312, 313
Lowery, Joe 112
Lulu 286–7
Luton Town 63, 167, 168, 310
Lynam, Desmond 258
Lynch, John 254, 255
Lynch, Kenny 183, 185–9, 221–2, 230, 231,
    252, 255, 283, 287, 291–4
Lynott, Phil 279, 280
Lynott, Philomena 157, 279

McAlinden, Bobby 143, 144, 146–7
Macari, Lou 102, 162
McCartney, Paul 283, 284
McCreadie, Eddie 132, 171
McDermott, Terry 65–6
Macdonald, Angie see Best, Angie
McDonald, Bobby 158
Macdonald, Malcolm 56, 119, 122, 157
MacDougall, Ted 43–4
McGuinness, Wilf 42–3, 48, 95, 178–9
McIlvaney, Hugh 205
Mackay, Dave 46
McKenna, Paul 68
McKenzie, Duncan 124, 230

McMenemy, Lawrie 161
Macmillan administration 111–12
McMurdo, Bill 316
McNab, Bob 26, 27, 165–6
McNamara, Jackie 315
McParland, Roy 106
McQueen, Steve 166
McShane, Harry 183
McShane, Ian 183
Madame Tussaud's 226
Mail on Sunday (newspaper) 317
Maine Road 9, 305, 307
Malta 211
Manchester City 5, 9–10, 36, 37, 42, 106,
    109, 110–11, 112, 136, 143, 146, 226, 236,
    273, 305, 307, 309
Manchester Evening News (newspaper)
    235–6, 317
Manchester United 7, 12, 19, 20, 22, 24,
    27–30, 31, 34–5, 40, 42–3, 48, 49, 50, 54,
    57, 62, 72, 82, 83, 91, 94, 95–6, 97, 99,
    102, 103, 105, 123, 126, 127, 130, 131–2,
    133, 141, 157, 160, 164, 168, 177, 183,
    185, 190, 191, 193, 196, 202, 209, 222,
    227, 235, 236, 255, 259, 262, 273, 275,
    276, 292, 295, 298, 304, 305, 306, 307,
    308, 310, 313, 314, 317
Manchester United Reserves 309
Mandaric, Milan 86
Manning, Bernard 96
Mannion, Wilf 14–15, 175–6
Marconi 315
Margaret, Princess 104
Margate 43
Markham, Ronald 68
Marks & Spencer 175, 200
Marsh, Rodney 5, 9, 35–6, 56, 113, 117,
    150, 157, 225–6, 230–1, 234–5, 259
Marsh, Tony 135–8
Mason, James 288
Match of the Day (TV programme) 127,
    168
Matthews, Stanley 12, 13, 14, 51, 121,
    175–6, 228
Maxwell, Robert 78–9
Meek, David 235–6
Melville Alemannia 315
Men Only (magazine) 112
Mercer, Joe 106–7, 110
Mermaid bar, Hermosa Beach 148
Mersey Tunnel 235
Metro Radio 259

Middlesbrough 15, 90, 91, 314
Milburn, Jackie 220
Miles, Sarah 272
Miller, Eric 86–7
Millwall 61, 62, 70, 218
Mindbenders 182, 186
Mirandinha 66
Miss World contest 155, 267, 309
Mitchell, Warren 255–6
Mods 174, 175
Money, Hy 113
Monkhouse, Bob 68, 228–9, 229
Montgomery, Marion 272
Mooney, Dominique 176
Mooney, Malcolm 174, 175, 176–7,
    179–80, 181, 182
Moore, Bobby 7, 9, 13, 87, 124–5, 126, 164,
    172, 173, 222, 254, 256
Moore, Brian 26, 74, 75, 257
Moore, Carolyn 287, 306
Moore, Dudley 212
Moore, Henry 221–2
Morgan, Willie 31, 102
Mortensen, Stanley 12–14
Morton 313
Moscow Dynamo 13–14
Moss, Jennifer 194–5
Motson, John 'Motty' 257
'Mountain of Love' (song) 186
Mulhearn, Ken 37
Munich air disaster 29, 30
Murphy, Jimmy 54, 183
Murray, David 85

NASL (North American Soccer League)
    297, 298, 310, 311, 312–13, 314
National Film School 255
Ndah, George 260
Neill, Terry 57–8, 68
Netherlands WC 299, 301
    see also Holland
Neves, Vivian 251
New England Teamen 313
New York Cosmos 129, 307, 308, 312, 314
New Zealand 212
Newbon, Gary 258
Newcastle United 56, 65, 66, 118, 220,
    260, 304, 306, 315
Newport County 314
News of the World (newspaper) 113
Nichols, Dandy 255
Nigeria 230–1

No Honestly (TV programme) 282
'No Milk Today' (song) 181
Norbreck Hotel, Blackpool 171
North American Football League 141
Northampton Town 125, 305
Northern Ireland 50, 56, 130, 132, 164,
    187, 301, 304, 305, 306, 307, 308, 311,
    312
Norton, Graham 269
Nottingham Forest 20, 60, 61–2, 98, 115,
    153

Oakes, Alan 37
Octopussy (film) 268
O'Farrell, Frank 43, 44–5, 95, 127, 141,
    307, 308
O'Keefe, Eamonn 56
Old Kent Road 61
Old Trafford 26, 29, 31, 42, 43–4, 48, 95,
    98, 168, 218, 239, 276, 286, 294, 304, 305,
    306, 307, 309
One Flew Over the Cuckoo's Nest (film) 131
Ormond, Willie 162
O'Rourke, John 35
Osbome Park Galeb 315
Osgood, Peter 9, 40, 41, 78, 149–50, 310
O'Shea, Tessie 228
Owen, Michael 9
Oxford United 79

Paisley, Bob 54, 98, 101
Palm Beach (Booth) 287
Palmer, Harry 104
Parkinson, Mary 271–2
Parkinson, Michael 120, 121, 183, 237,
    241, 271–2, 283, 293, 308
Parkinson (TV programme) 237
Parry, Mike 258
Partick Thistle 258
Partizan Belgrade 302
Partridge, Pat 73
Patrick Kielty Almost Live (TV
    programme) 318
Pavarotti, Luciano 186–7
Pearce, Stuart 61, 260
Pelé 129, 142, 254
Pentonville prison 315
Pete (barman) 88
Peter, Paul and Mary 191
Phene Arms, Chelsea 163, 282
Phil 202, 210
Philadelphia Fury 149–50

Philip, Prince, Duke of Edinburgh 29
Phillips, Brian 92
Pierre-White, Marco 190
Pierrepoint, Albert 282
Pigswill, Mike 106, 107
Platt, Jim 314
Playtex bras 249
Plymouth Argyle 309
Poland 14
Police 5 (TV programme) 26–7
Portland Timbers 311
Portsmouth 86, 160
Portugal WC 300
Prescott, Johnny 138–9
Presley, Elvis 186
Preston North End 76
Private Eye (satirical magazine) 257
Profumo, John 112
Puskas, Ferenc 16–17
Putney Bridge 118

Quatermass and the Pit (TV programme)
    247
Queen's Jubilee relay race, 2002 317
Queens Park Rangers 9, 35–6, 98, 117,
    306, 308, 309, 310
Queen's University, Belfast 317
Question of Sport, A (TV programme) 20
Question Time (TV programme) 227
Quixall, Albert 29–30

Racing Strasbourg 302
Racings Cars 182
Ramsey, Sir Alf 5, 77, 106, 112, 122, 124–6,
    234
Rapid Vienna 303
Rat Pack 174, 183
Ravel 176
Reading 167
Real Madrid 16, 25, 303
Real Sociedad 166
Reaney, Paul 47, 49
Redknapp, Harry 86
Reed, Oliver 229
Renault 251–2
Revie, Don 5, 54, 103–4, 106, 114, 122–4,
    127, 158
Richard, Cliff 186
Richard, Keith 156
Richmond, Fiona 112–13
Ridding, Bill 93
Rideout, Paul 142

Rioch, Bruce 90
Roache, Linus 254
Roache, William 254
Robbie, Joe 86
Roberts, John 69, 80, 306
Robertson, John 60
Robson, Sir Bobby 72–3, 77, 86–7, 117–18,
    119, 220, 313
Robson, Bryan 'Pop' 118
Rochdale 261
rock 'n' roll 174
Rolling Stones 141, 156, 175, 245
Romark (hypnotist) 68
Rooney, Wayne 8, 9, 82
Rotary Club 22
Rotherham United 97
Ruebens nightclub 308
Rush, Ian 142
Ryan, Jimmy 149

Sadler, David 102, 131, 134, 157
St George 315
Saint and Greavsie (TV programme) 39
St James Park 65
St John, Ian 258
St Mirren 313
San Jose Earthquakes 142, 149, 297, 298,
    311, 313, 314
San Lorenzo restaurant, London 277
San Sebastien Hotel, Spain 166
Sassoon, Vidal 182
Saunders, Ron 108–9
Scanlon, Albert 30
Scholes, Paul 7, 99
Scotland 17, 132, 227, 299, 300, 304, 305
Scottish Cup 85, 258, 313
Seaman, David 169, 170, 257–8
Seattle Sounders 311
Second Division 70, 79, 91, 97, 110, 114,
    115, 160
Seed, Jimmy 111
Seeler, Uwe 306
Selfridges department store, London 228
Setters, Maurice 22–3, 57
Sexton, Dave 40, 63, 87, 168
'Sha La La La Lee' (song) 186
Shakespeare, William 257
Shamrock Rovers 309
Shankly, Bill 54, 75, 98, 100–5, 106, 114,
    127, 160
Shape Up and Dance (LP) 267–8
Sharif, Omar 237–8

Shaw Theatre, Kings Cross 230–1
Shearer, Alan 79, 260
Sheene, Barry 287
Sheffield United 9, 261
Sheffield Wednesday 10, 57, 104, 128
Shelbourne 310
Shilton, Peter 19, 90
Shine, Betty 67
Shrewsbury Town 96
Simpson, Homer 202
Sinatra, Frank 127
Sinstadt, Gerald 260
Sirocco, David 135, 137–8
Sky 260, 261, 264
Slack Alice club, Manchester 309
Sloniecka, Stefanja 308
Small Faces 186
Smart, Billy 235
Smith, Iain Duncan 220
Smith, Sir Paul 244
Smith, Tommy 46
Southall 70
Southall, Neville 259
Southampton 34–5, 90, 143, 160, 161, 258, 275, 306, 307, 310, 311
Southend United 314
Southport 310
Southwark Court 205
Spain EC 300
Spice Girls 6
Sporting Club Lisbon 301
Sports Personality of the Year award 318
Sprake, Gary 48–9
Spring and Port Wine (film) 288
Springfield, Dusty 284
Stallone, Sylvester 254
Stamford Bridge 40, 51–2, 100, 204, 317
Star, Ringo 283
Stark, Koo 217
Stavin, Mary 155–6, 217, 267–8
Stephanie (girlfriend of George) 287
Stepney, Alex 19–20, 102, 294
Stewart, Eric 182
Stiles, Nobby 21–2, 73, 102, 294
Stock, Alec 167–8, 234–5
Stockport County 142, 295, 298, 310
Stoke City 9, 124, 310, 312
Storey, Peter 46
Storey-Moore, Ian 20
Strauss, Johann 106
Stretford Enders 168
Stubbs, Una 255

Suart, Ron 40–1
Sugar, Alan 89
'Sugar Me' (song) 282
Summerbee, Mike 37, 139, 146, 158, 176, 254, 275–6
Summerbee, Nicky 37
Sun (newspaper) 117, 232
    Page Three 251
Sunday Express (newspaper) 73
Sunday Night at the London Palladium (TV programme) 119
Sunderland 106, 111, 220
Superstars (TV programme) 63–4
Sutcliffe, Peter 117
Swan, Peter 91, 92
Swansea City 19, 310
Swindon 261
Switzerland WC 299, 304
Sydney Olympic 314

Talksport radio 258
Tambling, Bobby 204
Tambling's bar 204
Tampa Bay Rowdies 312
Tarbuck, Jimmy 183, 186–7, 202, 229, 272
Taylor, Graham 117
Taylor, Jack 73
Taylor, Peter 60, 116
Taylor, Shaw 26–7
Teddington Studios 146, 243, 244
Teddy Boys 174–5
Tesco 195
Thatcher, Margaret 241
Thaw, John 258
'They Shoot Horses Don't They?' (song) 182
Thin Lizzy 279
Third Division 43–4, 97, 117, 126
This Boy's Story (film) 255
This is Your Life (TV programme) 24, 243–7, 306, 318
This One's On Me (Greaves) 38
Thomas, Leslie 256
Thomas, Mickey 168–70
Thorpe, Jeremy 190
'thriller in Manilla' fight 147, 148
Tiler, Brian 86, 88
Till Death Do Us Part (film) 255–6
Tillman, Harold 244, 245, 246
Time and the Place nightclub 291, 292
Times, The (newspaper) 251
Tolly Cobbold 77

INDEX

Tobermore United 296, 298, 315
Tonbridge 309
Toshack, John 68–9
Tottenham Hotspur 30, 38, 46, 68, 89, 111, 207, 222, 304
Tramps nightclub 95, 217, 241, 245, 250
Trautmann, Bert 9–10
Trinder, Tommy 119
Tueart, Denis 226
Turf Moor 31, 83
Turkey WC 299
TV AM 24, 25
Two Way Stretch (film) 205–6

Ulster Television 316
Unc 148–9
Upton Park 223
Ure, Ian 227
Uruguay 299
USSR WC 300, 306

Valier, Suzanne 178–80
Vancouver Whitecaps 314
Venables, Terry 35, 171, 172, 259
Vicarage Road 62
Vienna 132–3
Village Barber, Manchester 181, 182
Viollet, Dennis 185
Virgin Soldiers, The (film) 256

Wagner, Malcolm (Waggy) 97, 135, 136–7, 138, 149, 157, 181–3, 194, 195, 250
Waite, Terry 105
Wales 143, 168, 299, 300, 305
Walker, Billy 138, 139
Walker, George 139
Walker, Jack 79
Walker, John 79, 81
Wallace, Marjorie 267, 309
Walsall 72
Washington Diplomats 312
Waterford 303
Watford 62, 117, 310
Weller, Keith 63
Wembley Stadium 15, 16, 17, 259, 305
Wenger, Arsene 98
West Bromwich Albion 49, 56–7, 304, 315
West Germany 17, 124, 257, 301
West Ham United 9, 38, 44, 73, 86, 87, 111, 158, 171, 172, 172–3, 223–4, 256, 306

Whirlwinds 181
White Hart Lane 13, 30
Wigan Athletic 314
Wilde, Marty 186
William Hill 194
Williams, Charlie 158
Williams, Graham 49–50
Williams, Kenneth 277
Williams, Professor 243
Williams, Robbie 210
Williams, Serena 111
Wilson, Bob 261–2
Wilson, Harold 220–1
Windsor, Barbara 269, 270
Windsor Park, Belfast 316
Wings 283
'Winter Wonderland' (song) 186–7
Winterbottom, Walter 125
Winters, Bernie 122
Winton, Dale 269
Wisdom, Norman 131–2
Wogan, Terry 238–40, 241
Wogan (TV programme) 229, 237–41, 316
Wolstenholme, Kenneth 257
Wolverhampton Wanderers 6, 42, 123, 306
Woodgate, Jonathan 260
World Cup Championships 14–15, 303
  1958 19
  1966 17, 38, 223, 257, 262
  1970 26, 126
  1994 127
  2002 220, 257–8
World Indoor Soccer League 308
World's My Football Pitch, The (Wright) 6
Worthington, Frank 229–30
Wrexham 168, 169–70
Wright, Billy 6–7
Wright, Ian 207
Wyman, Bill 175, 229

Yardbirds, The 181
Yeats, Ron 103
Yorath, Gabby 257–8
Yorath, Terry 257–8
York, Susannah 272
Young, Neil 107, 146

Zigger Zagger (play) 81

Copies of *Blessed* by George Best are available by mail order
at a price of £7.99 including FREE post and packing.

To order your copy phone
01624 677237

POST: Random House Books
c/o Bookpost, PO Box 29, Douglas, Isle of Man, IM99 1BQ

FAX: 01624 670923

EMAIL: bookshop@enterprise.net

Cheques (payable to Bookpost) and credit cards accepted.

Please allow 28 days for delivery.